An Alternative History of Britain

An Alternative History of Britain

Normans and Early Plantagenets

Timothy Venning

Pen & Sword
MILITARY

First published in Great Britain in 2014 by
Pen & Sword Military
an imprint of
Pen & Sword Books Ltd
47 Church Street
Barnsley
South Yorkshire
S70 2AS

ISBN 978-1-78346-271-1

A CIP catalogue record for this book is available from the British Library.

Typeset in 11pt Ehrhardt by
Mac Style, Bridlington, E. Yorkshire

Printed and bound in the UK by CPI Group (UK) Ltd, Croydon, CR0 4YY

Pen & Sword Books Ltd incorporates the imprints of Pen & Sword
Archaeology, Atlas, Aviation, Battleground, Discovery, Family History,
History, Maritime, Military, Naval, Politics, Railways, Select, Transport,
True Crime, and Fiction, Frontline Books, Leo Cooper, Praetorian Press,
Seaforth Publishing and Wharncliffe.

For a complete list of Pen & Sword titles please contact
PEN & SWORD BOOKS LIMITED
47 Church Street, Barnsley, South Yorkshire, S70 2AS, England
E-mail: enquiries@pen-and-sword.co.uk
Website: www.pen-and-sword.co.uk

Contents

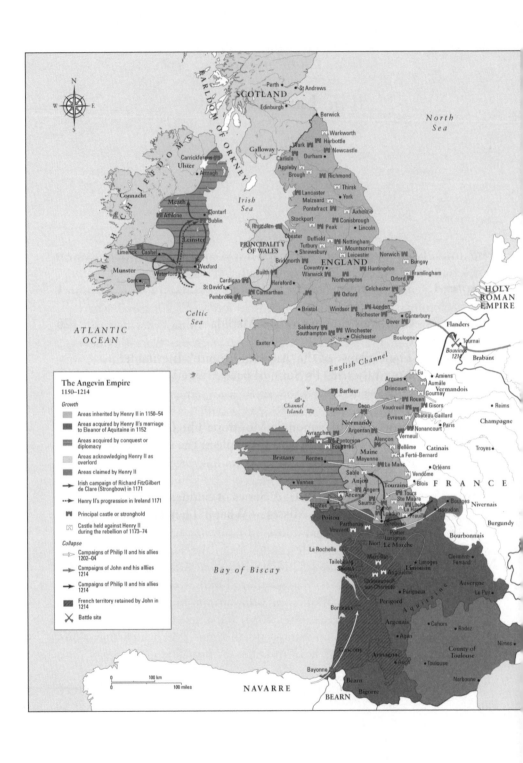

The Angevin Empire
1150–1214

Growth

Areas inherited by Henry II in 1150–54

Areas acquired by Henry II's marriage to Eleanor of Aquitaine in 1152

Areas acquired by conquest or diplomacy

Areas acknowledging Henry II as overlord

Areas claimed by Henry II

Irish campaign of Richard FitzGilbert de Clare (Strongbow) in 1171

Henry II's progression in Ireland 1171

Principal castle or stronghold

Castle held against Henry II during the rebellion of 1173–74

Collapse

Campaigns of Philip II and his allies 1202–04

Campaigns of John and his allies 1214

Campaigns of Philip II and his allies 1214

French territory retained by John in 1214

Battle site

SCOTLAND

Perth · · St Andrews
Edinburgh ·
· Berwick
Warkworth
Harbottle
Wark Newcastle
Galloway Carlisle Durham
Appleby
Brough · Richmond
Thirsk
Lancaster · York
Malzeard
Pontefract · Axholme
Stockport Conisbrough
Peak · Lincoln
Chester Duffield Nottingham
Rhuddlan Tutbury Mountsorrel
Shrewsbury Leicester Norwich
Bridgnorth Coventry · Huntingdon Bungay
Cardigan Builth Warwick · Northampton Orford Framlingham
St David's Hereford · Colchester
Pembroke Carmarthen Oxford
· Bristol Windsor London
Rochester · Canterbury
Salisbury Dover
Southampton Winchester Boulogne
Exeter Chichester

EARLDOM OF ORKNEY

North Sea

IRISH CHIEFDOMS

Carrickfergus
Ulster
· Armagh
Connacht
Meath
Clontarf
Athlone · Dublin
Leinster
Limerick · Cashel
Munster
Cork · Waterford Wexford
St David's

Irish Sea

PRINCIPALITY OF WALES

ENGLAND

Celtic Sea

ATLANTIC OCEAN

English Channel

HOLY ROMAN EMPIRE

Flanders
Tournai
Bouvines 1214
Brabant

Eu · Amiens
Arques · Aumâle Vermandois
Drincourt Gournay · Reims
Channel Islands Rouen Gisors
Bayeux Caen Vaudreuil Champagne
Barfleur Évreux Château Gaillard
Avranches Argentan Nonancourt · Paris
Normandy Verneuil
Dol Pontorson Alençon Bellême Catinais
Fougères Mayenne La Ferté-Bernard Troyes
Brittany Rennes Maine Le Mans Orléans
Sablé Vendôme FRANCE
Vannes Anjou Blois
Angers Touraine Ste Maure Bourges Nivernais
Ancenis Tours Chinon Issoudun
Nantes Saumur Loudun La Haye
Poitou Chenon La Preuille Burgundy
Parthenay Poitiers Bourbonnais
Vouvant Lusignan
La Rochelle Niort Le Marche Limoges Clermont-Ferrand
Taillebourg Melle Saintes Angoulême Limousin Auvergne
Châteauneuf-sur-Charente Aquitaine Le Puy
Périgueux
Périgord
Bordeaux
Argenais · Cahors · Rodez
· Agen Nîmes
Gascony County of Toulouse
Bayonne Armagnac · Auch
· Toulouse Narbonne
Béarn
NAVARRE Bigorre
BEARN

Bay of Biscay

Chapter One

The Norman State

The unlikely succession of Henry I: what if his older brothers Robert or Richard had ruled, and did he murder William II?

The succession to England from 1087 to 1154 owed a lot to fortuitous circumstances, in that it was unusual for Western Europe, where the major states more often descended through a 'father–eldest son' line – most notably in France, which did not deviate once from this between Hugh I's accession in 987 and John I's death in 1316. (The Holy Roman Empire descended more obliquely, but it was prey to the ambitions of competing families and was not a geographically compact 'bloc' of inherited lands.) The problem of female succession that afflicted England after Henry I's only son's death in 1120 was not apparent in Castile, where Alfonso VI's son also died unexpectedly (in battle) and his daughter Urraca was able to succeed in 1109 – as did Baldwin II's eldest daughter Melissende in the Kingdom of Jerusalem in 1131. The county – later kingdom – of Portugal, a minor part of Alfonso's realm, was inherited by his other, illegitimate, daughter, Teresa, and her husband. Those states ruled by a king that had irregular succession were usually due to civil war or repeated rebellion among a number of rival lines descended from the sons of one dominant ancestor, as in Denmark after 1134 (the line of Swein Estrithson) and Norway after 1130 (the line of Magnus 'Bare Leg'). A similar fate befell the weaker Duchy/Kingdom of Bohemia, while in the North-East of Europe, Poland (after 1138) and Russia (after 1054) remained technically one state but were in reality divided up into rival sub-states over which one senior ruler might from time to time have an honorary primacy.

The divided inheritance of 1087 – not the norm for the era in Western Europe?

The division of an expansionist ruler's lands among his sons on his death – on William I's death in 1087 in England – had a parallel thrice in Spain, where Ferdinand I (younger son of the King of Navarre) had inherited

Castile from his mother in 1035 and taken over his wife' s brother Vermudo's Leon by conquest in 1037. Ferdinand's father, Sancho 'the Great' of Navarre, had already divided his own lands among three sons – Navarre for one, Castile for a second, and Aragon for the third. On Ferdinand I's death in 1065 his united kingdom of Castile and Leon was divided between his sons Sancho and Alfonso, but the former disinherited the latter and was murdered, enabling his victim to take over both kingdoms (1072) – an approximate parallel with the fratricidal jealousy and possible fratricide among William I's sons. Alfonso VI passed on the reunited kingdom to his daughter Urraca and grandson Alfonso VII, but when the latter died in 1157 it was divided between two sons (Sancho and Ferdinand) again.

Dividing up the late ruler's lands among his sons was not standard legal tradition in William's homeland of northern France in the eleventh and twelfth centuries, with the Kings' Isle de France' patrimony and lesser dukes' and counts' dominions usually going to the eldest son. (The question of what to do with conquered lands did not usually apply as the political order was relatively stable.) The only repeated division within one family was of the counties of Blois and Champagne, which were not geographically contiguous anyway. Normally the younger sons could expect at best a minor sub-'state' that could not militarily rival their elders' lands – as with the lands given to younger sons of the Kings of France or Counts of Anjou. The largest bloc of lands, with the senior title, went to the oldest son unless he was incapable or a cleric (as, for example, with future King Stephen's oldest brother in Blois, William, who, according to historian William of Newburgh, was set aside by his mother due to deficiency in intelligence.) More often a younger son had to fend for himself and find an heiress, as future King Stephen, third or fourth son of Count Stephen of Blois, did with the county of Boulogne's heiress, Matilda. He then received the County of Mortain in Normandy from his mother's brother, Henry I of England and Normandy. Normandy had never been divided on the occasions when a Duke had two sons (e.g. William I's father and uncle in 1026); when new Duke Robert set up his younger brother Henry (the future king) in the Cotentin there as a powerful vassal c.1090 this was probably forced by Henry rather than voluntary generosity. Scandinavian kingdoms were divided at times – but between co-kings with one usually senior, e.g. Harald Hardradi's sons in 1066 and the sons of Magnus 'Bareleg' in 1103. The Normans' other dominions, in southern Italy, passed from one son of Tancred de Hauteville to another in the 1040s and 1050s rather than being divided, although this was due to pragmatism – a united state was needed to fight its many foes and the Count/Duke could not trust his brothers with mini-states of their own – and this new state lacked tradition. When Sicily was conquered by the family of Tancred in the late 1060s it became a separate state under the younger brother, Roger, of the current Duke Robert 'Guiscard' (for military efficiency in an ongoing war against the Arabs as much as out of Roger's 'rights'). 'Guiscard' notably disinherited his elder son, Bohemund, his most promising general and the likelier candidate to win the militaristic nobles' backing, from his mainland Duchy in favour of his younger son, Roger 'Borsa', and let him inherit only a minor county (Taranto). That incident, in 1085 so fresh in people's memories when William I died, was not, however, an exact parallel – the two young men had different mothers and Roger's was a local Lombard heiress, the warlike Sichelgaita who took part in battles, so the area's Lombards would obey him sooner than Bohemund. The latter, like Robert of Normandy in 1087, attempted to reverse the grant of a larger state to his younger brother by war but did not have the military resources to do so and had to give up; he consoled himself with the Duchy of Antioch when the First Crusade commenced and later made a bold bid to take over the entire Byzantine Empire (1107). Bohemund and Robert of Normandy, indeed, served as colleagues on the Crusade – where Robert showed that he did not lack military competence or bravery. Normandy's neighbouring North French states in Flanders, Maine, Anjou, and Brittany (the latter 'Celtic' by genetic origin and culture not French) usually descended as one polity, from father to son or from brother to brother – but were occasionally seized by a disgruntled relative in revolts. In the Scandinavian world from which the Normans' ancestors had come to France in the 900s, a divided inheritance was only common in the Jarldom of Orkney, held by the distant cousins of the Dukes of Normandy – the founding Duke Rollo/Hrolf 'the Walker', allegedly too fat to ride a horse, had been son of Jarl Rognvald of More in Norway. But there the sons of a deceased Jarl usually shared the – small – state out equally rather than having one as the dominant ruler, though the eldest was usually senior. Natural death or (more usually) fratricide duly elevated one contender to sole rule. There was one example of a youngest son in a seemingly hopeless situation triumphing as Henry I of England did by luck and his wits, namely Jarl Thorfinn 'Raven-Feeder' (r. 1015 to c. 1065) who had outwitted and outlived his feuding elder brothers and nephews. But there is no evidence of any influence of Viking Orkney dynastic practice on the Francified Norman state.

There was thus no decisive precedent for William to divide Normandy and England between two sons, except the geographical difficulty of ruling both at once and the likely anger of the second surviving son if disinherited. (He technically left England 'to God' as he had received it from Him, but by giving his second surviving son, William, the crown and telling him to go and take it he expressed a clear preference for his succession.[1]) He had held both states himself since 1066 rather than passing on Normandy to Robert once the latter was adult, which Robert may have resented given his rebellion in 1077 when he was aged in his mid-twenties. The King of France seems to have encouraged him, in order to split up William's dominions and make Robert his dependant protégé. Nor was a division of England itself in 1087 likely – though England was not a long-established unitary kingdom unlike hindsight can suggest. Local particularism and a possible threat of a 'breakaway' state were involved in the claims of King Harald 'Hardradi' of Norway on Scandinavian-settled York in 1066, which had benefited William by drawing Harold II away from the south coast to fight off this invasion. Swein Estrithson of Denmark, nephew of King Cnut of England and Denmark, attacked York on his own initiative in 1070, with some local support – whether he aimed for rule of just York or all England is unclear. (York had last been a separate state in 954, under ex-king Erik 'Bloodaxe' of Norway.) Eleventh century English tradition (played up in William's claims to be preserving the legal practices of the reign of King Edward) was in favour of a unified realm in recent decades. England had been divided among rival contenders once in the eleventh century, but only in the – temporary – case of a military stalemate between Edmund 'Ironside' and Cnut in 1016. The two feuding sons of Cnut in 1035–6 had failed to agree on any division after their father's death – all had gone to the nearest at hand, Harold 'Harefoot', and the loser Harthacnut's mother and faction-leader Queen Emma (William's great-aunt) had been driven out. The tenth century precedents for two sons of a deceased king ruling different parts of England – probably Aelfweard and Athelstan in 924 and certainly Edwy and Edgar in 957 – would have been a distant memory for the English administrative class that served William after 1066, if recalled at all.

In any case, the pragmatic William was hardly likely to divide up a hard-won unitary state wracked by rebellion in 1067–71 among two potentially feuding sons, or even give a substantial landed endowment to the third (Henry). William had made a point of confiscating the lands of any of his intimates, related or not, who posed a 'security risk' – such as his half-brother Bishop Odo, Earl of Kent, in 1083. He had carefully reduced the number of great lords who had a 'bloc' of territory in one area, which could be used as a centre for rebellion – as Odo's Kent could have been used as a landing site for an attack on England by a would-be usurper such as Robert. The creation of a contiguous 'bloc' of territory for one man was mostly restricted to the border areas where this was needed to lead defence – e.g. the earldoms of Hereford and Montgomery in the Welsh Marches (both of whose holders rebelled, in 1075 and 1101) and the North-East in 1067–70 (where his earls of Northumbria repeatedly rebelled or were overthrown).

The use of his personal 'trusties' for these fiefs was not a guarantee of long-term loyalty, as he had given Hereford to his foster-brother William FitzOsbern (1067) to face revolt once the latter's son succeeded (1075) and Odo of Kent (deposed 1083) was his half-brother. If he could not trust these men to be loyal to him, he could not trust his younger sons to be loyal to the latter's elder brother. William was hardly likely to create a new 'bloc' of English land in 1087 for a younger son, e.g. Henry within William II's realm, after the threat that Odo's 'bloc' had posed. The most that can be said is that if Henry's mother, Queen Matilda, a would-be peacemaker among the feuding youths in the 1070s, had not died in 1083 she might have persuaded her husband to increase Henry's legacy from money to a larger grant of land in England than he actually received.

Dividing England and Normandy was more logical, but also problematic. Giving one state to each of his two older sons would increase the chance of them fighting as each had enough resources for a prolonged war. The King of France, Philip I, was likely to encourage them to fight each other to weaken the dynasty's threat to his own domains 'next-door' in the Isle de France, as he had backed Robert against William I in 1077 – and as feudal overlord of Normandy he could declare the duchy forfeit (though this could be ignored by a strong ruler). It was safer to give a younger – or disinherited elder – son a smaller inheritance with which he could not mount a military challenge, and in this regard William did not leave his youngest son Henry any compact 'bloc' of land (he received Queen Matilda's scattered lands in the south Midlands plus five thousand pounds).[2] William's decision was hardly due to a sudden desire for 'justice' for all his sons as part of repenting for his past sins as he was dying, as he carefully prevented Henry from having enough resources to challenge the two older sons. He could, however, have left both states to his elder son, Robert, and a militarily powerless small district to the younger, William. If Orderic Vitalis' stories about his wrath towards the treacherous and rebellious Robert in the late 1070s are correct, he was capable of disinheriting him in William 'Rufus' favour – unless he was constrained by the promises he had made to the late Queen Matilda c. 1080 to pardon Robert. Matilda had apparently regarded Robert as her favourite, sent him money when he was living in exile after 1077 to her husband's annoyance, and successfully interceded for his restoration to favour after the rebellion. If Orderic is to be believed, William I had openly made belittling jokes about his eldest son's small stature before the revolt, which indicates contempt rather than confidence in him as a future ruler. Robert was also mocked for his pot-belly, and had a string of concubines.[3] Another of Orderic's possibly apocryphal stories has Robert driven to revolt in 1077 by being humiliated in front of his friends when his brothers William

'Rufus' and Henry poured water (if not worse) on him from a balcony with equal contempt.[4] If any of this is true – Henry was only eight or nine at the time – Robert was perceived as an easy target for teasing by his father and brothers, which may have undermined his confidence to hold down his future subjects by force. Did this mutual dislike between father and son make it more likely that William would give England to one of Robert's younger brothers, and did he do this as he thought Robert was not 'up to the job' of ruling such a large state? Or would Robert have stood a chance of gaining England if he had been in Normandy and reconciled to William at the time the latter died? He was currently in exile again, in neighbouring Ponthieu, after another row[5] – and William's death, at the age of probably fifty-eight or nine, was unexpected. It followed him rupturing his stomach against the pommel of his horse when the latter stumbled as the King was sacking the rebel Vexin town of Mantes – a rebellion backed by Robert's ally King Philip of France.[6] That circumstance was not likely to encourage the hot-tempered William to forgive Robert and give him England. But if the accident had not intervened Robert might well have had more difficulty in acquiring a pardon from his father after 1087 than he had done after 1077, without Matilda to aid him. Thus William I could have disinherited his exiled heir – at least from England – had he died naturally in the 1090s.

The quarrels over William I's inheritance – an unlikely chain of events

In the first instance, although William I's apparent plans for the succession were adhered to initially (the eldest son, Robert, having his paternal ancestors' patrimony of Normandy and the next surviving one, William II, England) the succession of Henry I to England in 1100 and his seizure of Normandy in 1106 were unexpected. William 'Rufus' saw off his elder brother's attempt to take over England in 1088, although both of their half-uncles, Odo (restored to Kent by William I's will) and Count Robert of Mortain, backed Robert of Normandy. Indeed the latter had the strategic advantage that Odo could raise his vassals in Kent to gain him a port there and Count Robert could offer him access to England via his castle of Pevensey – adjacent to William I's landing-site in 1066. But a mixture of bad weather and lack of money meant that Duke Robert could not muster a fleet quickly (he had to sell the Cotentin in western Normandy to Henry for ready cash), and William II blockaded the rebels' castles into surrender as they waited in vain for Robert to arrive to aid them.[7] Thus William I's settlement was not overturned, and Robert's reputation for bad luck (or slackness) was begun or reinforced. But William II did not settle the succession by marrying quickly and providing a son, though Robert did not either. (Their father had married in his early twenties; Robert did not marry until he was nearly fifty.) William II remained unmarried for whatever reason, despite apparent interest in the niece of Edgar 'Atheling' and daughter of Malcolm III and Margaret, Edith/Matilda (then living at Wilton convent) in the 1090s.[8] Over a decade younger than him, she had come south from her parents' court to be educated by her aunt Christina – allegedly a hard taskmaster – at Romsey Abbey in 1086, and had moved on to the less austere Wilton (which was effectively a school for noble girls). She had been betrothed to Count Alan of Richmond, premier baron of the North Riding of Yorkshire, but he had run off with her fellow-pupil Gunnhilde (a daughter of King Harold II). The fact that she had been forced to wear a nun's veil by her aunt, who wanted her to become a nun, later presented a legal problem for Henry I in marrying her in 1100 as this could amount to taking preliminary monastic vows – but that would not stop the irreligious William who delighted in shocking clerics. She was able to argue convincingly when objections were raised to her marrying Henry after wearing a nun's habit that she had been forced to wear it by her aunt, when under the age of normal consent to becoming a nun.[9] Indeed, in legal terms the number of Saxon heiresses hiding from heiress-hunting Norman lords in convents after 1066 (and wearing habits to discourage their pursuers) led to careful consideration of the whole issue of what exactly constituted taking irrevocable holy orders. It was decided that consent at an adult age was essential to make it legal, and Edith/Matilda had not been adult (she was born c. 1074/8) or consenting. The same argument would have been used had William II chosen her as a wife. However, Henry (and clearly Edith too) had an added advantage over the marriage that William would not have done. In 1093 the confident and uncompromising new Archbishop Anselm had insisted that Edith had taken vows and should stay in the cloister; in 1100 he had spent years in exile and was anxious to co-operate with Henry after his recall.

William was rumoured to be homosexual according to (Church) chroniclers, to which the effeminate conduct of his young aristocratic supporters at court with their long hair and trailing cloaks gave credence.[10] This may only be a slanderous inference by his enemies or opponents of their fashions – short hair was the fashion of William I's elite, as shown by the Bayeux Tapestry. His brusque treatment and eventual exile of his belatedly appointed Archbishop of Canterbury, St Anselm, ensured that the latter's hagiographers would be hostile. Indeed, his mysterious and violent death – without time to confess his sins – showed eager Church critics after 1100 that God had repaid his blasphemous behaviour as he deserved and made any slander seem believable.[11] William was at most forty-four, probably only forty, when he died, although most adult male rulers had acquired a wife (or bastards) much earlier; diplomacy and acquiring useful foreign allies by matrimony usually impelled a royal marriage and it may be that the King saw no need of this in the 1090s. He seems to have had at least one bastard son in the 1080s, though fewer than either of his brothers had. Henry was notorious for his mistresses – and could use his illegitimate children as political pawns, the more promising sons being given lordships and the daughters married off to political allies. (William I had himself been illegitimate, as his enemies reminded him.) But William II seems to have been careless of this potential usefulness of having children out of wedlock, unlike the calculating Henry. Possibly he was more fastidious, or possibly he preferred male comradeship without being much of a womanizer or being homosexual. Until he was regent of Normandy for Robert in 1096–1100 he had no need of Continental entanglement, the obvious reason for acquiring a wife. Robert was also unmarried in his forties, although he had been due to marry in his father's lifetime until his fiancée died.

The ongoing crisis in Scotland after Malcolm III was killed attacking Alnwick Castle in autumn 1093 led to William interfering to back the part-English (Saxon, not Norman) claimant Edgar, fourth son of Malcolm and St Margaret, against the 'isolationalist' incumbent Donald Ban, his uncle, in 1097. This expedition, entrusted to Edgar's uncle and namesake the 'Atheling' and assorted ambitious Anglo-Norman volunteers, placed the friendly Edgar on the Scots throne as an English client and was thus an obvious occasion for William to marry his sister Edith/Matilda, usefully available at Romsey then Wilton. As has been mentioned, he had already been to inspect her. The fact that he did not proceed with any marriage may suggest carelessness about hurrying to do something distasteful rather than any sexual reason – he had not bothered to appoint an Archbishop of Canterbury for four years after Lanfranc died, finding the see's revenues useful for his treasury. Allegedly homosexual kings married for State reasons – Edward II was to marry Isabella of France and have four children while emotionally entangled with Piers Gaveston in the 1300s. If anything can be read into William's reluctance to marry and beget an heir apart from carelessness, it may have been the lack of an obvious candidate – and he had no urgent State reasons to provide an heir. When he and Robert came to an agreement in 1091 it was proposed that the surviving brother have the other's dominions on his death, excluding their younger brother Henry. His carelessness about taking politically sensible action was evident in other areas, as when he rudely ignored the visiting Malcolm III of Scots at his autumn crown-wearing in Gloucester in 1093 and caused him to invade England in a rage.[12] If this had not happened not only Malcolm (then probably over sixty) but his eldest son by St Margaret, Edward, would not have been killed in the invasion at Alnwick and presumably Edward would have inherited Scotland. That would not have prevented any rebellions and thus an English intervention in Scotland, however – traditional 'Celtic'/Gaelic Scots inheritance-laws favoured the succession of a younger brother rather than a son so Malcolm's younger brother Donald Ban was likely to have challenged Edward. There was also the question of Malcolm's son by his first, Orkney, marriage, seemingly disinherited in the 1070s–80s by being held as a hostage in England – Duncan (II). In real life William II used him to challenge and overthrow Donald, temporarily, in 1094; but if Malcolm's son Edward had been an Anglophile king in the mid-late 1090s or 1100s this would not have been necessary.

William took charge of Normandy while Robert was absent on the First Crusade in 1096–1100, and the latter was returning to Normandy with his new wife, Sybil of Conversano, when William was suddenly killed hunting on 2 August 1100. The timing of the accident, as modern historians have commented, was seemingly useful for Henry. Henry's prospects of taking over England would have been reduced once Robert returned and had a son to continue the Norman ducal line, unless William fell out with his elder brother again and left England to Henry to spite Robert. The existence of an extra heir for Robert's line was not, however, decisive, as the choice of King or Duke lay with the magnates – and the Norman barons had rejected Duke Richard III's infant son for the adult Robert 'the Magnificent', William I's father, in 1035. (The pre-1066 English precedents for sidestepping an under-age heir mattered less, as their lay and ecclesiastical magnates had been removed from power.) Henry's swift seizure of power on William II's death – he rode straight for Winchester and the treasury – gave him the opportunity to defy Robert's inevitable attempt to invade England in 1101 and in due course to take over Normandy too. Had William had an Archbishop of Canterbury 'in situ', not in exile, in 1100, and that man backed Robert, his refusal to crown Henry could have been crucial. The exiled incumbent, Anselm, was a man of strict principle and unlikely to have been intimidated by Henry into breaking an oath to accept Robert as William II's heir – though Henry could have made another cleric crown him as the Archbishop of Canterbury did not always crown the eleventh century kings of England (the Archbishop of York had crowned Harold II and William I).

Seemingly abler than Robert at controlling the turbulent barons, Henry has been seen as a stronger king than Robert would have been had the latter returned to Normandy with William still alive and had succeeded him later. There have been recent attempts to rehabilitate Robert, arguing that the turbulent state of Normandy after 1087 owed much to factors beyond

Robert's control – especially the existence of a troublemaking rival able to stir up revolt and receive exiles – and even their ferocious father had faced minor revolt in 1077–9. If a neighbouring ruler (King Philip of France in 1077, William after 1087) was stirring up revolt, was any Norman ruler – however fierce – safe? By contrast, after 1106 Henry faced no rival in Normandy until his eldest brother's son, William 'Clito', was an adult in the late 1110s – when revolt broke out again. Henry also faced revolt from disaffected magnates in 1101–1103 as William (in England) and Robert (in Normandy) had done – though arguably any new ruler, competent and ferocious or not, faced revolt if a rival was available. Dissatisfied baronial 'chancers' were always ready to strike at a time of uncertainty, hence the usual eleventh and twelfth century occurrence of a ruler's death causing nervous magnates to hurry home and await disorder from a safe, fortified residence. So is it unfair to present the assorted revolts in Robert's Normandy as evidence of his weakness?

But the fact remains that Robert's Norman nobles felt able to defy his authority in 1087–97 and 1100–1106 unlike they did to William I in 1053–77 or Henry I after 1106. Both men faced major challenges from defiant local magnates on their accession, and William (aged seven or eight at the time, in 1035) could not stop the anarchy of his minority until he was old enough to fight; but once they had made examples of leading offenders their realms quietened down quickly. Both made a point of mutilating opponents – William notoriously did so to insolent rebel townsmen who had hung out tanners' hides on their walls as a gibe at his mother's lowly origins, but Henry mutilated a few nobles too. Among the victims of one blinding of hostages were two of Henry's own grand-daughters, handed over by the King to a noble whose son had been blinded by their father. (The girls' mother, his illegitimate daughter Juliana, then tried to shoot him with a crossbow but missed.[13]) Mutilation was seen as perfectly acceptable by contemporary standards, and by not killing the victims it gave them time to repent of their sins and so enter Heaven.

Both men also held their most dangerous State prisoners for many years, William's including Harold's brother Wulfnoth (for over thirty-five years?) and Earl Morcar and Henry's including Robert himself (for twenty-eight years). The anti-Robert disaffection did not halt after the early successes of his ducal reign (1088–91), and it cannot be put down solely to his having two troublemaking brothers ready to aid rebels, Henry within and William 'Rufus' outside Normandy. Both men may have been less pleasant individuals than Robert, but their known ferocity and killings and mutilations of enemies served to keep their Norman barons in line and Robert failed to do so. Ruling an eleventh- or twelfth-century state was not a popularity contest, and a sovereign had to be feared to secure order. The nearest equivalent to Robert's Normandy in terms of regular turbulence was Brittany, but the latter had no such tradition of long-term central control and its provincial 'decentralization' into semi-autonomous districts run by ancient families was far older. Ducal control from Rennes by a strong ruler had only (re-)emerged in the tenth century after expulsion of the Vikings, lapsed at times, and was the exception rather than the norm. There was regular defiance of central control by minor local lords in the late eleventh and early twelfth century 'Isle de France', but there Louis VI as heir and as king warred ceaselessly against it – unlike Robert did. Henry's scoffing claim after he took over Normandy that Robert could not keep order in his own household, let alone in his duchy, may have been opportunist but was hardly likely just to have been invented by Robert's detractors to please Henry. Nor was the claim that Robert's wife, Sibyl of Conversano, who died inopportunely in 1103, was a more capable ruler than him.

It is not a sufficient argument to allege that Robert had unique problems in Normandy from his accession in 1087 and return in 1100, in that rebels knew they could count on his ambitious brothers for help. The same could be said of William II in 1088 and Henry in 1100–1102, and they both faced down their challengers successfully. The argument of a 'reversionary interest' encouraging rebellion applies equally to William I, threatened in Normandy by his eldest son in 1077, and Henry, faced by his nephew William 'Clito' in the early 1120s. The former could put down the 1077 revolt despite the setbacks of defeat and personal worsting in combat by his son at Gerberoi, and the latter never faced the same level of anarchy from William 'Clito's faction as Robert did from his enemies. Both also had to contend with a hostile king of France backing rebels and fugitives. The most that can be said for Robert is that the victory of his rival Henry in 1106 made it certain that the latter would ensure that history was written by the winners and that his rule of Normandy would be presented by pro-Henry writers as anarchic. English, or Anglo-French, writers such as Eadmer and Orderic Vitalis also had the obvious contrast between a well-ordered England (good) and a turbulent Normandy (bad) to draw on, with weak governance of the latter the obvious reason for it.[14] Robert was a brave warrior and an adequate commander, as seen by his actions on the First Crusade – but did he have enough energy in controlling his barons? He could be defended more convincingly if he had the reputation for tireless aggression towards defiance that Louis VI did.

William I might nevertheless have named Robert as his heir to England as well as Normandy – it is not certain that 'feudal law' was coherent enough by 1087 to make it necessary for the paternal inheritance to go to the eldest son and the 'conquests' to younger ones. But did 'feudal law' apply to the inheritance of crowned states as well as ordinary landed possessions? As we have seen, there are no parallels with other states in France, and the lands divided among several sons in eleventh and twelfth century Spain had been inherited not conquered. Indeed, the situation as of 1087 was not that of the early years of William I's reign. Until his mysterious death in a hunting accident in the New Forest c. 1074 William's second surviving son was not 'Rufus' but his elder brother Richard (born c. 1054/6). Had he not been killed he was also ahead of Henry in the succession–stakes. There is no indication of Richard's capacity and he was probably killed while still in his teens, though later stories (written with hindsight?) have implied that he was capable and chivalrous.[15] It appears that while Richard was alive William 'Rufus' was being educated, at a rather advanced academic level for a secular ruler, by Archbishop Lanfranc, which may indicate an intention for him to enter the Church.[16] One source claimed that he took preliminary holy orders as an oblate, and it is not impossible that his father intended him to take over the role of the family's episcopal 'strongman', keeping the Church friendly, from Bishop Odo. But it is unclear if there was any such intention, or if it ended with Richard's fatal accident. Henry's reputation for being 'bookish' and erudite, deriving from William of Malmesbury, was once seen as implying that Henry 'Beauclerc' had new 'modern' concepts of the monarch's administrative role that William I and II did not; it has been 'downplayed' by modern research.

Robert as ruler of England after 1087?

The turbulence in Normandy under Robert gives a fair guide to what he would have been like as King of England, with the 'caveat' that the King had more resources to deal with rebellion easier than had a Duke of Normandy (whose rebels could always retreat across the border into the 'Isle de France' and launch raids, as Robert himself had done in 1077). The possession of more central resources in England than in Normandy would have helped Robert to keep rebellion at bay, if he could satisfy or marginalize William 'Rufus' and Henry. But can any parallels be drawn between his character, and what it might have implied for England, and the real-life defiance that met the equally courageous but lackadaisical Stephen after 1135? The latter faced repeated defiance and defections from 1136, which he failed to halt by decisive action – most notably by not capturing his challenger Matilda at Arundel in 1139 (see below). If Robert had faced one or two brothers stirring up trouble, would he have fared any better than Stephen did? The likeliest places for open defiance of the King would have been the more compact and larger lordships far from London – the Marcher lands on the Welsh Borders, where the ambitious lords acquired new lands and tenants in occupied parts of South, Central, and North Wales (Dyfed, Brecon and Radnor, and Clwyd) in the late 1080s and early 1090s, and the Scots Borders. Their distance from Winchester and London meant that royal visits there to check up on and overawe the great barons were rare, and even under the ferocious William I there was a major Marcher plot in 1075. The active and successful William II, who had already seen off the most serious potential threat to unseat him in 1088, faced a Northumbrian revolt in 1093; a less energetic or feared Robert would have been likely to face either revolt or a slipping away of his authority to local magnates unless his centrally appointed sheriffs could contain this. The capable administrator Archbishop Lanfranc died in 1089 so he would have needed a viable replacement – though he might well not have kept the archbishopric vacant and used its fiscal resources for as long as the anti-religious William II did (to 1093).

Robert's reign (he died in 1134, aged over eighty) would probably have seen blatant defiance of the King by powerful individuals and groups of lords as under Stephen – and possibly also a revolt in William's or Henry's favour. Younger brothers resenting their lack of power were a perennial nuisance to monarchs, as faced by Richard I as late as 1190–4, and if King Robert had departed on Crusade in 1096 he would have had to decide whether to allow William and Henry to stay behind as regent or to insist that they accompany him. As with Richard I in 1190–94, leaving an ambitious brother in England or Normandy would run the risk of rebellion. But Robert, unlike William II, seems to have had no major problems with the Church for alleged contempt of their 'mores' – and was backed in real-life 1088–9 by his uncle, Bishop Odo. The ruthless Earl-Bishop, who had fought at Hastings, would have made a good regent for England during the Crusade if Robert could not rely on his brothers; in real life he was by then living in Normandy after William II drove him out of England, and he accompanied Robert on Crusade and died in Sicily. Another potential episcopal regent was the able and extortionate Ranulf Flambard, Bishop of Durham and treasurer to William II and likely to have worked for Robert too had he been king. Like Richard I's extortionate episcopal regent William Longchamp in 1190–91, he could easily have faced a baronial revolt once his master had left England.

Murder or accident? The events of 2 August 1100
The useful timing of William's violent death has led to accusations that Henry and/or his adherents planned it. The supposed firer of the arrow that killed William by 'accident' on 2 August 1100, one of his hunting party called Walter Tyrrell, fled the scene[17] – but he had every reason to flee even if innocent. Henry was capable of killing him as a scapegoat, particularly given

the number of Henry's friends among the hunting party (assorted de Clares and Robert FitzHamon). Tyrrell could have been, or feared that he would be, 'framed' for a killing done by Henry's men. He was still denying that he had shot the King years later on his deathbed. He even denied that he had been in that part of the New Forest at the time,[18] while the party in attendance on the King included a number of men (e.g. FitzHamon, given the lordship of Glamorgan, and the de Clares of Tonbridge) who Henry was to reward as his close allies as King. That has led to modern claims that these men could have arranged the killing to do him a favour, with Prince Louis of France an alternative choice as a man who would have been glad to have the aggressive King out of the way and replaced by a conflict between Henry and Robert. Tyrrell, married to a de Clare, could have collaborated with them to kill William, and Emma Mason has suggested that his possession of the castellanship of the French town of Pontoise on the Norman border (in the gift of the French King) and friendship with Prince Louis was suspicious.[19] According to one chronicler, Geoffrey Gaimar, he was asking William about the route of his forthcoming campaign in northern France before the killing – was this spying for Louis, and did that extend to regicide?[20] William had been showing recent interest in expanding his interests in the duchy of Aquitaine, acting as regent while the Duke was on Crusade – which could give him the resources to challenge the King of France.

The convenient timing of claims that William was warned by a monk on the day of the killing that he had had a dream portending his death – involving an arrow?[21] – is not reliable evidence of a plot. This could be coincidence, or later gossip. The portents allegedly seen before the accident, such as a lake of blood, and other dreams hinting at immanent Divine vengeance on the blaspheming, Church-despoiling King were a common contemporary phenomenon around the time of a major disaster.[22] Nature was supposed to reflect important politico-religious crises, and stories to confirm this were collected eagerly by the impressionable. No value can be placed on a story that William allegedly gave Tyrrell an arrow on the day of the accident and told him to see that justice was done[23] – if the detail was remembered accurately he was presumably referring to 'justice' on the deer and it was an irony that the King was the one who was killed. The site of the King's residence, which he left that morning to hunt, is unknown and the nineteenth century suggestion, Castle Malwood (taken up by the novelist Charles Kingsley), was not even a hunting lodge at the time. The forest had only been taken over for hunting as a royal game preserve in the 1070s and the later main royal hunting lodge at Lyndhurst may not have been built; the largest local settlement in the 'Domesday Book', which probably had a royal hall, was Brockenhurst.

Indeed, the site of the killing is still uncertain despite a 'definitive' identification using local stories when the 'Rufus Stone' was set up near Stoney Cross, in the north of the forest, in 1745. An alternative site has been suggested, far to the south near Beaulieu – and the site of the killing was supposed to have been near that of a demolished church and there were no settlements at Stoney Cross.[24] Any 'reconstruction' of the events is thus futile. The exact circumstances of the King's killing have to be taken at the word of those at the scene, who subsequently backed Henry as his successor – and according to them William stepped into the line of shot of another hunter as a stag passed, with the setting sun dazzling them. By the usual custom William, as host, should have had the sole shot at this first deer but perhaps he had conceded this to a comrade.[25] It thus remains possible that one of Henry's men shot the King, possibly using one of Tyrrell's arrows (purloined?) and then showing this as evidence that Tyrrell had done the deed – and the sources agree that the hunting party dispersed in panic to protect their lands from a possible civil war rather than staying to hold an investigation.[26] But this is only a plausible scenario, and it would mean that Henry was prepared to gamble on surviving attack once Robert returned to Normandy in a few months' time. Whatever the truth behind the shooting, it must have seemed unlikely as of 1 August 1100 that both the King (aged between forty and forty-four) and his elder brother would be superseded by Henry.

If there had been no accident or Henry had not gambled on fratricide, then the chances are that either William or Henry would have been trying to remove Robert from his dukedom again within a few years. William was an ambitious and restless man who was prepared to become involved with faraway Aquitaine to expand his interests, and Normandy would have remained a tempting target – particularly if disorder continued there after 1100, as it did in real life. Whether it was a 'weak' Robert to blame or a meddling Henry of England or Philip of France (or Philip's son Louis) encouraging dissidents, barons continued to defy Robert until Henry finally invaded and deposed him. The same temptation may have seemed irresistible to William, encouraged by Henry – but William is unlikely to have given Henry any major power within Normandy once he took over lest his brother try to seize the entire Duchy. With Scotland ruled by an ally from 1097, the other main target for an expansionist William within mainland Britain would have been Wales, where much of lowland Gwynedd had been conquered by his vassals (led by the Earls of Chester and Montgomery) in the early-mid 1090s but mountainous Arfon and remote Anglesey were still resisting. Possibly the embattled native dynast Gruffydd ap Cynan, lord of Anglesey and a former but escaped prisoner of the Earl of Chester at that town, would have been a target for a campaign to secure all of Gwynedd and reinforce the precarious castles built on the coast at Rhuddlan and Caernarfon. William II could thus have anticipated Edward I's campaigns of 1277 and 1283–4, with less likelihood of long-term success as by 1100 castle-building had not produced such complex and secure structures as it had by the 1280s. The probability is that the Welsh would have held out inland until he ran out of supplies and had to patch up a truce leaving the mountains (and most of the coast west of the Conwy?) to them as faced invading King John in 1210. Alternatively, there were pickings in far Western Dyfed where the barons of the middle Marches had penetrated to Ceredigion (Cardigan) and set up castles since the killing of King Rhys ap Tewdr in 1093. But would William have seen his Continental French foes, fellow-knights not 'backward' Celtic dynasts, as a more worthy foe? In the latter case, if he had taken over Normandy the next logical targets were either Brittany (invaded by his father in 1064/5, as seen on the Bayeux Tapestry) or Maine and thence Anjou. The crucial question was whether he would have finally married and produced an heir, and if not which brother he would have settled on as his heir. If he had deposed Robert from Normandy and imprisoned or exiled him, then Henry was a more probable heir.

Robert's failure to dislodge Henry, 1101
Similarly, as of 1100–1106 the possibility remained that Robert would still reign as King of England, by succeeding Henry; on his return to Normandy he invaded England successfully, which he had failed to do in 1088, and landed in Hampshire. He had the advice of the refugee Bishop Ranulf Flambard of Durham, William II's brutal and acquisitive chief minister, who Henry had arrested but who had escaped from the Tower of London. He only seems to have had around 200 ships, as compared to his father's 1,000 in 1066, but this was enough to carry several thousand men and he evaded Henry's army at Pevensey, landing safely at Portsmouth with the advantage of surprise and some time to strike before his brother arrived.[27] It was on the cards that enough nobles would defect to him to enable him to win the conflict; he was a Crusader, though Archbishop Anselm had rallied the Church to Henry's side and pressurized the nobles to support him,[28] and unlike Henry he had recent experience of battle (in the testing conditions of the Middle East). Henry's marriage to the royal Saxon heiress Edith/Matilda was popular among the English people, arguably encouraging them to rally to his army, but led to some mockery from his nobles;[29] could they even have deserted him? The mass-levy of the English that Henry ordered would have been ineffective if enough senior landowners – the cavalry who had won in 1066 – had deserted him.[30]

The Saxon chronicler Eadmer implies that there were substantial noble desertions when Robert landed, and certainly these included Robert of Belleme (head of the Montgomery dynasty, lords of Shrewsbury and the central Welsh Marches) and William de Warenne of Lewes. Luckily for Henry enough nobles remained loyal for him to meet Robert on virtually equal terms, and the latter failed to seize nearby Winchester with its treasury (possibly out of chivalry as the Queen was in residence). The armies confronted each other east of Winchester, probably in the Meon valley, and their near-equal numbers would have made cautious nobles wary of fighting. Possibly Flambard, Robert's principal adviser, was persuaded by the offer of reinstatement by Henry (which he secured in the subsequent treaty) to talk Robert out of fighting. The stalemate was ended with a treaty at Alton which confirmed that Robert would renounce his claim to England but be Henry's heir if the latter had no children – a 'climb-down' for which he has been much criticized.[31] He threw away his best chance of securing England, whether betrayed by Flambard or not, though from the perspective of 1101 he may well have been too disappointed by his lack of English support to run a risk of defeat when he thought he could attack again later. We have the advantage of hindsight, and know the result – he ended up deprived of Normandy too and in Henry's prisons for twenty-eight years. But William and Robert had manoeuvred around each other warily without either achieving full success for thirteen years, and Robert would have expected that there were other chances of success. As events turned out, Henry could destroy the pro-Robert faction within England in 1103, stir up trouble in Normandy, and in 1106 invade to defeat and capture his brother.

William 'Clito': potentially more than a footnote to history?

Thereafter the only chance of depriving Henry's line of England or Normandy lay with his brother's son William 'Clito' (the name is the French equivalent of the English 'Atheling', meaning 'Throne-Worthy', and thus indicates onlookers' belief that he was a potential successor to Henry.) He was a refugee protégé of the King of France in the mid-1120s and the French nominee to rule the neighbouring county of Flanders. His candidacy may have been suggested to Henry after the death of the latter's son and heir William in 1120, the succession of a female (Henry's daughter Matilda) being unprecedented in England and Henry having no children by his new wife, Adeliza of Louvain. Some nobles seem to have backed him at the council of 1126, which discussed the issue, and 'Clito' significantly received glowing praise in the chronicle of Henry of Huntingdon, clerical deputy of Bishop Alexander of Ely (whose uncle Bishop Roger of Salisbury was Henry's chief minister and Matilda's foe).[32] Did this praise imply that

Alexander and Roger preferred the 'Clito' as the next king, in 1126, and was it significant that Henry I now removed the captive Duke Robert from Bishop Roger's castle of Devizes to his own custody? The 'Clito' was backed by his and Henry's Continental overlord King Louis VI of France[33] – though appointing him as heir would imply Henry's recognition that Robert had had a superior claim to the throne he had usurped in 1100. But in 1127 Henry ordered an oath of loyalty to be taken to Matilda, and the 'Clito' did not dare to come to the King's court but stayed in Flanders – where Henry backed the revolt of his rival Thierry of Lorraine. The 'Clito's fatal wounding during a siege in July 1128 ended the possibility that he would succeed to England. If he had been alive in 1135, it is possible that the controversy over Matilda's unpopular marriage to Count Geoffrey of Anjou would have helped him to invade successfully, as it did his cousin Stephen of Boulogne in real life. But it would have been politically risky for Henry to promote the 'Clito' as his heir (at least until Robert was dead in 1134), given the chances of the young man bearing a grudge for Robert's arrest and so staging a revolt. In a parallel case in the Eastern Roman Empire seventy years later, lackadaisical Emperor Isaac II Angelus was deposed and imprisoned by his abler brother Alexius III (1195) who lacked a son. Isaac's son Alexius, at liberty but politically excluded, then escaped to Western Europe to collect allies to invade his uncle's realm – resulting in the Fourth Crusade attacking the Empire. Logically, the politically astute Henry could well have feared a similar fate from the 'Clito'.

The unexpected identity of Henry I's successor: The 'White Ship' disaster of 1120

Notably, Henry I's daughter Matilda (born 1102?) only became his heiress due to the accidental drowning of her brother William the 'Atheling' on 25 November 1120. The prince, probably aged seventeen and recently married to his sister's future husband Geoffrey's sister Matilda of Anjou, had been accompanying his father to the peace-conference with Louis VI of France. This ended the kings' contest over Normandy since 1116 and led to William doing homage to Louis as heir to Normandy. (It is possible but uncertain that he was technically now co-ruler of the Duchy and also 'rex designatus' of England.[34]) The ship in which he was returning to England, the famous 'White Ship', loaded with junior members of the Anglo–Norman aristocracy, ran aground on rocks off the harbour – due to a drunk captain and crew trying to overtake the King's own ship, according to Orderic Vitalis. Henry himself had refused to sail in her but had given his son to the captain's care. The prince had foolishly encouraged both crew and passengers to open some casks of wine according to Orderic – who presumably received the story via the only survivor, a Rouen butcher. The state of the drunken crew (and passengers) and the unsafe number of people crowded aboard had allegedly caused some wiser young nobles, crucially including Henry's nephew the future King Stephen, to disembark before the ship left the harbour. Almost all of those on board were drowned.[35]

If this avoidable accident had not occurred William would probably have succeeded to the throne of England and the Duchy of Normandy in December 1135, aged thirty-two (?), and could have reigned for decades. There would have been no civil war or Angevin succession – though his Angevin wife should have provided a half-Angevin heir. Moreover, if Stephen had not been so alert he would have drowned and thus not been available to seize the throne on his uncle's death, providing Matilda with an unchallenged succession. (His elder brother Theobald was preoccupied ruling the County of Blois; his younger brother Henry was a cleric and so invalidated from succeeding.) At the worst, if she had proved unpopular and an attempt had been made to remove her and her husband (whose Angevin dynasty was an old rival of the Normandy barons) the absence of Stephen would have meant a search for an alternative candidate. Unlike in the eleventh century, English law was now more aligned to Southern European practice and serious claimants to the throne had to have a dynastic claim – which Cnut and Harold Godwinson had not done. Thus the death of Henry I's elder brother Robert's son William 'Clito' in 1128 left no dynastic challenger within the Norman dynasty, and the best claim lay with the descendants of Queen Margaret of Scotland. Her surviving son, King David, had strong English baronial links as husband to the heiress of Huntingdon, Earl Waltheof's daughter Matilda (the widow of Simon de Senlis, Earl of Northampton). He was an ally of Matilda, to whom he had sworn allegiance in 1128; a claim by his son Henry, heir to and later enfeoffed with Huntingdon, was possible but unlikely without David's support. The only claim outside his family would lie with any children that Stephen had had by his wife, David's sister's daughter Countess Matilda of Boulogne.

Chapter Two

Civil War: Stephen Versus Matilda

The identity of the successor: Stephen's luck in being in the right place in December 1135

The Angevin era nearly began in 1135 or 1141 not 1154. If Henry I had not died when and where he did in December 1135 in southern Normandy, with Matilda – his chosen heiress to whom he had made the magnates swear allegiance – further away from England (Anjou) than her cousin Stephen (Boulogne), Matilda could have got to England first and secured the Crown.[1] If Matilda had been in England with Henry at the time there would have been no contest, with his senior advisers – especially Bishop Roger of Salisbury – on hand to ensure that the magnates kept to their oath of allegiance to her. This would have been the case had she not remarried after the death of her first husband, Emperor Henry V, in 1125 – though her father was likely to have pushed her into remarrying to gain grandchildren and heirs. She would also have been in England had she married an Anglo-Norman noble – though that would have led to jealousy of her husband by his local rivals and King Henry was unlikely to have risked this political problem. She would have been in England too had she been married to a younger son of a Continental ally of Henry's – another possible solution for him, which did not entail her husband's county or duchy uniting with England/Normandy as was the case when she married the Count of Anjou. But was any husband of an 'inferior' rank, i.e. non-ruling, or a younger son likely to be acceptable to Henry or to the haughty Matilda (who may have regarded even a count, i.e. Geoffrey as socially inferior)?[2]

A woman ruler was a new phenomenon to the great lords who had expressed disquiet at Matilda being named as heir[3] – but once William 'Clito' was dead they could not threaten to transfer their allegiance to an obvious male rival. (Henry does not seem to have thought of Stephen, his sister's son, as a threat.) But it was not unique in Europe as Alfonso VI's daughter Urraca had succeeded him in Castile and Leon in 1109. Similarly, Alfonso's illegitimate daughter Teresa had transmitted the dynasty's claim to the county of Portugal (then part of Castile) to her son Afonso. In all cases, the identity of the heiress' husband was of prime importance. Alfonso VI also faced his son's unexpected violent death – in battle – and like Henry had to adjust to his daughter being the new heir; he married off Urraca to Raymond the brother of the Count of Burgundy (from a junior line of the royal house of France) who moved to Castile. Like Henry, Alfonso then faced his son-in-law dying before him and as a result Urraca's second husband was a neighbouring ruler, King Alfonso of Aragon (1109); this resulted in the Castilian nobles resisting Alfonso as a potential threat just as the English and Norman nobles resisted Count Geoffrey, and Urraca and Alfonso's marriage broke up. Urraca then ruled alone until she died and her son by Raymond succeeded (1126). Did this give ideas to the Anglo-Norman nobles about the feasibility of Matilda divorcing Geoffrey?

The identity of Matilda's husband was one of her main weak points as heiress – and if Matilda had still been married to her first husband, Emperor Henry V (d. 1125), her father would have had the problem of an Anglo-German union. As Matilda and the Emperor had no children there was no complication of a son of theirs having a claim on the Imperial throne as well as on England – though the imperial title was elective and at this point not always hereditary so the child would have had little chance of gaining election against adult German princes. It would have been impractical for a surviving Henry V, with a multitude of German princes to supervise, to exercise any authority in England after Matilda succeeded in 1135 even had the barons allowed it; her quarrelsome character would have made it possible that she preferred to separate from Henry and return home to govern alone (perhaps on behalf of a child from the union between Matilda and Henry).

Alternatively, had Henry V still been Matilda's husband in 1128 her father might have turned to Stephen, his elder sister's son, as his heir. A lesser possibility was legitimizing his most prominent and able (and eldest?) illegitimate son, Earl Robert of Gloucester, born around 1090 so probably two or three years older than Stephen. The succession of a bastard was frowned upon by the Church, but could occur to hold a state together – William I had succeeded to Normandy in 1035 despite being a bastard and aged around seven, for lack of an alternative. An alternative male choice to them both was Stephen's elder brother Theobald, Count of Blois, but the geographical difficulties of ruling both states would have been serious as Blois had no port to enable easy sea-access to England. Blois had access via a narrow corridor of land to Normandy, but its ruler's route down the Loire to the Atlantic lay at the mercy of Count Geoffrey of Anjou, Matilda's husband and so Theobald's rival.

Matilda's husband: A likely cause of revolt? If she had been with Henry on his death, would she have succeeded anyway? Or divorced Geoffrey?

The political coup that Henry I brought off by ending Norman-Angevin tension with his daughter's marriage to Geoffrey of Anjou in 1128 may not have been as controversial at the time as it seemed later. It is arguable that the presumed Norman baronial hostility to Anjou, cited as a cause of opposition to Matilda's succession, only became serious after her husband's brutal invasion of Normandy in the late 1130s and was not serious in 1128–35. Border disputes were always possible, but at this time the Count of Anjou was no more a potential threat to Norman lords than their other southern neighbour, Count Theobald of Blois – Stephen's brother. Geoffrey, a decade younger than Matilda, was the son of Count Fulk of Anjou, who left his county to Geoffrey in 1128 on departing to Jerusalem to marry its heiress – the widowed Empress Matilda thus married a ruling count not a landless heir, but still may have considered her husband too low for her rank. According to Geoffrey's biographer John of Marmoutier and Henry of Huntingdon, Geoffrey was intended as co-ruler of England and Normandy after his father-in-law, not just consort; William of Malmesbury implies that Henry I intended this but changed his mind when he was dying.[4] In a contemporary case, Fulk was always intended to be co-ruler of Jerusalem with his wife Melissande; the Moslem- surrounded state needed a warrior-ruler. It was normal practice for an heiress' marriage in a 'feudal' European state to see the bride's husband become co-ruler or even sole ruler, as with King Alfonso VI of Castile's daughters, Queen Urraca of Castile and Countess Teresa of Portugal. (This was logical to give them full authority to lead the army by outranking its great lords.) There was no differing English law or precedent to counter this. By the time of Henry I's death, Matilda and Geoffrey were at odds and she was spending much time with her father not in Anjou; it was thus unusual that she was back in Anjou when her father died rather than with him ready to inherit. Ironically, Henry's presence in Normandy was due to his dispute with Geoffrey over keeping control of some Norman castles promised to Geoffrey in the dowry-agreement of 1128.[5] Matilda's absence in Anjou was probably connected to her third pregnancy, her son William being born in July 1136. However, if Henry had been in England not Normandy when he died and Matilda in Anjou news of the event would still have reached Stephen, in his wife's county of Boulogne, quicker than it would have reached distant Anjou.

In retrospect 'pro-Stephen' personnel claimed that their oath to Matilda had been invalid as extorted by intimidation, and even that Henry accepted that.[6] This was incorrect. Nor is it likely that Henry would have married

Matilda to another candidate who would have been settled at the English court, as he was set on Geoffrey – a vital potential ally – as his choice from the start.[7] If Matilda cavilled at marrying a mere count, she would have found an Anglo-Norman noble or a younger son of a ruling French count or duke even more beneath her. The only available royal candidate on the British mainland was her first cousin, Henry of Huntingdon, son of her uncle King David of Scotland (acceded 1124) – too close a relative for the Church to grant a dispensation for the prohibited consanguinity. Henry was probably some years younger than her, like Geoffrey; if he had had available younger brothers the age gap would have been even greater.

But Matilda would have secured the Crown in December 1135 had she been closer to hand, which was likelier if she was not pregnant – or if Henry I had died after her son's birth in July 1136 when she had had time to quarrel with and leave Geoffrey again. Stephen would have been unlikely to challenge her at once, even with his wife's Boulogne resources. If Henry had persisted in his grudge against Geoffrey into 1136, a possibility considering their belligerent characters, he could easily have encouraged Matilda to leave him now that she had three sons to succeed to England. An arrangement could have been made for Matilda to bring one son, probably her eldest (the later Henry II, born in March 1133) to England and leave the others in Anjou as Geoffrey's heirs. Given her haughty temper and habit of alienating people, whether or not the quarrelling Matilda and Geoffrey had been together at her accession a later revolt was a possibility as one had followed the previous disputed successions in 1087 and 1100. The chances of Henry I (sixty-four at his grandson's birth) living until the latter was old enough to inherit directly were not great – though his brother Robert did live to over eighty.

The unprecedented (English) circumstances of a female succession made it logical to grant some territory and titles to the new Queen's husband, if only for the sake of his ability to maintain prestige. It is possible that Henry had decided against such a grant to Geoffrey on his deathbed,[8] as William of Malmesbury says; in that case Geoffrey could have turned up in England later demanding his 'rights' and cited the case of his father's co-rule in Jerusalem as justification. If the quarrel between him and Henry had been patched up and he had been with his wife as she succeeded to England, Matilda granting Geoffrey estates and strategic castles appropriate to his rank (with an earldom?) could have led to trouble from disappointed rivals and/or men with whom he clashed personally. Lords with estates or relatives in Normandy who were denied grants due to those made to Geoffrey were likeliest to intrigue against him. It is probable that Matilda would have used the excuse of trouble in Normandy, logically encouraged by Stephen from

Boulogne, to send Geoffrey to Normandy to act as her representative – and for him to have the rank to issue orders and grants without constant referral to her, he would have needed full ducal status. But as he lacked partisans in Normandy he would have needed to rely on his own – Angevin – lieutenants, a probable source of local anger. His only local ally was William Talvas, son of the disgraced Norman rebel Robert of Belleme, who he was asking Henry I to reinstate as of autumn 1135;[9] giving William high rank and lands would alienate those lords who had benefited from the eviction of William's family by Henry in the 1100s.

If Matilda brought her husband to England rather than using the excuse of turbulence in Normandy to require him to reside there, he would have been likely to ask for English favours for his Angevin vassals. The promotion of some of Geoffrey's trusted senior lords to office and fiefs in England would have been a focus for grievance by excluded Anglo-Norman barons feeling that they had a greater right to them, or for Matilda's half-brother Earl Robert of Gloucester and other local supporters to encourage her to resist Geoffrey's claims for patronage. Robert, lord of Glamorgan and the most powerful of the Marcher barons whose geographically contiguous estates gave them an advantage over other magnates in raising private armies, would have been a crucial figure at court. He was a possible leader of a 'coup' to force Geoffrey's exile if it came to a clash between Geoffrey and local English lords – possibly with Matilda's connivance if her husband had been showing his ambitions to dominate her government. But Geoffrey had no brothers or adult sons to whom to delegate rule of his own domains, and it is logical that the task of ruling his own Anjou and Normandy would have been enough to keep him out of England for most of the time.

The nature and timing of a civil war: Would different timing to the outbreak have made a quick decisive blow more likely?

Stephen's real-life supporters by the late 1130s were mostly in the centre and east of England, though we should be cautious about assuming that men who backed him against Matilda in the late 1130s would have been prepared to revolt against an incumbent Queen Matilda on his behalf. He had to win over the most crucial senior magnates in this region – men like the Beaumont brothers (lords of Warwickshire and Leicestershire), their Warenne half-brother (lord of Surrey), Geoffrey de Mandeville (Essex), and Hugh Bigod (Norfolk) – in 1136–40 with a series of concessions.[10] Usually the landed magnate dominating a particular county received the earldom of that county, thus reversing the Conqueror's careful avoidance of making any one magnate powerful in a particular geographical area apart from the Marches. Indeed, the grants of blocs of territory to closely related allies –

Worcester went to the Beaumonts, already dominating the Midlands – raised the danger of the emergence of substantial areas becoming dominated by one family to the detriment of the King. This creation of local 'principalities' was the norm in feudal France and was logical for the Blois noble Stephen to pursue, but it was not usual in most of England.

Stephen did initially keep William de Roumare, needing a reward as his loyal governor in rebel-affected Normandy in 1137, out of the earldom of Lincolnshire (close to his half-brother Ranulf's Cheshire lands) and place him in Cambridge instead. But this was resisted as such a role needed appropriately large estates in the county,[11] and most of William's lands were in Lincolnshire not Cambridgeshire. It was more suitable from recipients' points of view to give them control of a county where they had inherited estates and could support their administrative role adequately, and when Stephen finally gave William the earldom of Lincolnshire without the county town's castle (1140) the latter tried to seize it by force and precipitated the battle in which Stephen was captured. Matilda would have had this problem too, leading to the threat of revolt from disappointed applicants with claims on particular districts. Any accession after 1087 meant a new 'share out' of lands and offices and the probability that disgruntled losers would turn to the new sovereign's rivals, sparking off revolt – Matilda's alleged arrogance or Stephen's alleged weakness were not the causes of revolt in a political system geared to armed competition for power on each accession. Revolt would have been implausible only if there was no potential rival monarch ready to strike against the new sovereign. That was most likely had Henry I's son William lived and succeeded in 1135 as 'William III'; a monarch's sole, adult son was virtually unchallengeable.

Matilda would have had to grant similar concessions to Stephen's to make up for a weak position as a female ruler, and be even more generous to the Church under its papal legate, Stephen's brother Bishop Henry of Winchester. Indeed giving in to the Bishop's demands on local grants for himself as Abbot of Glastonbury in the south-west would have caused discontent from rival landowners. These grants – in real life by Stephen, but probably made by any new sovereign in 1136 – went beyond the usual promises to rule more justly and cancel oppressive laws that a new king made, e.g. Henry's promises concerning the laws in 1100.[12] They laid the ground for a concentration of local power in the hands of a small number of powerful magnates across the country, raising the possibilities of the latter being able to develop virtually autonomous powers under a preoccupied ruler – and to blackmail the latter into leaving their power intact by threatening to back a dynastic rival. When demands were not met or the ruler sought to claw back lost powers of local patronage (e.g. over appointments to sheriffdoms) or seized royal lands, revolt would follow. Matilda would have faced this as Stephen did, with her husband's claims to land or office in England or Normandy as her consort a potential 'flashpoint'. The difference is that her uncle King David would have been less likely to encroach on the kingdom of England's northern frontier in 1136 and 1138, demanding more lands and titles for himself or his son Henry and effectively blackmailing Stephen until he was taken on militarily at Northallerton by the Northern lords and Archbishop of York. David had a claim on Carlisle, as part of Cumbria, which had previously been Scottish until William II had evicted Earl Dolfin and built Carlisle Castle in 1092, and may have governed part of Cumbria for Henry I as well as governing his neighbouring 'appanage' of Strathclyde and Lothian for his brother King Alexander of Scots before 1124. Logically he would thus have had personal ties with the local lords to call on an in invasion, quite apart from the links in Northern England of his own Norman vassals in Scotland – houses including Fitzalan/Stewart, de Brus, and Morville.

Given the opportunity for discontented lords to back an invading claimant to the throne – as in 1088 and 1102 – Stephen would have been likely to receive support from Matilda's or Geoffrey's enemies within a few years of her accession. An invasion would have followed, though he might have concentrated first on Normandy if the alienation of the Norman barons from their local Angevin enemies led to a conspiracy to deny Geoffrey power over the duchy. The first plan of a France-based potential challenger to the ruling King of England/Duke of Normandy was usually subversion in restless Normandy, an easier matter than intervening in England as it had a land not sea-border. Also, the King of France was usually ready to intervene to undermine the Norman ruler – though in 1137 the King of France was the young and relatively timid Louis VII (born 1121) who had his hands full with his marriage to Duchess Eleanor of Aquitaine. His help for a revolt was unlikely for a year or two. Thus William I's eldest son, Robert, had acted to stir up Norman revolt with French aid in the late 1070s and William 'Clito' had acted similarly after 1120.

The 'new men' magnates of Henry's reign who had been closest to the King, such as the Beaumonts, might well have remained loyal to the Crown – and to their late patron's wishes for Matilda's succession – provided that they were bought off, and Matilda would have had the backing of Henry's justiciar Bishop Roger of Salisbury (with his Wiltshire castles) and his nephew Nigel of Ely (with his castles of Newark and Sleaford). Lords with geographical 'power-bases' usefully close to the East coast could have been tempted to defect to Stephen and been encouraged by him. Logically the ever-acquisitive Geoffrey de Mandeville, controlling the Tower of London as well as Essex and later able to perpetrate a reign of terror in the early 1140s as a classic 'robber baron', was a candidate for this reaction. Earl Ranulf of Chester, a Northern foe of any claims by King David, and his half-brother William de Roumare had ambitions in Yorkshire and Lincolnshire under Stephen, and denial of local power to them in favour of the Scots King, his son Henry, a 'loyalist' Angevin newcomer, or the Beaumonts (who Stephen was to use to counter their power) was a possible cause for revolt.

Matilda could not have satisfied all claims to local influence in areas where magnates' interests clashed, and was as likely as Henry to attempt to claw back some power after her initial grants by taking on potential traitors. He had challenged the disloyal Montgomery family, possessors of a dangerous bloc of territory and body of armed retainers on the Marches, and driven them out of England; the weaker position of the new sovereign in 1135–6 would have meant more royal concessions then than in 1100 and so a greater risk of local control slipping to magnates.

Even if Geoffrey had been in Normandy as Matilda's governor – their marriage was not noted for connubial affection – and Earl Robert been her lieutenant in England that could have sparked off revolt across the Channel. Distrusting the prospect of a union between Anjou and Normandy, the new King Louis VII of France was married in 1137 to the heiress of Aquitaine, Duchess Eleanor, in a massive boost for the reach of the French Crown – and was capable of accepting the homage of a meddling Stephen for Normandy and denying his backing as overlord to Geoffrey and Matilda. Could he have persuaded his wife to send her vassals in Poitou to attack Anjou from the south and take Geoffrey in the rear? That would spark off revolt against Geoffrey in Normandy, with the rebels able to receive support from Stephen's Boulogne to the north-east and from the French King's lands in the Vexin to the south-east. Matilda was to be accused of excessive haughtiness and a refusal to grant politic concessions to potential supporters who then unnecessarily turned on her (e.g. Simon de Senlis) in her hour of triumph in 1141. Given the probability of similar attempts to enforce her control of her vassals as Queen (or 'Lady of England'?) in the late 1130s, contenders who lost out in demands for lands and office were as likely to revolt against her as they did against Stephen in real life.

Had Matilda not Stephen succeeded Henry I? The probable course of Stephen's attack on an incumbent Matilda

Stephen could have invaded from Boulogne to Kent, East Anglia, or the Humber (to link up with Roumare and/or the Earl of Chester) in the late 1130s if he had not been preoccupied with fighting Geoffrey over Normandy. The aged Archbishop of Canterbury, William of Corbeil, was a political nullity and died in 1136 so the leadership of the Church would have been disputed between Bishop Roger of Salisbury, Henry's justiciar (and accused in real life in 1139 of supporting Matilda), and Stephen's brother Henry, Bishop of Winchester and Abbot of Glastonbury. An ambitious politician and in 1139 the new papal legate, Henry was not automatically a supporter of his brother and was rumoured (and said by Matilda) to have been among the aristocrats who invited her to invade England.[13] Matilda was capable of quarrelling with Bishop Roger and seeking to diminish his power as Stephen did in reality, though as he was her father's closest adviser and he had backed her claim to the throne since 1128 this was not that likely. But the Bishop's advancing years in the late 1130s and Bishop Henry's role as the new papal legate (which rank he gained in 1139, independently of Roger's disgrace) would have made Henry the main political actor in the episcopate. Keen on adopting papal-instigated measures for Church 'reform' – and dimunition of secular influence – Bishop Henry would have been seeking a more independent role for the Church than Henry I had allowed it. He was capable of trying to force strict terms out of Matilda for her support, and a clash followed whether or not Matilda had forcibly taken over Bishop Roger's secular power-base of castles. Henry would then have been tempted to seek better terms for the Church from his brother Stephen, and used his own castles in his Winchester bishopric to let Stephen into Hampshire if he and Matilda failed to come to an agreement. Stephen would have been likely to land around Portsmouth Harbour and head for Henry's Winchester on his arrival to start a revolt, as in real life in 1139 Matilda headed for her stepmother Adelaide of Louvain's castle of Arundel in nearby Sussex.

Once Bishop Henry was suspected of disloyalty the Angevins would have been keen to deprive him of his strategic castles, especially his fortified palace of Wolvesey in Winchester, but he would have resisted an Angevin attempt to curtail his power. As in summer 1141, Winchester would have been a likely site for an armed clash between the rival factions – even if Stephen had not landed by then. In real life Stephen besieged the suspect Bishop Roger's castles to remove his secular power; Matilda (or Earl Robert of Gloucester or Geoffrey on her behalf) would have ended up besieging Bishop Henry's castles. Henry was capable of decoying Matilda and her army down to Winchester for a confrontation while Stephen crossed from Boulogne to Kent to march on London, with the attitude of Geoffrey de Mandeville at the Tower crucial for the invader's success. If Matilda had by then quarrelled with her Angevin husband, or he was preoccupied in Normandy, she would have needed another reliable commander to fight Stephen for her. Earl Robert of Gloucester, as the principal pro-Matilda magnate in the Welsh Marches, his brother Earl Reginald of Cornwall, and

Baldwin de Redvers (lord of Devon and the Isle of Wight) were the logical leaders of an army to tackle Bishop Henry at Winchester.

But if Matilda had alienated enough lords in the Midlands and East of England with her initial appointments and land-grants an invading Stephen could have had the benefit of more support for an invasion than the would-be usurper Duke Robert of Normandy had had in 1101–1102. Controlling London thanks to de Mandeville, a victory over Matilda's army as it marched back from Winchester would then have given him a solid bloc of territory and concentration of castles to continue a long-term war. Crucially, he could have been crowned as rival sovereign had the Church in Canterbury come over to his side – and the lack of English precedent for a female being crowned would have provided the new Archbishop of Canterbury (Theobald of Bec as in real life?) an excuse to withdraw allegiance from Matilda.

The barons in Normandy included a number of opportunists and brigands willing to play off rival members of the ducal dynasty against each other. Men had risen against the easy-going (or weak) Duke Robert between 1087 and 1096 and after 1100, and had tried to use his son William 'Clito' against Henry's strong rule after 1106. After 1136 some of them plotted against Stephen. The rule of the neighbouring Count of Anjou, on behalf of his wife Matilda would have stirred up discontent, with the French kings ever willing to support rebels in order to diminish his main rivals for control of the North of France. By 1137 or 1138 Norman barons could well have risen against Geoffrey's rule, and Stephen invaded from Boulogne to act as their leader. This would have required Matilda to send troops to Normandy to fight him, accompanied by Geoffrey if he had been in England when the rising occurred. Diverting troops to Normandy would have weakened her position in England and made her open to pressure for grants of land and office by 'power brokers' such as Bishop Henry, and Matilda was clearly not known for her emollience so her angry refusal to be blackmailed would have sparked off revolt.

Her dependence on her uncle King David of Scots would have weakened the loyalty of Northern barons, particularly if she had had to accede to David's demands for Cumbria and Northumberland (which he forced out of Stephen in real-life 1136). David had ruled from Carlisle as viceroy for his brother Alexander of Scotland in the 1110s, and was unlikely to give up his claim to Cumbria – the southern part of the old kingdom of Strathclyde, united with Scotland in the early eleventh century – to ease his niece's problems. At best he could have avoided claiming Northumberland (once part of the Anglo-Saxon Earldom ruled by his wife's father, Waltheof, son of Siward), though he would have been asserting his son Henry's right to the Northamptonshire and Huntingdon lands (and the earldom of the latter) that Waltheof had also held. The ambitions of Earl Ranulf of Chester and William de Roumare in the North made them the likeliest local rivals of the Scots, and if Matilda had sought to deny them control of important lands and castles on behalf of a third party (a Beaumont?) instead of David or Henry of Huntingdon revolt was equally possible. If Matilda had sought to build up Henry of Huntingdon's role by giving him neighbouring Lincoln (earldom or county town's castle), or appointed a 'new man' there, it would have turned William of Roumare against her. That would have led to him and his half-brother Ranulf of Chester revolting, as in real life they did against Stephen, and possibly Stephen sailing to the Wash or the Humber to join in. The attitude of Earl Hugh Bigod of Norfolk, who in real life auctioned his loyalties throughout the turbulence of Stephen's reign and revolted against Henry II as late as 1173, would have been crucial to Stephen's chances. Even if there was no quarrel between Matilda and Bishop Henry, leading to a confrontation at Winchester that benefited an invading Stephen, the situation in the East Midlands could have led to a confrontation over Lincoln as in real-life 1141.

'Nineteen long winters when Christ and His Saints slept': Inevitable? How Stephen or Matilda could have won at an early date. Was Stephen's initial position in 1135–8 no worse than William II's or Henry I's, and worsened by his leniency?

After Stephen was captured by Matilda's men in early 1141 at Lincoln the indecisive civil war could have been ended. The stalemate that an evenly balanced situation between the supporters of the two claimants to England had created by 1140 was enhanced by the nature of twelfth century warfare – it centred around sieges of castles, and with an endless round of sieges it was rarely decisive unless one power had overwhelming military superiority and/or the capture of important castellans forced their supporters to surrender their castles.

The crucial event in the outbreak of civil war was Earl Robert of Gloucester's decision to renounce his fealty to Stephen and claim that his oath to Matilda in 1126 took precedence. This was announced by his messengers to Stephen in late spring 1138, as the King was either in Hereford (a rebel town and castle recently forced to surrender) or en route back to Gloucester.[14] The Earl himself appears to have been in Normandy, where he had stayed on to force a truce on the duchy's threatening neighbour Geoffrey of Anjou (Matilda's husband) after Stephen ended his own campaign there in 1137. Robert had had qualms about swearing allegiance to Stephen after the latter's surprise coup, and had stayed away from his court as long as he dared until forced to come and swear allegiance on pain of war in 1136. It is unclear if he swore allegiance unconditionally or, according to one source, on condition that he would be maintained in his current status – presumably meaning the same honour and influence at court that his father Henry I had granted him.[15] If this is true, it indicates that he was 'touchy' as to his security and power – and an alert king would have been careful to conciliate and to watch him. His potential for revolt was thus already an issue, and his participation in the 1137 Norman campaign had seen him at odds with royal favourites such as the mercenary commander William of Ypres. Apparently, the Archbishop of Rouen had to mediate between him and his enemies,[16] and it is possible that his 'semi-detached' status at court and the threat of mischief-makers denouncing him to the King pushed him over the brink into revolt. Quite independent of his 'conscience', he may have feared being sidelined from power or even deprived of his lands and decided to strike first. It was impossible for a ruler to please all contending factions at his court indefinitely and a grant of lands, office, a wife, or a royal ward to one contender could cause defeated rivals to revolt in favour of a pretender. This was a normal hazard, and was not restricted to allegedly 'weak' kings whose vassals were not afraid of reprisals if they revolted; even the ruthless William I and II had not been secure from plots in the years of their greatest power (1075 and 1093 respectively). Keeping Earl Robert at court in the King's entourage for a few years as a 'hostage' and/or offering him reassurance and riches would not have worked for Stephen 'long term'; a great lord was expected to be free to come and go as he pleased. Once he did revolt, he had the quantity of castles and men to make his rebellion dangerous and a 'bloc' of territory weeks' march from London. But most acts of armed defiance were usually containable if the king acted quickly; in 1138 he was able to regain rebel-held Hereford and Shrewsbury with swift action. (The local Marcher rebels on these occasions, Gilbert de Lacy/Geoffrey Talbot at Hereford and William FitzAlan at Shrewsbury, were prompted by the usual matter of private grudges over landholding not by loyalty to a rival claimant to the throne.[17]) Similarly, in 1136 Stephen had moved quickly to besiege Exeter when Baldwin de Redvers revolted there and the revolt had not spread. This was normal procedure for a new king facing 'tests' from defiant nobles, and swift and harsh action with overwhelming force had worked for William II and Henry I in parallel cases in 1088 and 1101–1103. The action of Earl Robert in declaring for a rival claimant to the throne in 1138 was no worse than that of those nobles who defected from the incumbent kings in 1088 and 1101–1103, with the 1088 rebels having control of an even more strategically dangerous castle (Rochester) than Robert's Bristol was in 1138. The advantage that Bristol possessed for its rebel garrison was access by river, which enabled supplies to be brought in easier than the rebels had been able to do at Rochester in the parallel case of 1088. But in both cases the strength of the castles' walls and the poor state of development of siege-artillery meant that the rebel strongholds could not be stormed easily. The de Montgomery family, defying Henry I in 1102–1103 in the Northern Welsh Marches, had been further away from the King's centre of power but had not had such semi-impregnable castles; it had taken Henry time to invade their remote estates but once he did so he had less difficulty than Stephen did in 1138.

The failure of Stephen to press forward west and blockade Bristol successfully was thus excusable and not just due to his alleged weakness of resolve. He faced a serious problem in retaking Robert's principal stronghold; though it can be argued that his main fault was allowing Robert to remain in Normandy in 1137–8 rather than keeping him at court under surveillance. The views of contemporary chroniclers are vital evidence on how the crises that faced him were viewed at the time – and on why so many of his vassals felt it safe to take up arms and his dangerous inability to make his vassals fear him. On this issue, opinion is clear that he was seen as weak and ineffective after his failure to punish the rebels who had seized Exeter and been blockaded into surrender in 1136. The rebel garrison held a strong-walled castle in a walled ex-Roman town, which had already revolted against William I in 1068, and the siege took three months and cost much money. But the castle well's water was running out when they sued for terms, so they could not have held out much longer. They were granted easy terms and nobody was executed or deprived of their lands – de Redvers was obliged to leave England – whereas Stephen had had the option of waiting another week or two to force surrender on harsher (or no) terms and making an example of the rebels. Apparently, his brother Bishop Henry of Winchester advised this, but was ignored. Both Henry of Huntingdon and John of Worcester say that Stephen's leniency was much criticized and was counter-productive.[18] Certainly contemporary opinion was that this action was important in presenting an image of a king who could be defied safely, and this may well have added to the number of those prepared to assist Earl Robert in rebellion in 1138. It is doubtful if Robert himself would have been too careful to avoid rebelling at some point, and he certainly presented his decision to defy Stephen as driven by his conscience (over his oath to Matilda in 1126) and approved by Churchmen who he had consulted. The historian William of Malmesbury believed that he was sincere.[19]

Stephen could already have stopped the civil war in its infancy when he managed to corner the newly arrived Matilda at her stepmother's second husband William d'Albini's castle of Arundel in 1139. The castle – a large double 'ward', one to either side of a central tower on a 'motte', as at

Windsor – was blockaded into offering terms, but Stephen allowed Matilda safe passage to her half-brother Earl Robert at Bristol rather than requiring Matilda to surrender, which was the logical outcome of a longer siege. This was a political disaster of the first order, and showed his difference of temperament from his ruthlessly effective grandfather William I, uncles William II and Henry I and mother, Adela. One interpretation of this apparent over-confidence has it that imprisoning a woman would have been to the detriment of his chivalric instincts, though more plausibly he was unwilling to continue the siege for another few weeks with the current revolt spreading. Her half-brother Earl Robert (lord of Glamorgan) held Bristol, and another revolt was underway in the south-west as the exiled Baldwin de Redvers (of Wight and Christchurch as well as Exeter) returned to his Devon lands. Stephen needed to march against the rebels in person as he could not trust his leading 'loyalist' magnates; he could afford to let Matilda go free from Arundel to concentrate on military victory. The author of the *Gesta Stephani* subsequently claimed that Bishop Henry had advised Stephen to let Matilda leave unharmed and advised that it would be easier to tackle and capture Matilda and Earl Robert when they were together. (Robert had already left Arundel for Bristol before Stephen, who had been guarding the Hampshire or Dorset coast, arrived.) The question must arise if the devious Henry was playing a double game and was not as loyal to Stephen as he pretended – the longer the war went on the higher price both claimants would pay for his support. Henry had intercepted Earl Robert, en route to Bristol, on his way to Arundel and let him travel on after a friendly discussion and kiss of peace – was this cousinly courtesy or double dealing?[20]

Whether or not Matilda reached Bristol to lead the revolt would not matter, provided that Stephen could stamp the latter out quickly as he had done earlier risings. The sooner he reached Bristol to besiege the rebel leadership, the less the chance of other castellans taking the risk of rising against him. He had adequate troops with him, as he had been expecting to intercept the rebels on landing – possibly at Wareham or Southampton. He had showed that he could be ruthless in punishing the defenders of a rebel town, and thus terrifying other rebels into abandoning their resistance, at Shrewsbury in 1138 – a change from his action at Exeter in 1136 – and could repeat that tactic.[21] Doing this at Arundel was unlikely from a chivalrous point of view – it was the property of the late King's widow Queen Adeliza, who needed to be won over more subtly and was probably by now married off to the royal official William d'Albini. Stephen needed to follow Matilda to Bristol, blockade the castle there, and prevent her from rallying her supporters. Another round of mass-hangings of (low-class) rebels at Bristol, as at Shrewsbury, and throwing some of Earl Robert's knights in prison for a lengthy term would have served as a warning that he was not to be defied. In that sense, the personal possession of Matilda was less important than a quick campaign to overawe her supporters – and a delay at Arundel to ensure her unconditional surrender would frustrate that aim. Stephen was not to know at Arundel in autumn 1139 that this rebellion would spread too far for him to achieve the success that he had done against risings in 1136–8. But his failure to follow up his 'success' at Arundel by attacking Bristol was a serious mistake. It had its military logic as the town and castle of Bristol were strongly walled and had river-access down the Avon to the Bristol Channel, enabling supplies to be brought in; a siege would have needed a large army and a lengthy blockade.

If Stephen had attacked Bristol in later 1139 or spring 1140, it would have diverted his attention from nearer London and so enabled more potential defectors to risk abandoning him. He could thus have lost the strategically vital adherence of Brian FitzCount, lord of Wallingford Castle, as in real life. But at least his military presence in the Bristol region would have shown that he was not to be defied – as he had shown in 1138 by an equally risky advance far into the turbulent Marches to attack rebel-held Hereford and Shrewsbury. (Both had surrendered.) He had at least some trustable foreign mercenaries already – men from his wife's county of Boulogne, brought in by her in 1138 to take Dover Castle.[22] Psychologically, an offensive against Bristol was therefore likely to have impressed 'waverers' more than being cautious as he was in real life. Instead, within weeks of the Empress' arrival there two more major magnates – Miles of Gloucester, whose lands around that town could cut Bristol off from Earl Robert's lands in Glamorgan, and Brian FitzCount of Wallingford – had defected. Stephen proceeded to besiege Wallingford instead, but soon moved off to attack Trowbridge whereupon Earl Robert relieved Wallingford by driving off the remaining besiegers.[23] From now on Matilda had major castles in the middle Thames and Wiltshire regions inhibiting any attack by Stephen on her base at Bristol.

Significantly, when faced with a similar threat from two – male – claimants to his throne in 1106 Henry I had imprisoned his brother Duke Robert for life but not imprisoned the latter's young son William 'Clito'. The latter had been at liberty to escape to Henry's enemies and pursue his claim to the throne as an adult. Imprisoning a woman, even one already in armed revolt, was contrary to current social 'mores' among the knightly class as William of Malmesbury makes clear. It would have raised the chances of her sympathizers attempting to free her, or rallying to Earl Robert at Bristol out of (real or opportunistic) indignation; the difficulty of a quick resolution in a conflict centred on siege-warfare meant that the more castles were seized the longer the revolt would last. But Stephen had a chance to use this opportunity to secure Matilda in person and attempt to induce her to renounce her claim to the throne in return for her freedom. The accounts of his character show that if she refused he was not the man to imprison her for life as King John would do to his potential rival Eleanor of Brittany (and in effect Henry II did to his wife Eleanor after she took part in their sons' rebellion in 1173). At a later stage in the civil war, Stephen memorably threatened a rebellious Wiltshire castellan, John Fitz Gilbert the Marshal, with throwing the latter's captive son over the walls from a trebuchet if he did not surrender but was not able to go through with it.[24] The boy survived to be the most famous knight in England – and as King John's chief general arguably saved the English throne for John's nine-year-old son, Henry III, when John died in the middle of a French invasion in 1216. William Marshal, regent of England in 1216–19, thus owed his life to Stephen's scrupulousness.

Matilda was a stubborn character, insistent on her rights throughout, and later had the courage to escape from besieged Oxford castle across enemy lines during a snowstorm.[25] She would no doubt have renounced any promise later as given under duress with Church absolution and started another revolt. But Stephen could have attempted to use the opportunity to seize her and then bargain with Earl Robert, possibly exchanging her for Bristol and thus neutralizing the main centre of rebellion for the moment, or shipped her back to Anjou. The latter would have postponed her next invasion until she had enough time and money to build a new army. As events turned out, the concentration of rebel power in the Marches and the Severn valley was boosted by her arrival and apparently many local magnates swore allegiance to her. She was able to set up her base at Gloucester and secure most of Wales, while the rebellion in the south-west similarly prospered. Despite the adherence of most of the south-east and Midlands and a useful army of mercenary Flemings, Stephen was unable to take decisive action against so many rebel castles and 1140 saw effective stalemate between two evenly matched sides. Compared with the situation in pre-Norman England where revolts and civil wars were rarely long-drawnout affairs, the nature of Anglo-Norman defensive architecture thus aided the ability of post-1066 rebels to hold out in unstormable castles and threatened royal authority.

Matilda fails to win despite capturing Stephen, 1141

The continuation of the civil war – now at a virtual equilibrium – depended on the failure of two rounds of peace-talks that Bishop Henry took the lead in arranging in 1140. First he used his authority as papal legate to call a meeting near or at Bath around midsummer, with him, Archbishop

Theobald of Canterbury, and Queen Matilda representing Stephen and Earl Robert the only high-ranking representative of Matilda. This failed, and Bishop Henry proceeded to France to consult the new king, Louis VII, his adviser Abbot Suger of St Denis, other leading churchmen, and Stephen's brother Count Theobald of Blois. He brought back a set of proposals, to which the Empress agreed but which Stephen refused. Details then are unknown, but the participation of the King of France – overlord of Normandy, Blois, Boulogne and Anjou – and people such as Theobald and the Queen suggests that the family interests of both Stephen's and the Empress' families in the long term were being considered. The Pope had backed Stephen's election, coronation, and right to the throne as all legal and it is very unlikely that he would ever have abdicated his Crown voluntarily; but the future of Normandy was another matter. It has been suggested that the eventual terms of settlement in 1153 give a clue to what was intended, with the Empress' son Henry (II), aged seven in 1140, succeeding Stephen in England so that her claims of 'right' were upheld via her son (who would probably be adult by the time that Stephen, now in his late forties, died). Normandy, however, might well have been assigned to Stephen's son Eustace, with the French King pleased to keep England and Normandy divided; Boulogne would go to Eustace's younger brother and Anjou to the Empress' second son.[26] This was logical, and the war seemed at a stalemate; but Stephen seems to have preferred to gamble that he could use his advantage of having a majority of the English magnates on his side to wear the enemy down. The war continued.

The capture of Stephen at Lincoln in February 1141 seemed a 'tipping-point', as a quarrel with Earl Ranulf of Chester, custodian of the Royal castle there, led to Stephen dismissing him and Ranulf appealing to Earl Robert for aid. Stephen marched quickly up from London to besiege the castle, and Robert brought a large army to the rescue, including both landowners forfeited by the King who had nothing to lose (such as Baldwin de Redvers) and Welsh mercenaries led by King Madoc of Powys and Cadwaladr, brother of Owain of Gwynedd. Numbers seem to have been around equal and the battle-site is unclear so any royal mistakes cannot be identified, but it is possible that Stephen was over-confident (fighting against the King in person was treason so some rebels might be hesitant) and the 'disinherited' and the Welsh fought more ferociously than the royal knights were used to. For reasons of prestige declining battle was not a viable option for Stephen, but his cavalry wing – led by six earls – proved deficient and was routed by Earl Robert's charge. The more 'professional' mercenary army under William of Ypres drove the Welsh back but was unable to save the day and once the royalists were in disarray they prudently withdrew, unmolested.

Rather than entrusting himself to them the valiant but naïve Stephen, who did not have a horse handy, carried on fighting on foot with a battle-axe until he was overwhelmed, and then refused to surrender to a 'commoner' who overpowered him and insisted on doing so to Earl Robert instead.[27] His prowess as a knight outmatched his strategic competence.

The possibility of Stephen being killed in the melee at Lincoln was relatively small, as he would have been identifiable by his heraldic surcoat and he was a potential source of a huge ransom to whoever captured him. It was rare for 'high-status' individuals to be killed in twelfth-century warfare, as there was a 'culture' of knightly restraint in such matters; capture and ransom was the established practice among the upper classes. (The lower orders were another matter.) Those kings who were overthrown and killed in battle were Scandinavian, operating in a starker world than that of international chivalry. It was very rare for a king or senior lord to be killed in battle in the 'chivalric' world, except in the Crusades or in Spain where they were fighting the 'infidel'; several rulers of the principality of Antioch were killed in Syria in battle at this time (Roger in 1119 and Bohemund II in 1130) but no kings were killed in western Europe. The next king to die in an inter-Christian battle was Peter II of Aragon, killed fighting the 'Albigensian Crusade' at Muret in southern France in a bitter struggle for land and faith where his opponents viewed him as an apostate ally of 'heretics'. Richard I of England was to be mortally wounded by a crossbow-shot from the walls of a minor castle in Poitou, which he was besieging in April 1199; the chances of Stephen being killed by a fluke shot or sword-stroke in a siege was higher than the danger at Lincoln. Perhaps his most dangerous moment was when he was leaping forward close to the walls of Ludlow Castle to slice through a grappling-iron that had entangled his protégé Earl Henry of Huntingdon (son of King David of Scotland and so his cousin) in May or June 1139. He rescued Henry from being hauled up into the castle as a prisoner, but could easily have fallen to an arrow-shot from the walls in the process.[28] This incident rather than the battle of Lincoln in February 1141 is the most obvious occasion for asking 'what if Stephen had been killed in the civil war?' In either case, the answer must be that the Empress would have been likely to secure victory on easier terms than she did in spring 1141, when Stephen was still alive and potentially ransomable so his wife and his remaining landed adherents could hope to remedy the situation. Matilda had to negotiate for assorted magnates to accept her rule after her adherents captured Stephen; if he had been killed their focus of loyalty would have been his eldest son, Eustace, at most a teenager. Queen Matilda, his mother, Stephen's wife and the Empress' cousin, would possibly have held out on his behalf, with William of Ypres and his army; but most magnates are likely to have deserted to the winner quickly provided that they were promised pardon and guaranteed their lands.

In real life, the battle of Lincoln was not enough to tip the balance of fortunes immediately in Empress Matilda's favour but it opened the pathway to her victory if it could be followed up. William of Ypres and the Queen remained at large in Kent with a substantial force, but the war seemed lost with the person of the King and most senior lords could be expected to negotiate terms for their surrender as the only realistic option. There was no sense of 'blood-feud' caused by assorted executions and extra-judicial killings of the 'losing party', as in the civil wars of the period 1455–71 where each swing of fortune led to the deaths of assorted unlucky nobles caught fighting for the loser. This civil war was certainly not more genteel for the ordinary citizenry or those caught in the path of a marauding baron such as Geoffrey de Mandeville, but among the elite the struggle hinged on whether the oath taken to Matilda by the magnates in 1126 was legal or breakable. (This matter of 'conscience' was the explicit excuse for Robert of Gloucester deserting Stephen in 1138 and was probably sincere on his part.[29]) Practical politics led to a considerable number of magnates switching allegiance to Matilda, and in Normandy most of the magnates accepted the claim of Geoffrey of Anjou after their first choice – Stephen's and Bishop Henry's elder brother Count Theobald of Blois – turned them down. Theobald attempted to get Geoffrey to back releasing Stephen on condition that the deposed King received a guarantee of the lands he had held of Henry I as of December 1135, one possible solution to the civil war had Stephen seen his position as hopeless and so agreed.[30] In this case, Stephen would have had to agree that he could seek absolution for his anointing at his coronation and his coronation-oath from the Church. 'Cancelling out' an act of coronation would have been legally difficult and unprecedented, but the Archbishop who had performed it (William of Corbeil) was dead so it could be alleged that Stephen had tricked him and the coronation was thus invalid. Theobald was apparently annoyed in 1135/6 that the argument that the oath to the Empress in 1126 was invalid so a son of Adela of Blois was rightful king should have given him, not Stephen, 'first refusal' of the Crown.[31] Fraternal jealousy could have led to him acting as mediator between Matilda and his younger brother and offering Stephen rich landed rewards for renouncing the Crown but would Stephen have listened? Would Stephen's wife have eventually backed Theobald in order to save a large inheritance for their sons, perhaps part of Normandy added on to Boulogne?

Other English lords held out, most notably the Beaumonts and Simon de Senlis who controlled the central Midlands, but they could have been dealt with piecemeal once Matilda was crowned. It is probably only special pleading for the author of the *Gesta Stephani* to allege that Bishop Henry, leading the Church, only negotiated with and seemed to accept Matilda to win time[32] – political reality would have had to be recognized if Stephen's partisans did not rally. It is true that the Norman magnates turned to Geoffrey, not Matilda, as their choice of ruler once Count Theobald turned them down. But already one female ruler, Melissande of Jerusalem (as the heiress of her father like Matilda) had been accepted as co-ruler of her kingdom on her accession in 1131 – ironically, her husband and partner was Geoffrey of Anjou's father, Fulk, who had left Anjou to Geoffrey in order to take up the marriage.

In 1143 Melissande was to continue as Queen on Fulk's death, with her teenage son Baldwin III as co-ruler until he deposed her in 1152, and was advised by the Church leader St Bernard to make up for her inability to conduct warfare by acting like a male ruler in all other matters. The most prestigious cleric (and moralist) of the era did not think a female ruler unacceptable, and Bishop Henry promised his support to Matilda at their meeting in March provided that she consulted him on Church business. Archbishop Theobald attended her court temporarily during her ascendancy despite his oath to Stephen, once he had secured the latter's permission. The chroniclers such as William of Malmesbury claim that most of the magnates came over to Matilda that spring while Stephen was captive, and a more concrete list of her adherents was given by her long-term 'loyalist' Brian Fitz Count (of Abergavenny and Wallingford) in a subsequent letter to Bishop Henry. This and the lists of witnesses to charters Matilda granted show that the Beaumonts and de Senlis held out, while the absence of Ranulf of Chester and William de Roumare – who had backed her earlier by attacking Lincoln, leading to Stephen's capture – could be explained as due to fears of King David's intentions in the North.[33] There is no indication that the pro-Stephen faction would have fought on for years in all circumstances even if their candidate had agreed to give in, and Bishop Henry could use his Church rank as legate to ask the Pope to invalidate Stephen's coronation on a technicality if this was required.

Matilda's victory in 1141: Would it have weakened the Crown?
The cause of Stephen's adherents would have seemed to be losing as long as Stephen remained in captivity – though Queen Matilda and William of Ypres would have had to be defeated first to end hopes of a revival of fortunes. Earl Robert of Gloucester (Matilda's chief commander) would have needed all the troops that their uncle King David of Scotland could bring south to secure a decisive victory. Without that, the pro-Stephen castles and lordships in the east of England would have had to be reduced by

a round of sieges and, supported across the Channel by Boulogne, places like Dover could have held out for months as it held out for Henry III against Louis of France in 1216. Great landed magnates entrenched as governors of localities for Stephen would have done their best to bargain hard terms for an early surrender and secured semi-autonomous positions, with the cost in time and resources of besieging each of them into surrender being prohibitive. Ranulf of Chester and de Roumare would have demanded backing against claims to their lands by King David or his son Henry of Huntingdon. Most notably, magnates would have been seeking the control of the sheriffdoms of their counties (possibly as their families' hereditary rights) to weaken royal control. The real-life autonomous 'gangster state' which de Mandeville was said by chroniclers to have set up in the Fenlands in the anarchic 1140s might have been replicated elsewhere, with parts of England coming to resemble decentralized areas of France.[34] Possibly Matilda would have had to grant all that was demanded to break up the pro-Stephen faction, which would have been temperamentally difficult for her and only been granted grudgingly.

Given her character and the need for a strong sovereign to be seen to outface challengers, the new ruler would have been seeking to reverse dangerous alienation of land and office in favour of men she could trust as soon as practicable. But if Stephen's Queen and his elder son Eustace – a bloodthirsty ravager of 'enemy' lands by 1153 in real life, as remembered by his victims at the Abbey of Bury St Edmunds[35] – were still at large in the mid- and late 1140s they would have been the focus for discontented nobles in the event of any new revolt. Had ex-Queen Matilda and Eustace had to retreat to the former's lands of Boulogne they would have been well-situated to invade Kent or East Anglia later.

The semi-autonomy of the Marcher lordships from the Severn to the Dee, where local administrative and judicial power lay with a hereditary lord not a removable royal official, would have been extended to other areas by agreement with the weakened Crown unless Matilda and Geoffrey had wanted – or been able – to engage a substantial army on a long campaign to reduce Stephen's loyalists. The claims of Anjou and Normandy on Geoffrey's time and their resources make this unlikely in the immediate aftermath of 1141. Matilda would have been in as weak a position as sovereign as Stephen was in those areas that he controlled after 1141, though the situation of local semi-autonomy for entrenched dynastic lords is unlikely to have lasted. The English Crown would have maintained its potential to overawe its great lords, due to its financial and legal administration, even if the local sheriffdoms had been temporarily ceded to Matilda's feudatories. It would have been able to reassert its power later, and

Matilda had the determined character to insist on this and the will to supervise campaigns in person even if she could not command troops in battle. Assuming that her principal captain, Earl Robert, had died in 1147 as in real life the main burden of leading royal armies against recalcitrant Earls and junior lords would have fallen to her son Henry (born in 1133) as soon as he was old enough.

Matilda's blunders: When did her victory slip away? Avoidable?
As it happened, Matilda managed to secure the temporary allegiance of Bishop Henry – now legate – and the Church, though her award of the Bishopric of Durham to David's candidate in defiance of the legate's candidate (and thus the Pope) was a blunder.[36] But her conduct on her arrival in London to negotiate the city's adherence and start preparations for her coronation apparently roused resentment. She had had experience of the need for flattery and caution in dealing with civic authorities with her first husband Emperor Henry V in Italy, but had clearly learnt nothing. (It is uncertain if she ever claimed to be 'Queen' as opposed to 'Lady of the English': the evidence is unclear.) On 24 June 1141 a sudden rising by the Londoners drove her out of Westminster back to her main bases of Oxford and Bristol.[37] The east of England passed back into the hands of the Queen's army, which otherwise could have hopefully been kept out of London until Matilda had enough troops to force a decisive battle. Matilda's position was still strong, as shown by new adherents such as William de Beauchamp (claimant to control the earldom of Worcester) that summer, and her husband's triumph in Normandy was a reason for lords such as the Beaumonts with lands in both countries to come over to her to protect their position. Waleran de Beaumont, Stephen's choice as Earl of Worcester, had to accept his deposition in Beauchamp's favour and back Matilda once the family's Norman lands were under Angevin control.

When Matilda was unable to rely on Bishop Henry's allegiance, she advanced on Winchester in August with a substantial force including King David's Scots and according to the *Gesta Stephani* the Earls of Gloucester, Devon (de Redvers), Cornwall (her half-brother Reginald), Hereford (Miles of Gloucester), Dorset (William de Mohun), and Warwick (Roger de Beaumont), plus Brian FitzCount and John the Marshal. Earl Ranulf of Chester, David's enemy, was present but ineffective and Geoffrey de Mandeville (Earl of Essex) defected to the Queen. Given that Stephen was still captive and the initiative seemed to lie with Matilda, this force was a sign of her widespread but not overwhelming support. Besieging Henry in Wolvesey Castle in Winchester, his retaliatory bombardment against her forces up the hill in the royal castle led to much of the town being set afire –

with comment on the novelty of a cleric causing this sort of destruction. The Queen's troops came to assist Bishop Henry, and cut off Matilda's supply-route with the capture of Andover and Wherwell. Facing defeat or being starved out by William of Ypres' Fleming force, Matilda and the rest of the leadership had to flee; it is unclear how much the dramatic account of their escape in the biography of William Marshal is romanticized but evidently the situation was desperate enough to require a speedy flight in preference to risking a battle. The Empress' rearguard was caught up with and attacked at Stockbridge, though she escaped across Danebury Down while Earl Robert held up the enemy; valuable members of her leadership including Robert were captured. The advantage now lay with the Queen; she traded her hostages for Stephen, he was re-crowned and secured extra support from people Matilda had alienated, and the stalemate resumed.[38] Arguably the less risky course for the Empress' men at Winchester would have been to pull back from the city as the Queen approached and either withdraw in good order or fight a battle on the open Downs, either east of the city on the line of the Queen's advance or above Stockbridge to the north-west. Was Earl Robert over-confident that the Queen's force was too small to break the siege, or did Bishop Henry's insistence on fighting in the city draw the Empress' men into an exhausting clash in the streets that tied them down unnecessarily?

No decisive success resulted for either candidate throughout the rest of the 1140s, though Stephen had the advantage across central and Eastern England and Matilda's main supporters were isolated in the west and south-west – especially the crucial Marcher lordships held by Gloucester and his allies. They were unable to advance their cause significantly until her son Henry arrived in 1149 with the resources of conquered Normandy to assist his army. The only chance of a quick resolution might have been when Matilda was besieged in Oxford by Stephen with little chance of relief late in 1142. Earl Robert had been collecting aid in Normandy and on hearing of the siege tried to distract Stephen by attacking Wareham, a leading south-western port; Stephen refused to leave Oxford and clearly intended to capture *and* hold Matilda this time.[39] Oxford was isolated from her main areas of support in the south-west and the Marches, so relief before her supplies ran out was unlikely – and the snowy weather that enabled her to escape on foot meant that Oxford was not protected from attack on two sides by the usual winter flooding of the Thames and Cherwell rivers. Thus Stephen could blockade Oxford at leisure and bring up troops across the frozen rivers, while the roads were too snowed-up for a swift cavalry relief-force sent by Earl Robert to hurry across the Cotswolds from Bristol to draw him away and allow her to flee. What if she had had to surrender? At the least she could have been exchanged for several crucial castles, such as her Thames valley stronghold of Wallingford, which held up Stephen's threat to her easternmost base in Wiltshire. It would have given Stephen an advantage comparable to that which Matilda had held in 1141, without bringing the war to an end. But she escaped on foot across the frozen Thames in the snow, and the stalemate continued. The King's failure on this occasion was due to the cold; his guards at the outposts surrounding Oxford were too busy shivering round their camp-fires to note a few shadowy figures in white cloaks slipping past in the snow.[40]

The results of a victory for Matilda in 1141

What if Matilda had not alienated the Londoners and Bishop Henry in 1141 and kept her coalition united long enough to be crowned? And Earl Robert and King David mustered enough men to defeat William of Ypres' Flemings at Winchester and so tipped the scales in Matilda's favour? The military defeats at Winchester and Stockbridge were more important than the loss of London, though the latter had given people like Geoffrey de Mandeville the chance to return to the Queen's side while Matilda was still besieging Bishop Henry in Wolvesey Castle. Presumably the pro-Stephen castles and lordships would have been reduced over the next year or two in a gradual process and the civil war come to an end in the mid-1140s, or more likely Matilda and Earl Robert would have had to negotiate the transfer of allegiance of all but 'die-hard' loyalists. The terms of surrender would have included no reprisals and probably some new earldoms and grants of local sheriffdoms to secure loyalty. The abortive charters granted to de Mandeville and Aubrey de Vere, who received a tranche of extra lands and offices in return for support in mid-1141,[41] give an indication of the sort of demands that Matilda would have had to satisfy – with the danger that those stripped of the lands in question would have rallied to the Queen as long as she remained a military threat.

The captive Stephen, as a crowned king, would have been an embarrassment and murder would have blackened Matilda's name so he might have had to be locked up for life like Henry I did to his brother Robert from 1106. If released on a forced abdication and sent back to his wife's county of Boulogne, Matilda could not be sure that he would not start another war if her behaviour caused trouble in England or there was an anti-Angevin rising in Normandy – but Bishop Henry could have used his Church position to get Rome's support in forcing Stephen's eventual release once he had sworn allegiance to Matilda. As proposed by Stephen's other brother, Count Theobald, in 1141, Stephen could have been offered undisputed rights to the lands he had held across Henry I's domains as of

1135, plus a guarantee of no attempt to deprive him of Boulogne. Like Richard I's disgraced ex-rebel brother John in 1194, he could then have been required to remain on the Continent and merely draw revenues from his lands in England. As Richard I showed when held prisoner in Germany in 1193 to Philip II's disappointment, a captive sovereign with enough powerful backers (Churchmen included) had the 'lobbying-power' at Rome to make his continued detention embarrassing if not impossible for his captor. The international situation in 1141 had moved on from that of 1106–34 when Henry I could hold Robert 'Curthose' prisoner for twenty-eight years, and Stephen had more powerful allies who could appeal to the Pope (Bishop Henry and Count Theobald) than Robert had possessed. Matilda would have been in a weaker position than her father had she endeavoured to ignore this pressure, as she had to secure acceptance of her takeover of England and Normandy from an anointed king whereas Henry I had been crowned and 'legitimated' before he took his rival captive.

Was Matilda likely to have faced baronial resentment over her arrogance and handicaps by being a woman and thus expected to take second place in warfare and judicial matters to her husband? The queenship of her husband's stepmother, Melissende, in Jerusalem in 1131–52 is relevant here as the only other equivalent – Eleanor of Aquitaine, succeeding her father Duke William in 1137, had not been a queen and so had been in a weaker position. (It had been taken for granted that her husband would govern her domains in more than name, hence the haste of Louis VII of France to secure her.) Melissende was co-ruler with her husband Fulk (Geoffrey's father) to his death in 1143 but Fulk took the lead in politics and warfare. She was then co-ruler with and regent for her son Baldwin III until a coalition of barons exploited a quarrel between her and her son and encouraged the latter to depose her.[42] Matilda was a more active and forceful personality than Melissende, but her relations with Geoffrey were not good – and he would have needed to spend a lot of time at home in Anjou to deal with his own lords and in conquered Normandy to prevent a revolt.

Presumably Earl Robert would have been her chief adviser in England, though with a risk of clashing with Geoffrey when the latter was in the country, and Bishop Henry would have been insisting on leaving all clerical matters to him and would have tried to become as powerful as Roger of Salisbury had been under Henry I. Would Northern barons resenting the handover of all Cumbria and Northumberland to Matilda's uncle and ally King David have been likely to revolt, even if Stephen was not available? Was Geoffrey de Mandeville, Earl of Essex and castellan of the Tower of London – and the arch-'brigand' baron who rampaged across East Anglia unhindered in the real-life stalemate of the early 1140s – likely to overplay his hand, insisting on virtual autonomy, and have to be dealt with?

The need to win over pro-Stephen adherents rather than campaign year after year against them and reduce castles, a slow process, could well have seen Matilda and Earl Robert having to accept assorted 'illegal' castles and local autonomy for men like the Earls of Essex and Chester, and a far weaker central government than Henry I had been able to exercise. The brigandage and extortion would have caused discontent and a desire for strong government, but attempts to punish defiant local lords have required military action – meaning high taxes to hire a large army and a siege-train – and if Earl Robert had died in 1147 then Matilda would have been short of commanders unless her husband was on good terms with her and in the country. Geoffrey's priorities would have been defending his enlarged Continental dominions.

Matilda and Henry II: A potential parallel between them and what happened to Queen Melissende at her son's hands in Jerusalem in 1152?

Probably an increasing role as military commander would have been taken, as in real life, by Prince Henry from c. 1149. He came to England as much on his own initiative as on his mother's, and launched an active campaign (and secured knighting from his great-uncle King David) that foreshadowed his restless peregrinations across his dominions for which he was later to become famous.[43] Henry was likely to have taken an active part in politics and war from his mid-teens if his mother was already Queen/'Lady' – and it is possible that assorted lords, alienated by his mother, would have been thinking that an adult male could rule England without her. His leadership in warfare to reduce local lords and their illegal castles would have won him support and he would have been seen as more effective in keeping law and order than Matilda, especially if she had been unable to be militarily effective in touring the country after Earl Robert died with Geoffrey abroad and that had encouraged some local brigandage. There would have been demands that Matilda abdicate in his favour once he was adult, and the possibility of a coup to force her hand if she refused. The death of Geoffrey in 1151 would have required Henry to secure Normandy and Anjou and then he would have been in pursuit of Eleanor of Aquitaine and her lands to thwart Louis VII as in real life. It is also possible that his absence in England in the later 1140s would have encouraged plots to divide the family inheritance in France among his younger brothers, at least to the extent of giving one of them Anjou – which occurred in real life but would have had added impetus had he been primarily resident in England when Geoffrey died. Had he been in England in 1151, would rebel barons in Anjou have succeeded in installing his younger brother Geoffrey as their new count before Henry could reach the area? And Henry have had to evict him later with Anglo-Norman troops?

Matilda lived until 1167, but once Henry was adult it is possible that a coalition of nobles in England could have acted with him to at least make him co-ruler. England had never had two sovereigns before, and Matilda could have ended up deposed and/or forced into retirement like Melissende in Jerusalem. In real life she mainly lived in Normandy once Henry was king from 1154, and if she had had to be deposed rather than just being superseded in her claim her son might have preferred to deport her to Normandy or Anjou rather than letting her stay in England. As shown by his relations with his wife Eleanor, Henry was not the type of ruler to accept a partner – his good relationship with his mother after 1153 in real life is no guide to their relationship had she been ruling queen as Matilda seems to have spent most of her time away from court in retirement. Had she been co-ruler it is probable that tension between them, exacerbated by her foes, would soon have arisen.

Chapter Three

The Collapse of the 'Angevin Empire': Inevitable? Would Richard I's Survival have Avoided the Angevin Collapse of 1203–4?

Richard I's accession: Not the original plan of his father.
He was the second surviving son, intended for Aquitaine.
What was intended to happen in 1152–83? Angevin family
plans – and the importance of Henry's 1152 marriage to
Anglo-French wars over 300 years

It should be noted that Richard I's position as King of England, Duke of Normandy and Aquitaine, and Count of Anjou and Poitou in 1189–99 was not the original arrangement for inheritance of the Angevin lands made by his father, Henry II. The latter had intended England, Normandy, and Anjou to go as a 'bloc' to Richard's elder brother, Henry, the 'Young King' (born in 1155). The creation of this 'bloc' – a 'union of crowns' rather than a 'state' as all kept separate legal and administrative systems – had been Henry's main international achievement. It had probably been planned by his father Geoffrey 'Plantagenet', assuming that we can dismiss one contemporary allegation (repeated later by the chronicler William of Newburgh) that Geoffrey only intended Henry to keep Anjou until he had won England. Once that had happened he was supposed to pass on Anjou to his younger brother Geoffrey, whose patrimony at their father's death (1151) was three important castles in Anjou – Chinon, Loudoun, and Mirabeau. It is unlikely that the elder Geoffrey made Henry promise to do this and he reneged on it with Church help;[1] the creation of the England-Normandy-Anjou 'bloc' was probably intended by father and eldest son alike in 1151. The younger Geoffrey proved as treacherous as William I's sons, allying with Louis VII against Henry in 1152 – probably hoping to gain Anjou with the King's support – and revolting again later. Henry seized his castles in

1156 and repositioned him as Count of Nantes in war-torn Brittany, probably intending him as the family vassal-ruler of all Brittany; his death in 1158 left that role vacant until Henry's third son (another Geoffrey) was old enough to assume it.[2]

Had the King's brother lived on as ruler of Brittany there was clearly a possibility that his ambition would lead him to challenge Henry again later, possibly in alliance with Queen Eleanor and her sons in 1173 and no doubt backed by the meddling Louis VII. His survival and presumed siring of an heir would have kept Henry's son Geoffrey from ruling Brittany as in real life, meaning that Henry needed to find a new role for his third son. Would the younger Geoffrey have been given the task of acting as royal lieutenant in restless, semi-conquered Ireland, which in real life went to Prince John in 1185? There were no other obvious family tasks for a vigorous young prince to take on, given that Henry showed no interest in installing a son in any of the Welsh states to replace untrustworthy local rulers and any division of the duchy of Aquitaine would have infuriated its heir, Richard. Had Geoffrey been in command in Ireland in 1186 he would not have been visiting Paris to be killed in a tournament as he was in real life, so would he still have been alive to succeed Richard in 1199? (His posthumous son Arthur lost out then in real life as he was under-age.) The chances are that the ambitious and not too scrupulous Geoffrey would have been unwilling to stay in a political (and social) 'backwater' such as Ireland throughout his career, and that he would have secured a grant of some land (or a bride with lands?) elsewhere in the Angevin domains before 1199 and made sure that he spent much of his time in England or France instead. Thus there is a chance that he would have played John's real-life role in 1191–4, trying to overthrow Richard while the latter was on Crusade.

Henry's second son, Richard, born in 1157, was intended to receive his mother Eleanor's lands of Aquitaine and Poitou, which were titularly transferred to him in 1170–72 under the King's continuing effective governance. The duchy was hereditary, having been inherited by Eleanor from her father William X in 1137, and Henry had no rights there except as consort – a role that he had swiftly taken over from the infuriated Louis VII by allying with Eleanor when the King's marriage to her collapsed in 1152. The dramatic extension of French royal resources by Louis' 1137 marriage to Eleanor, swinging the political/military balance of power sharply against the Angevins, had been transformed into an Angevin coup by the breakdown of Louis' and Eleanor's relationship (first apparent on the Second Crusade in 1147–8). Henry's marriage to Eleanor within weeks of the divorce brought Aquitaine into the Angevin orbit, and into the English orbit too once he assumed the English throne in October 1154. Without this reversal of fortunes for Louis VII, the French Crown would have overshadowed the Anglo-Norman state on the Continent in terms of military strength in the 1150s and 1160s and the possibility arises that it would have been Louis rather than his son Philip Augustus who took on the conquest of Normandy and Anjou. Louis did have significant military experience, having led his troops across Asia Minor and in Palestine in the Second Crusade in 1147–8, but was generally thought of as a more pacific ruler and less of a violent warlord than his father, Louis VI. Eleanor was rumoured to have left him because she despised his religious enthusiasm, which was encouraged by his mentor, Abbot Suger of St Denis. It can be assumed that Henry would have been the victor in any conflict. Quite likely the independent-minded Eleanor would have tired of using her Aquitaine vassals as 'cannon-fodder' for Louis' wars against Henry even if she did not divorce Louis as a result and the Aquitaine nobles were always resentful of 'central' control by an overlord so they would have been unwilling too. A defeat by Henry's armies as the Aquitaine lords tried to invade Anjou at Louis' behest could have sparked off revolt against the ties between Aquitaine and France, to Henry's benefit – and to Eleanor joining in and leaving Louis to save her reputation as defender of her people's interests? Thus the survival of Louis and Eleanor's marriage after 1152 might still have worked for Henry's benefit in the long term.

In real life it was Henry not Louis who was the Duchess' 'Consort' in Aquitaine after 1152, and the duchy duly passed to his second surviving son, Richard. The fact that Henry's nominees rather than Eleanor, its duchess, usually acted as governor in Aquitaine until she separated from her second husband in 1168 and set up her court in Aquitaine may indicate the King's centralizing instincts – but it may be merely convenience by both parties. While the Queen was living with her husband and regularly producing children it would be inconvenient for her to have to spend months at a time in distant Aquitaine to oversee her administration and her turbulent vassals; her return home may indicate an agreed strategy with Henry so that she could prepare the ground for her favourite son Richard's assumption of (titular) power as duke. There may also have been an element of the end of her child-bearing years making Henry more willing to do without her – and the birth of her final son John (December 1166), when she was several years over forty, was apparently unwelcome to her. Her assistance to the untried teenage Richard in his first years in power in 1170–72 was not necessarily a rebuff to Henry's alleged 'centralizing', though it may have been welcome to her if his 1166–7 garden-works at his favourite residence, Woodstock, indicates (as in legend) the start of his notorious affair with Rosamund Clifford. The Queen's and Richard's backing for her eldest son Henry's revolt in 1173 is unlikely to have been planned far in advance, though the Rosamund Clifford affair would logically have encouraged her to try to depose her husband in revenge. Without Louis VII recognizing the younger Henry as rightful Duke of Normandy – his legal right as suzerain – the revolt would have been far more difficult to organize. Louis' meddling was in the tradition of his grandfather King Philip backing William I's rebel son Robert in 1077–9 and his father, Louis VI, backing William 'Clito' against Henry I in the 1120s – and if Louis had stayed married to Eleanor and had been able to call on Aquitaine for military aid his assistance to any rebel son of Henry's would have been even more dangerous.

Despite Henry's and Eleanor's turbulent relationship and eventual estrangement, it made the Angevin dynasty the politico-military superiors of the French kings and gave them extra resources and lands that were invaluable to England as late as 1453. Aquitaine had been destined for Louis' and Eleanor's eldest daughter, the younger Eleanor, and her husband Count Henry of Champagne; now it was the backbone of English power in France for 300 years. Without the marriage of May 1152, the Angevin loss of Normandy could have been fatal to English power in France – and Anglo-French relations would not have been complicated by the requirement that the English Duke of Aquitaine do homage to the King of France. It might not have prevented Edward III and Henry V endeavouring to seize the throne of France, but it would have significantly altered the relationship between the two states. The kings of France would not have had the excuse of using their rights as suzerains of Aquitaine to confiscate it from 'disobedient vassals' whenever they wanted to put pressure on England, as in the 1290s and 1330s.

John and Ireland

Henry II's and Eleanor's third son, Geoffrey, was intended to receive Brittany to whose heiress Constance he was married; the youngest son, John, would receive Ireland (and at one point some castles in Anjou and/or Maurienne). John had shown his fecklessness or incompetence as a teenager on his first visit to Ireland in 1185, alienating the Anglo-Norman and Irish nobles alike instead of building up a loyal following that could have helped him in the power-struggles of 1188-94.[3] (His young age was no excuse; Henry and Richard were successful military leaders at the same age.) The Prince was clearly bored and possibly felt insulted at being packed off to a 'backwater' – he was supposed to have pulled the beards of some local Irish chieftains at a meeting, despising their 'uncouth' appearance. But what if he had made a success of the post and Henry had asked him to stay on (i.e. until Henry died in July 1189)?

The main problems that a more successful John, ruling as overlord of the Anglo-Norman barons in Ireland in Dublin during the mid-late 1180s, would have had were these men's lack of large forces of trained knights (as opposed to half-armed Gaelic infantry 'kerns') to aid him in any war with his elder brothers and their unwillingness to risk revolt while they were overseas by following John to England. Like Geoffrey in isolated Brittany, his location would have put him at a disadvantage in intervening in the power-struggles in England and Normandy. It is also possible that Henry would have married him off to the daughter and heiress of the baronial leader Richard de Clare, Earl of Pembroke ('Strongbow'), a powerful Marcher lord who had led the Anglo-Norman expedition to assist the exiled king of Leinster in retrieving his lands in 1169–70 and then take over his kingdom. This would have gained the de Clare lands in Ireland for an Angevin prince and so secured them for the sovereign's control, with the bonus that Earl Richard had married the Leinster heiress so John's children would have royal Irish blood and be able to call on 'native' loyalty. (In real life, Earl Richard's heiress was married off to the senior loyalist courtier knight, William Marshal.) As of 1173 Henry II had planned to marry John to the eldest daughter of the Count of Maurienne in Savoy, as part of their mutual alliance against Toulouse; this would have put John out of the 'market' but she died.

John would thus have become Earl of Pembroke after Richard de Clare and had lands straddling the Irish Sea, in Pembroke and Leinster, as his father's Irish Sea coastal 'strongman' – though his wife would have been rather younger than him so no children could have been expected soon. He would, however, have had a good chance of sons from this marriage, who would be adult before he died in 1216 – in real life his first marriage (1189) ended in divorce (1199?) and his first son by his second marriage was not born until 1207. Thus John would have had an adult son to succeed him in 1216, not a boy, and the 1216 baronial rebellion to replace him would have been weaker – and might even have led to the rebels asking John's son to lead them rather than calling in his French nephew Louis (VIII). The real-life role of John as husband of the heiress of the Earldom of Gloucester after 1189 – based in the Southern Welsh Marches and castles in Wiltshire and Derbyshire – made him more of a threat to Richard than he would have been had he been based in Ireland.

The main 'bloc' of Angevin lands – for the eldest son

The intended structure of the so-called 'Angevin Empire' – a misnomer, as it was only a grouping of independent dominions with separate legal systems and no central control apart from the personal rule of Henry II – has been disputed, particularly regarding King Henry's intentions. But it is clear that he intended to keep his father's and mother's lands (i.e. Anjou and England/Normandy) together, with his wife's Aquitaine being held separately.

The first 'bloc' was intended for the 'Young King' Henry, who was uniquely crowned King of England in his father's lifetime (May 1170), aged fifteen, to confirm the English inheritance and did homage for the rest to their overlord Louis VII of France. The practice of coronation of an heir in a father's lifetime was Byzantine in origin, and had been adopted in France to secure the succession. Did Eleanor, who had been married to the French King and travelled across the Byzantine Empire on Crusade, suggest it to Henry? Unfortunately, it seems to have added to the 'Young King's' arrogant sense of 'entitlement' and he was reported as showing off his new rank and implying that he wished his father would hand over some lands to him permanently.[4]

Richard, heir to Aquitaine, was supposed to do homage to the 'Young King' as his overlord, keeping up the personal link to the senior Angevin ruler, which Henry II had established for Aquitaine as its Duchess' husband from 1152.[5] This amended the King's original dispositions of 1169 whereby Richard did homage directly to King Louis of France and was thus equal, nor junior to his elder brother.[6] The Duke of Aquitaine was not historically a vassal of anybody but the King. Thus the Angevin domains would be preserved as a sort of 'family business', with the 'juniors' bound by legal and personal obligation to the 'senior executive', the eldest son – which did not take account of individuals' personal resentments and the quarrels of a brood of Henry's headstrong sons. Unfortunately for Henry II, Richard refused to pay homage to his elder brother – and neither he nor the 'Young King' were willing to grant any territory of theirs to John whatever their father wanted. The problem was exacerbated by the refusal of Henry II to trust the arrogant and feckless 'Young King' with any serious independence of authority in any of his future territories, and by the constant competitive bickering of the King's three elder sons. Henry has been criticized for not allowing the restless youngsters any real power, and being too 'controlling'; but their unstable characters suggest that the 'Young King' and Geoffrey, if not Richard, were incapable of behaving wisely if so treated. If he had allowed his eldest son control of Normandy or Anjou, the latter could still have linked up with Louis VII to defy him – and the heir's response when thwarted was still to sulk and indulge in aimless ravaging when he was twenty-eight (1183). The 'Young King's' arrogance towards his father, no doubt egged on by his knightly hangers-on, suggests that he was likely to lack political ability as a ruler unless he matured rapidly; the fact that his father's resources far outweighed his (making a sole revolt futile) did not stop him from a pointless demonstration of his dissatisfaction by looting and burning at will in a second revolt in 1183. The character-sketches given of him by contemporaries suggest his petulance, immaturity, and habit of following bad advice, which balanced his charm and generosity[7] – though the future Edward I, John's grandson, was to be equally headstrong and violent as a youth and he matured well enough. The added facto of Queen Eleanor encouraging her sons against their (adulterous) father may have 'tipped the balance' into revolt in 1173. Unlike most queens, she was a ruling dynast with her own loyal followers to use in the conflict. After being caught riding to rebellion dressed as a man, she was locked up for fifteen years – adding to the family's dysfunction. Their turbulent relationships have made them a favourite for fictionalization, e.g. in James Goldman's play 'The Lion in Winter'.

Henry II sought to retain a degree of control of Aquitaine for his lifetime, or at least as long as possible after Richard had taken over in name as Duke. That led to Eleanor and Richard seeking to regain control by force in 1173, while the 'Young King' complained that he was given no power or authority as titular co-ruler and listened to the blandishments of his father's enemies led by Louis VII. In 1173–4 Henry II faced the threat of, Lear-like, being deposed by his ungrateful children. A mural commissioned for Westminster Palace allegedly showed a symbolic picture of an eagle being attacked by its eaglets. Henry apparently had no illusions about his sons being grateful or loyal after this, John included.[8] The feuding of father and older sons continued until the 'Young King' died suddenly of dysentery during the course of his second rebellion in June 1183, bringing his domains (England, Normandy, and Anjou) to Richard. It was Henry II's intention for Richard to take his older brother's place and hand over Aquitaine to John, but he refused to do so. Lacking the power to coerce Richard (who was evidently supported by the Aquitaine and Poitou barons), Henry had to give in and seek to compensate John elsewhere.[9] In the meantime Henry and Richard's relationship was further soured by the King keeping possession of Richard's intended fiancée, the French princess Alice, who was rumoured to be his mistress.[10]

The tension was encouraged by the new king of France (1180), teenage Philip Augustus, who lacked the martial skills of Henry and his sons but made up for it in deviousness and fully used his role as titular overlord of all of them for their French lands. If Henry would not grant lands in France to one of his sons, they could gain them equally legally from Philip as overlord – and Philip and Richard were close friends at one point, though the fact that that they once shared a bed was not evidence of a homosexual relationship despite modern claims.[11] The surprise death of Geoffrey in a tournament in

1186 did not alter the central struggle between Henry and Richard, given that Geoffrey had been intended to rule only Brittany and this duly passed to his posthumous son Arthur, but it was to affect the question of who was Richard's heir. Had Geoffrey been alive in 1199 his succession to Richard would have been undisputed, and there would have resulted a union of England and Brittany. Given Geoffrey's combination of vanity, fecklessness, and deceit, he is unlikely to have been a capable king; in the 1180s he had a reputation as a mischief-maker.[12] But it is unlikely that John would have been able to secure much support from Norman or Angevin barons to challenge Geoffrey's succession at the time or revolt against him later, despite the probability of aid from the opportunistic Philip Augustus. In terms of past record John was seen as a 'loser' in 1199, having failed in his revolts against Richard, and would thus have been in a weaker position as a challenger to the incumbent new King than Geoffrey's son Arthur – arguably the next heir by line of descent – was against the incumbent (John)in real life. Moreover, the failure of local barons to fight for John in Normandy as Philip invaded in 1203–4 can at least partly be attributed to their disgust at John having (probably) murdered the missing Arthur. Had it been Geoffrey on the throne and John invading with Philip's support, the invader's position would have been weaker. So would Geoffrey's son Arthur (born in 1187) have succeeded to England sometime in the 1200s or 1210s – and would Geoffrey have bequeathed Brittany to him too or given it to his daughter Eleanor?

What nearly happened in 1189

The inheritance of the 'Young King' and Aquitaine were combined in one (personal) dominion for one candidate when Henry II died in July 1189, contrary to the King's intentions in 1183. Henry had been suspected by Richard of seeking to deprive him of at least part of this inheritance – England and Normandy? – on John's behalf in the interim, and had notably not been crowned as co-king. He made the worst interpretation of rumours that Henry intended to marry his fiancée Princess Alice of France to John, encouraged by her brother Philip Augustus, and when the fall of Jerusalem led to papal demands for another Crusade in 1187–8 he refused to go on it unless Henry sent John with him. He clearly anticipated that if he was still in the East when Henry died and John was 'on the spot' he would suffer the same fate as Duke Robert had at William II's death in1100, this time with the dying King assisting the usurpation. He was in rebellion again, with Philip's support, when Henry died in July 1189. Having just been driven out of Le Mans by Richard and Philip, Henry was openly threatening vengeance on the two of them when they forced him to accept their terms – which they could not have done had he followed his original intentions to withdraw north from

Maine into Normandy out of their reach. It was only because Henry turned south again to his birthplace, Chinon (because he wanted to die there?), that he was cornered and forced into peace with Richard. The latter was thus reinforced as legal heir to all the Angevin dominions (except Brittany, now ruled by his brother Geoffrey's widow, Constance) before Henry died.[13] But this agreement would have been unlikely had Henry taken a different route away from Le Mans and evaded Richard's and Philip's armies.

Had the sickening King died in Normandy without having had to reach accommodation with Richard, or recovered from his unexpected physical collapse (he was only fifty-six), he might have reached the point of disinheriting Richard in favour of John. The young Prince was only twenty-two to Richard's thirty-one in July 1189 and, unlike him, untried in battle or as a leader of powerful noblemen; he had only had one undistinguished campaign, in Ireland in 1185. Notoriously, John had alienated almost everyone he came into contact with there and ended up pulling the Irish nobles' beards; he showed no signs of the vigour and military skills that Richard had developed at an early age. As events turned out, Henry died within days of having to accept Richard's terms and did not attempt to grant part or all of his lands to John – who apparently took the prudent and self-serving course of hurrying to Richard's side as soon as his father was clearly dying.[14] In any case, Richard had armed support at his call and any bequest from Henry to John in July 1189 would have been hopeless. But had Henry recovered to live for another year or more Richard's succession could not have been guaranteed despite his attempt to ensure that if he had to carry out his expected duty of leaving on Crusade John went with him. The King would have been in a problematic situation if his own health enabled him to evade going on Crusade and he had to send both sons to ensure Richard's participation, not least as Philip (on Crusade too) could return early if he heard Henry was dying and attack the Angevin dominions. Richard would not trust John to return to protect the 'empire' on his behalf for fear of an usurpation.

There were no other legitimate Angevin males to govern England in the interim between Henry's death and his sons' return; if Richard had insisted that John join him in Palestine in 1190 Henry would have had to rely on the men who in real life joined John on the 'regency council' after Richard's regent Bishop Longchamp was deposed. The most prominent of them was Henry's illegitimate son Geoffrey, a reluctant cleric made Archbishop of York by Richard before he left for the East (possibly to end that ambitious character's hopes of secular power). Did Geoffrey hope that his father might turn to him not to John in 1188–9 as an alternative to Richard? This was a 'long shot' as the last bastard to succeed to any of the family domains,

William I in 1035, had not faced legitimate claimants. In real life Longchamp, fearing Geoffrey's ambitions, required him to stay out of England and arrested him as soon as he landed, but Geoffrey would have been in a stronger position as Henry's favourite son had that King been alive to back him up in 1189–90 and Richard and John both been absent on Crusade. Henry might well have had to end his cynical delay in nominating a new Archbishop to York for years (to use the see's revenues) in order to give Geoffrey an appropriately powerful see to consolidate his role as regent. Henry would have needed Church acquiescence for him to avoid carrying out his own Crusading vow in 1189–90, and Richard (as in real life) would have wanted Geoffrey to take irreversible ecclesiastical vows to end his secular ambitions. Whatever Geoffrey hoped, it was not realistic to expect Henry to have disinherited both the disliked Richard and the hopelessly inexperienced John in his favour in 1189–90. Nor could Henry have turned to the infant Arthur under the regency of Constance, whose primary interest was Brittany and who lacked English or Norman noble backers.

If Henry had attempted to disinherit Richard on John's behalf in 1189–90 a war would have resulted, probably involving Richard attacking Anjou and Normandy from Aquitaine with Philip's support. Richard – and Philip – was unlikely to have gone on Crusade without a resolution of the conflict in favour of Richard's confirmation as heir, and the Church would have been eager to see an agreement in order to obtain the maximum amount of royal participation in the Crusade. Henry is likely to have had to reinstate Richard at the request of the Church, having been in a weak position for defying the Pope ever since the murder of Thomas Becket and being at risk of an interdict. A papal order absolving his barons from their allegiance to force his submission would have given Richard the backing he needed to stage a more successful revolt than the 'Young King' had done in 1173–4. Needing Richard's presence in the East, the Church leadership would have been keen to see Richard feel secure enough over the succession to leave France. Logically, Henry would have had to swear a Church-sponsored oath to name Richard as successor if the occasion arose in Richard's absence, with the clergy guaranteeing that they would insist on Richard's accession. Ironically, with Archbishop Baldwin of Canterbury heading off on Crusade the leading role as guarantor would have fallen to Geoffrey as Archbishop of York.

John's accession, April 1199: The timing. A surprise to all. The question of Richard's childless marriage, which gave him a chance at the throne

The death of Richard at Chalus Castle on 6 April 1199 was totally unexpected, ending the career of one of the most noted and feared warriors of his time – a man regarded by contemporaries as more than a match for his unmilitary rival Philip II of France. Philip, whose personal domains in the 'Isle de France' were easily outmatched by Richard's possessions, although he had the legal and psychological advantage of being Richard's titular overlord in an intensely legalistic age, had been trying to divide the Angevin dynasty and break up their 'empire' ever since his accession in 1180, without much success. Having used Henry II's jealous and impatient sons – including Richard – against their father in the 1180s, he had sought to benefit from Richard's capture by the Duke of Austria as he returned from the Third Crusade and holding to ransom by Emperor Henry VI, by using the King's brother John to start a revolt in England and Normandy. He had shamelessly tried to bribe Henry to keep Richard prisoner permanently.[15] But Richard had returned unexpectedly soon despite John's efforts to seize the ransom money, defeated the rebels, and pardoned John; he had retaken the small gains that Philip had made on the Norman frontier and had now built the huge new castle of Les Andelys ('Chateau Gaillard') to defend the Seine valley.

Despite the humiliation of being held to ransom by a fellow sovereign and the fact that his prolonged absence on Crusade had nearly lost his kingdom, Richard held the military advantage in 1199. In an age where kings personally led their armies into battle, his humiliating ransoming was not that unexceptional or seriously damaging – his father's vassals had captured the King of Scotland, William I, in an ambush during the siege of Alnwick in the 1174 rebellion. The sheer effect of his reputation as the foremost warrior of his age should not be underestimated when considering the reactions and loyalties of the Western European warrior nobility, and his 'leading from the front' (unlike Philip) in the Crusade had added to this. In an age where 'elan' was admired it was to his credit that he had risked his life on numerous occasions, in impressive 'set-pieces' such as his charging ashore from his ship at the head of his men to reverse the fall of Jaffa to Saladin without waiting to see the odds against him. However, the defensive nature of warfare in a castle-filled landscape gave less scope for permanent success through victory in battle in Western Europe than in Palestine. There was less opportunity for him to win definitive victories as he struggled with Philip on the long Norman/Angevin-French frontier – and his reputation meant that his enemies often avoided battle and shut themselves up in castles that had to be stormed or starved out. But he was a far more attractive magnet for the ubiquitous mercenary captains of the era, both as a competent commander and as a solvent employer in charge of massive resources from the Scottish borders to Gascony. His current mercenary captain Mercadier was a formidable asset in ravaging countryside and denying the enemy supplies in any conflict, though military power in the field could be countered by a determined and well-supplied stronghold that had the defences to require a long blockade or risky undermining.

Given that Richard had been married to Berengaria of Navarre for eight years and had had no children, there has been speculation that this was due to his alleged homosexuality. The timing of events – accession in July 1189 and marriage in April 1191 – might suggest a lack of hurry to marry and father an heir at his accession, despite him being nearly thirty-two already and the risk of him being killed in the imminent Crusade or some other military conflict. But there are two logical explanations. A royal marriage was an occasion for complex diplomacy to secure the most 'useful' as well as suitable princess from a neighbouring state by a formal treaty, and was thus bound to take some months to arrange – and longer if there were disputes between the two countries to settle in the treaty. A dowry had to be haggled over and often a military alliance against disgruntled opponents to be arranged. Given the King's priorities, acquiring a bride who could secure advantage for his duchy of Aquitaine was probable – and the logical time to arrange this was when he was in Normandy in spring 1190 to settle his French lands before his departure and to arrange the Crusade with Philip. Richard's choice of a bride from Navarre represented an alliance between the Angevin state and one of the three Iberian monarchies across the Pyrenees who could invade Aquitaine (Castile, Navarre and Aragon). Castile was already an ally, with Henry II having married off a daughter to King Alfonso VIII in 1173. The larger and most useful of the other two was Aragon, whose King Alfonso II was at odds with Richard's enemy Count Raymond V of Toulouse – and as Raymond had not taken the Cross he could be intending to stay behind and invade Aquitaine when Richard was overseas. An Aragonese alliance in 1190 brought in Alfonso's ally King Sancho of Navarre too, and Richard applied to marry the latter's sister Berengaria; this was probably decided at the 'family summit' of the Angevin dynasty that Richard held in Normandy at Easter 1190.[16] But according to a song presented by the troubadour Bertrand de Born to King Philip back in 1188, Richard had already been interested in Berengaria as a bride then – when he was still formally engaged to Philip's sister Alice, his father's alleged mistress.[17] At a 'summit' of Henry, Richard and Philip at Bonmoulins in November 1188 Philip, then Richard's ally, had promised to return all conquests if Henry married Alice to Richard and had fealty sworn to him as his sole heir[18] – so had Richard still been promising to marry Alice then?

Alice is the other explanation for the delay; if the unwelcome engagement was to be abandoned her brother Philip would have to accept it, and this could be difficult. Rejecting Alice would imply that she was either not good enough or was 'damaged goods' due to her apparent relationship with Henry II. Securing this agreement needed a personal meeting between Richard and Philip, which occurred after the 'family summit' in Normandy.[19] By this argument, had Alice's 'past' not been an issue then Richard might have married her after all in autumn 1189 or spring 1190 to secure his relationship with Philip before the Crusade – and they could have had a son aged around eight by the time Richard died, a block to John's accession. Setting aside a late ruler's under-age son would be more difficult than, as in real life, setting aside a nephew in 1199. Even after this, Richard left for the East before the King of Navarre had made arrangements to send Berengaria to him, and Queen Eleanor collected the Princess and took her to Southern Italy where they caught up with Richard's party at Messina at the end of March 1191. Due to it being Lent when marriage was prohibited, they did not marry until April, at Limassol in Cyprus.[20] They seem to have been apart not only during the resultant campaigns in Palestine and journey to England, which was perhaps to be expected, but for much of Richard's subsequent reign. Richard was apparently being criticized for his lax private life and (anonymous) love affairs by the moralist Bishop Hugh of Lincoln several years before he died.[21]

But it is more likely that Berengaria was barren than that normal marital relations were infrequent out of Richard's sexual leanings. He had at least one bastard, Philip (later made much of as a 'peg' for patriotic speeches by Shakespeare in his play 'King John').[22] It has been suspected that there was more to his love of the camaraderie of chivalric warfare and knightly 'bonding' and neglect of his wife than a mere refusal to accept his political responsibilities. The statement of the chronicler Roger of Howden that a hermit rebuked him for the 'sins of Sodom' and threatened him with a similar fate seems superficially more important than his apparently once sharing a bed with Philip Augustus.[23] But did this phrase mean exclusively 'sodomy' rather than general sexual licence, and did it just reflect gossip? A parallel case can be drawn with Alexander the Great, an equally charismatic military hero who was careless about arranging an early marriage to provide an heir, had few proven female attachments, plus a similarly powerful mother, and was supposed to have a homosexual attachment to his friend Hephaistion. Richard was not sterile, so if he had a son by an equally fertile Berengaria John would probably have had to make do with the regency in 1199. There had not been one in England since 978 and in Normandy since 1035, so its nature cannot be reckoned by past experience in either state; but in 1216 John's nine-year-old son was to be placed under a 'one-man' regency held by the nation's best general, William Marshal, Earl of Pembroke. (This was in wartime, but the arrangement continued after the French were expelled in 1217.) A regent might be bound to accept the advice of a council or, more likely, have full powers; but by feudal custom like the holder of a 'minor's wardship he was required to hand over his charge's estates to them intact when the latter became adult. By this reckoning, John would have had every legal excuse to refuse to hand over any lands to King Philip of France if the latter attacked or occupied them. And if Richard had lived into the 1200s, would he have risked alienating Navarre by having his marriage annulled and marrying a second time to gain a son?

The loss of the Angevin domains in France: Inevitable by 1199, or due to John's failings? An analysis using the evidence of John's leadership and character from events in 1189–1216
Some historians in the twentieth century, looking back from the quick collapse of Richard's empire in France north of Aquitaine to Philip's assault in 1203–1204, have argued that this catastrophe cannot be entirely blamed on Richard's successor John. He has been seen as unlucky rather than incompetent, and the (mainly Church) thirteenth-century historians as biased. The seeds of decline must have been evident in 1199 for the well-defended Angevin lands to crumble four/five years later, and the huge demands that Richard had made on his subjects to pay for the Third Crusade in 1189–90 and for his ransom in 1193–4 must have produced serious discontent. After these seriously draining payments, was the Angevin state able to raise enough money to pay for its defence – or were its leading barons unwilling to fund royal demands any longer?[24] The English magnates may have been unwilling to pay for or take part in warfare on the Continent, as they mutinied when John attempted to raise armies to retake Poitou in 1205 and their discontent with his financial demands helped to cause the revolt of 1215.[25]

Was this factor likely to undermine any king – Richard, John, or even Arthur of Brittany – whenever he had to cope with a French assault on Normandy? Would this have affected Richard as badly as it did John in real life? The failure of an English army, or major Norman landed interests, to rally to John in defence of invaded Normandy in 1203–1204 was noticeable, as Philip was able to mop up towns and castles at leisure; John was inactive at Rouen as Chateau Gaillard was under siege.[26] Was this an example of English and Norman weariness with the cost of defending Normandy, and lack of will to fight – which would have afflicted Richard as well as John? Was John powerless rather than lazy or depressed when he failed to intervene in 1203, and would Richard have faced a similar reaction from his Norman vassals? This, however, does not take account of the exact circumstances of 1203 – John's nephew Arthur had recently disappeared in custody after the

King had captured him to end his challenge for the throne. John was failing to produce Arthur, at the request of the latter's overlord King Philip, and was widely assumed to have murdered him. The most plausible story is that he had struck him down at a confrontation in Rouen Castle and thrown his body, weighted down, into the Seine. Indeed, he had earlier sought to use the methods of Henry I a century before in making Arthur ineligible for the throne by having him blinded and castrated[27] – which would have produced equal anger among his vassals. Moreover, John had made his political/military position in Normandy and Anjou repeatedly worse by calculated actions in 1200–1203 – first annoying the strategically vital Hugh of Lusignan by marrying his fiancée, Isabella, then alienating his Norman ally William des Roches by breaking his promises on Arthur's fate, and then by releasing the arrested Lusignans (who like des Roches defected to Philip). He thus fractured the local elites mid-crisis. Thus it cannot be said that John in 1203 only faced a 'war-weary' refusal to fight by overtaxed barons that would have undermined any defender of Normandy.

The 'revisionist' approach to John's reign sought to put much of the blame for the disasters of 1203–1204 on Richard for his endless wars and his long absence on Crusade, and his dismissive attitude to England – where he spent a bare six months in ten years as king – could be used against him. As the military ethos and chivalric ideals that had made him a fashionable figure in the nineteenth century came under severe criticism, he could be portrayed as a bloodthirsty and irresponsible warmonger who failed to see that his peoples needed peace and his kingdom needed a resident king. By this reckoning, John – resident in England for most of his reign and concerned to enforce his power over Wales, Scotland, and Ireland in person – was more 'patriotic' and aware of the kingdom's strategic needs. The contemporary criticism of Richard's deviousness, greed and jokes about clerical failings could be recycled and 'Richard yea and nay' seem an inappropriate character to be celebrated with a prestigious equestrian statue outside the Palace of Westminster.[28] Richard could also be accused of failing to marry until he was thirty-three and thence to provide his kingdom with a son and heir, though his fiancée in the 1180s (Alice of France) had been withheld by her guardian, his father.

At most, the strains of Angevin royal financial demands and strong legalistic administration on their subjects was producing growing discontent among Richard's vassals by 1199. This was not the same as open revolt, and any strong and financially demanding king could face a revolt from opportunists aiding his ambitious relatives as Henry II found in 1173. The crises of 1199–1204 were not foreshadowed by any rising arc of baronial discontent or 'war-weariness', but followed the sudden change of national leadership in April 1199. Richard's sudden death followed an avoidable incident where he ventured within arrowshot of the battlements of a rebel castle at Chalus in Poitou, held by the Viscount of Limoges, without adequate protection from mail or a padded surcoat. A lucky crossbow-shot caught him in the shoulder, and the wound turned septic. Subsequent writers made much of the story that the greedy Richard had been in pursuit of a buried treasure that the Viscount had found but had not handed over to Richard, his overlord, as legally required under 'feudal' practice. But from the most contemporary account it would seem that the dispute was a more conventional case of rebellion (probably backed or inspired by Philip).[29] Nor was it a French 'master-plan' to kill Richard off; the King's venturing out unprotected to survey the state of the siege at Chalus was a case of unforeseen carelessness. Richard's posthumous literary critics were mostly in Philip's pay. This sort of revolt was the norm for turbulent Aquitaine, with armed defiance of the Duke the normal reaction by an affronted, jealous, or rival-seduced noble, and Richard had often faced it since 1173.

Was John more 'responsible' and 'statesmanlike' than Richard? And could John have taken the throne earlier than 1199 by revolt?

Thus Richard's able but controversial brother John, already renowned for his disloyalty to his family, was able to seize the throne in place of the younger but dynastically closer contender, their nephew Arthur of Brittany. He did not lack military skills and a share of the family energy, as seen by his dramatic advance across Anjou to rescue Queen Eleanor and capture her besieger Arthur at Mirabeau. But this example of his 'potential', often cited by his defenders, and his concern for exerting English royal power against the reviving state of Gwynedd in 1210–11 must be set against his failures. His energy was not consistent, unlike Henry II's and Richard's; indeed in Normandy in 1203 he showed no sense of strategy in endeavouring to halt Philip Augustus' advance (e.g. by relieving Chateau Gaillard). He clearly did not inspire the sort of loyalty that Richard did, although his defenders have sought to excuse the extent of revolt in 1215 and the long list of complaints about governmental abuses of power and heavy taxation as an indictment of the Angevin 'governmental machine' rather than him personally. By this reckoning, the intrusive bureaucracy of Angevin government had been over-taxing its subjects for decades and after the loss of Normandy and Anjou John had to make up for the reduction in his income by redoubling his demands on his remaining subjects. He was thus in the 'wrong place at the wrong time' in facing revolt in 1215 as any current king, even Richard, would have faced this problem; and any king with a sense of his rights would have sought to overturn the humiliating forced settlement at Runnymede. Appealing to the Pope to annul it was perfectly legal, albeit taking a risk that any armed challenge to the settlement would face stiff military resistance. And had John's strategy to invade France in 1214 succeeded and his Low Countries allies not Philip won the battle of Bouvines, leading to a march on Paris, would it have suppressed baronial criticism? Would John have seemed too successful to face a winnable revolt? Indeed, Philip came within inches of being killed by a pike-thrust at Bouvines – humiliatingly, by German spearmen not lordly knights – and had to be helped to safety by his men. Given the usual collapse of an army if its leader fell, Philip being killed would probably have caused a French retreat – though his adult son Louis (VIII) was capable enough to halt a subsequent invasion of Normandy by John in 1215, with fortifications aiding the defence.

John's actions in undermining Richard in his absence on Crusade in 1191–4 with the aid of Philip were arguably no worse than Richard's in turning to Philip for aid against Henry II in 1187–9, or the 'Young King's' in waging war on his father in 1173–4 and 1183. But this time it occurred during the Crusade so it incurred the institutional Church's (and assorted Christian idealists') displeasure. There are indications that some lay opinion was critical of John too and this undermined his search for support; he achieved more backing in the first stage of his plans, in 1191, when he was not aiming for the throne (yet) but at removing the loathed regent Bishop Longchamp. When it came to an open challenge to Richard as king he had less support, and the fact that his brother was now a captive gave him the appearance of a shameless opportunist. The fact that John had little support in England against the regency in 1193–4 was, however, not necessarily just a sign of him being disliked – few people would back a probable 'loser' against a vigorous government for fear of punishment, and the regency was politically stronger in 1191–4 once the greedy and unpopular Bishop Longchamp had been removed. John's self-interested treachery to father (June 1189) and brother (1191–4) was not that unusual or condemnable in the context of his family and times, and his parents had been at war with each other when he was six. Psychologists have suggested that he was affected by being an unwanted child, given that he was born much later than his siblings when Eleanor was already either forty-two or forty-four. All Henry II's attempts to grant him lands within his elder brothers' domains had been frustrated by them, and his desertion of Henry as he was dying at the end of June 1189 was practical in securing his new sovereign's goodwill if rather sordid.

John's actions in 1191 to lead the deposition of Longchamp had public backing from his peers, not least as the arrogant regent had recently violated sanctuary by having Archbishop Geoffrey of York dragged out of sanctuary at Dover.[30] But taking advantage of Richard's capture by Leopold of Austria as he returned from Crusade to try to have Richard imprisoned indefinitely and take his throne was another matter. The action of attacking a Church-backed Crusader by taking advantage of his absence was a breach of contemporary 'mores', and when John's ally Philip attempted to invade Normandy his own barons refused to support him.[31] In particular as John (already recognized as heir by the English secular and religious leadership in 1191) went beyond claims of regency – in case the disappeared Richard was dead – to seek the Crown. Queen Eleanor and the Church sent out envoys to find out if Richard was still alive as rumours spread, with or without the mythical participation of Richard's minstrel Blondel; John immediately claimed the Crown. This time the majority of the magnates remained loyal, and John's rebel castles across England were isolated and blockaded.[32] His visit to France to do homage to Philip for Normandy, followed by Philip's invasion of Normandy on his behalf and capture of the strategically vital Gisors (whose castellan surrendered without a fight)[33] had no serious justification even if Philip was accepted as being entitled to transfer his 'fief' of Normandy to a new holder. Transfer of a fief was supposed to have legal justification, and Philip's action against an illegally kidnapped Crusader was blatantly opportunistic; he was justifiably believed to be encouraging Emperor Henry to keep Richard in prison for life.

Richard's captivity was unprecedented for an English monarch, and the crisis that resulted has been seen as part of his general lack of a sense of responsibility for his role as King of England. His absence on Crusade and his captivity from 1190 to 1194 was followed by a brief visit to England and then spending the rest of his nearly-ten-year reign on the Continent. This could be compared with the way in which John, in contrast, spent a far greater part of his reign in England. John, indeed, raised the domestic power of the King over his baronial vassals and the princes of Wales to new heights by 1210 and his defiance of the Pope over accepting the papal nominee Stephen Langton as Archbishop of Canterbury could be portrayed as a 'nationalist' forerunner of Henry VIII's actions. A remarkable 'national' collection of major and minor vassals rallied to him on Barham Downs in Kent in 1213 to defy Philip Augustus' threatened invasion. By contrast, Richard enabled King William of Scots to buy his way out of the strict vassalage enforced by Henry II in 1174 and according to one account put all offices he could up for sale to raise money.[34] (Buying William off in fact stopped him from aiding rebels.) He was criticized (in retrospect) for forgiving and lavishing lands and an heiress on John, building up his power which was to aid his treachery,[35] and allegedly said that he would sell London if he could find a buyer (no doubt just a joke).[36] Was John therefore a more responsible English king compared with the warrior Richard's 'obsession' with a Crusade that was not in England's interests? This was the attitude of some patriotic historians, who deplored Richard's preference of Aquitaine, and it owes its origin to the presentation of the crisis of 1213 by William Shakespeare in his play 'King John' in 'pseudo-1588' patriotic terms. John stood up to the Catholic Church as Henry VIII and Elizabeth did later; he was thus a better king. Similarly, the survival of large amounts of governmental documentation from John's reign and his keenness for paperwork earned him the plaudits of modern historians for understanding and concentrating on governance rather than on warfare. John seemed not only a 'nationalist' but a responsible bureaucrat; Richard seemed a vainglorious thug.[37] But this was not the contemporary view, as Richard (unlike John) was treated to poetic lamentations on his death as the epitome of glory, success, and Christian valour[38] and even the sceptical monk Ralph of Coggeshall commended his piety and energy if deploring his greed.[39]

It could be argued that Richard – intended as Duke of Aquitaine until 1183 – neglected his kingdom. He chose to be buried at Fontevrault in Anjou – but this was a family monastic foundation where his parents were buried. John had some grounds for overthrowing him in his absence by this argument. But this neglects the fact that taking up the papal call to retrieve the Holy City from the infidel in the late 1180s was not seen at the time as 'neglect' of a practical duty to stay in one's own lands keeping order. It was accepted as part of a Christian king's religious duty to protect Christendom under papal direction, and the Crusade was joined by other rulers who had pressing duties at home such as Philip Augustus (although he left Palestine for home as soon as he had an excuse that he had fulfilled his vows, after the fall of Acre, and was criticized for it.) Philip, soon to be excommunicated by the Pope for abandoning his wife Ingeborg of Denmark in favour of his mistress Agnes of Meran and by all accounts ruthlessly pragmatic, was unable to evade taking the Cross in person in 1189–90 and Henry II's reluctance to leave his kingdom was subject to Church criticism. Nowadays, such preference of kingly duties at home to fighting the 'Infidel' has seemed more praiseworthy to commentators. But this argument is projecting modern 'mores' onto the twelfth century, and there is no sign in the evidence that John's greater sense of 'nationalism' or 'responsibility' was welcomed by his leading barons. If they were relieved to be rid of Normandy after 1204, why did John face repeated revolt? And why did he keep attempting to recover his lost domains, with a major campaign – hiring European allies at great cost –planned as late as 1214?

Richard: Crusade and captivity: Was his humiliating capture primarily due to his incompetence or his enemies' luck?

Any ruler of England in Richard's position in 1189 would have had difficulty in evading the requirement to save what remained of the Kingdom of Jerusalem; this would have applied to John had he been nominated as heir by a vengeful Henry II after the confrontation with Richard at Le Mans (perhaps if Henry had lived until the autumn). It was to Richard's credit as a responsible statesman that he stayed in Palestine into 1192 to attempt to take Jerusalem and then force a treaty out of Saladin stabilizing the revived Kingdom, as well as fulfilling his personal lust for glory as a warrior to test himself against the Moslem armies. At the time it was Philip who was seen as irresponsible for leaving for home before the Kingdom of Jerusalem had been secured, not Richard for staying.[40] Moreover, the English King's captivity was not the result of his own irresponsibility – except in so much as he angered his future captor, Duke Leopold of Austria, at the capture of Acre by pulling down his banner from the walls and denying his rights as first to enter the city.[41] Technically, Richard had a legal point in that Leopold was a vassal of the Holy Roman Emperor not a sovereign and so not entitled to the same martial honours of displaying his banner. It was more risky of Richard to leave for England with only a small escort in one ship and sail up the Adriatic, rather than assembling enough men and hire enough ships to voyage on a more south-westerly route via the Straits of Messina or the south coast of Sicily to Spain. But it appears that many of his army had already drifted home from Palestine, and that more had left earlier in autumn 1192 without waiting for their king.[42] Richard had been concentrating on the final settlement with Saladin at that point, not worrying about assembling a viable fleet to sail home in safety.

Given the strong currents in the Straits of Gibraltar, sailing home that way in a small, wind-powered sailing-vessel was very difficult (especially in winter). It would also attract the attention of North African Moslem pirates, who only a large fleet could fight off. He thus had to head for the European coasts and travel home thence by land – across other rulers' territory. Logically, given the number of his enemies controlling the north-western Mediterranean coasts between Italy and Aquitaine in 1192 Richard needed to consider his return route carefully. Philip was capable of having him kidnapped en route so John could seize his throne, whether or not Philip genuinely believed that Richard had wanted to murder him.[43] Philip was supposed to have asked Emperor Henry VI to intercept and arrest Richard if possible, and was claiming the Vexin, 'smearing' Richard to the Pope, and inviting John to Paris before Richard's seizure – his plots preceded and did not result from the King's arrest.[44] As with his trust of John, 'honourable'

Richard was caught by surprise. Duke Raymond V of Toulouse – a hereditary foe of the Dukes of Aquitaine – was hostile and had reputedly sent his son to Provence to intercept and seize Richard.[45] Toulouse controlled the Languedoc and the lower Rhone by holding the county of St Gilles, blocking the route up-river to Lyons. If Richard did not have enough men with him to force his passage across a hostile land like Toulouse or Provence, his legal inviolability as a Crusader was useless – as it was to be in Austria. The small size of his escort home from Palestine suggests that he had given no thought as to the enemies waiting on his return journey, which was naïve and possibly irresponsible but understandable given his recent priorities. This rashness is similar to that which he showed when he ventured within arrow-shot of the walls of Chalus in April 1199, but it is arguable if this would have been seen as incompetence on either occasion if his luck had not run out.

The timing of the conclusion of the Palestine campaign left Richard facing a winter sea-journey home, and his failure to order a substantial English naval contingent to wait for his embarkation added to the weather to make the Atlantic route impractical. He would thus have had to aim for the French or Italian coasts in any case. But he had a problem in his intended landfall; his own domains did not have a Mediterranean port. Landing at Genoa or Pisa, the main western Italian commercial shipping-centres, to return home overland would be risky as they were currently allied to his foe Emperor Henry VI and lending him ships for his imminent war against Richard's ally, King Tancred of Sicily. Even if he landed at Venice – a possible real-life destination had he not been shipwrecked in Istria – and travelled overland to Turin (in the county of Piedmont) or semi-autonomous imperial vassal Milan he still had to cross the Alps in midwinter, and risked being intercepted by Henry's men in lands owing allegiance to the Emperor. Dangerously close was Montferrat, home of the late Conrad who he was accused of having killed – would Conrad's kin ambush him? His best course would have been to have a large entourage, making interception difficult, but it seems that this was not available –probably due to the piecemeal nature of the English Crusaders' departure from Palestine. Nor was Richard a calculating character who would have sought to travel with other senior Western European rulers who had been on the Crusade, meaning that if Henry's men intercepted the party the Emperor would face complaints from a multitude of offended dynasts. As it turned out, his sister Joan (widow of William II of Sicily) and his new wife Berengaria did attempt to cross Italy northwards from Sicily to France and had to take refuge from Henry's and Philip's allies in Rome with the Pope. That would have been Richard's safest option, if rather inglorious –provided that he evaded ambush en route across southern Italy from people he had attacked during his brief war with Tancred there in 1190. Typically, he was supposed to have infuriated the locals in one town by seizing a falcon from a farmer on the grounds that such a lowly born person had no right to a hunting bird of prey (restricted to noble ownership in France).[46]

Richard's decision to avoid the snowy Alps, the pro-Henry ports of Liguria, or Languedoc and attempt to travel north-east across Austria in a wide arc to the Danube in secret had some logic – it would not be expected by his enemies. He was allegedly shipwrecked and could not come ashore where intended, but he made the best of his position. The alternative would have been to leave his ship at his first port of call, Ragusa/Dubrovnik, and head across Croatia for Hungary or Vienna; but this would entail crossing unfamiliar mountain-passes in midwinter. He travelled fast and quickly with only a small escort, leaving most of his men – enough to attract attention but not enough to guard him against a determined attack – behind. Rumour soon spoke of his presence, and some of the men he had left behind were mistaken for him and arrested by a local foe he had insulted on the Crusade, Count Meinhard of Gorizia. One of them was supposed to have pretended to be Richard to give his king more time to get across Austria before a search was instituted. Richard's eventual capture at the end of December 1193 was a matter of bad luck, with the possibility that illness held him up as his speed of travel had unexpectedly slowed near his foe Leopold's capital, Vienna. Supposedly his attendant pageboy attracted suspicion by selling unusually fine items of apparel to raise funds or by showing off Richard's expensive gloves while out shopping; Leopold's men arrested and interrogated him and called at Richard's inn. (Philip made the most of the ignoble circumstances of a king being found roasting meat in an inn's kitchen.) Leopold then handed him over to a minor vassal, who could keep Richard secure at the nearby castle of Durnstein on the Danube cliffs while he debated what to do; Emperor Henry heard what had happened and required Leopold to sell the captive to him.[47] It was not certain that Leopold would obey orders and hand Richard over, with the transaction taking several weeks to arrange; but if Henry had not secured Richard there was a danger that Philip would have paid Leopold to keep their mutual enemy in prison for years. Richard's arrival in Henry's hands meant that he could negotiate with the supreme ruler in Germany – a man who would want political concessions plus cash so that Richard would not interfere in his attack on Tancred – rather than with some minor prince who was more amenable to an offer of money from Philip to keep him locked up. Philip's responsibility for encouraging (or paying) Henry was believed even in France[48] – so would Richard have been released quicker, on easier terms, but for him? Henry's main concern (apart from money) appears to have been Richard's alliance with Tancred of Sicily, his Italian foe – both he and Leopold wanted to bind Richard to assist them, not Tancred, in Italy.[49]

Had Richard not been recognized and been captured it would have seemed another brilliant if daring gamble, like his headlong assault on Jaffa as Saladin's men were reoccupying it on 1 August 1192. Sooner or later he would take a risk too far, as he did in venturing within bowshot of the walls of Chalus without protection in April 1199. But at the time his rashness nearly paid off, though his disguise as an ordinary traveller does not seem to have been very effective. It was the rumours that he had been spotted in Austria that induced Duke Leopold to watch out for him in the first place, leading to his capture at an inn outside Vienna. It would have been far wiser for him to wait in Palestine until he had collected enough men and ships to make it difficult for any enemy to intercept him at sea or on land during a return journey to Languedoc or Aragon, or to travel up through Italy relying on an armed escort and the Pope.

The 1193–4 rebellion: John's miscalculation and defeat

John received minimal support in England or Normandy in 1193–4, and ambition outstripped sense in his taking the gamble that Richard would remain captive and his usurpation succeed. Only the arrival of the new Archbishop of Canterbury, Hubert Walter, from Richard to arrange a truce for the collection of the ransom saved his remaining English castles of Tickhill and Nottingham from conquest by Richard's loyalists in April 1193.[50] The attempt to encourage Emperor Henry in his breach of faith in holding Richard for ransom was equally bound to be detrimental to John's reputation, granted that he could not expect Henry to be politically able to defy the Church indefinitely in holding Richard captive even if John and Philip between them prevented a ransom being paid. Henry I of England had been able to hold his brother Robert captive for twenty-eight years, but the Church was now far more active, Richard was a major sovereign and a Crusader, and John had his mother, Eleanor, and assorted other royal partisans of his brother active in agitating for the King's release. Emperor Henry was not likely to hold Richard for many years even if John intercepted a ransom, given that he needed papal acquiescence for his planned attack on southern Italy to back his wife Constance's claim to Tancred's kingdom. The militarily difficult task of bringing a German army down through Italy to take over Apulia and then Sicily had defeated past Emperors, e.g. Lothar III in the 1130s, and the proudly autonomist Northern Italian city-states were always suspicious of German power – they had successfully defied Henry's father, Frederick, in the 1160s. Henry's plans would not be helped by having a furious Pope condemning him for holding a Crusader king captive – though he might well seek to keep Richard out of action until he had overthrown his ally Tancred. (In the event, Tancred died in 1194 so Henry could depose his young sons relatively easily.)

John may have genuinely thought Richard to be dead for a few weeks early in 1193, while Leopold of Austria and Henry VI were haggling over his custody. The Church emissaries finally found Richard in Leopold's custody, en route to the Emperor near Wurzburg, in mid-March.[51] Richard had named his late brother Geoffrey's son Arthur of Brittany as his intended heir in a private treaty with King Tancred while on Crusade,[52] and whether or not John's spies had informed him of this John could claim the throne in the event of Richard's death the same way that Henry I had claimed William II's in 1100. The English magnates' recognition of his claim in 1191 was a sign in his favour. But once Richard was known to be alive his continued plotting showed naked ambition and miscalculation of the level of his support. The option still lay open to him of backing down and pretending that he had only sought the Crown when he believed Richard to be dead, although his earlier actions would sour Richard's attitude to him anyway.

In military terms, John (lord of Tickhill and the Peak District area of Tutbury, and in control of Windsor, Wallingford, and Nottingham) did not have enough lands and castles within England in 1193 to mount an effective revolt without major backing by other magnates. He clearly ignored the military lessons of 1173–4, when the rebel 'Young King' had also failed to overthrow the incumbent regime despite being the crowned heir (or co-king) and having the loyalty of the Bigods in East Anglia so he could land mercenaries from the Continent. John's lands were too scattered to serve as a secure 'bloc' that could not be reconquered easily, as the rebel coalition of 1139 had been able to defy Stephen from their south-western territories; nor did he have Scots help, as those rebels and the 'Young King' had done. The royal justiciars, backed by Queen Eleanor, held John at bay and he had to hand over all his castles but Tickhill and Nottingham to the Queen as part of a truce-settlement. Richard took them in 1194. Nor did his allies win much ground in Normandy or Poitou, though Philip – more interested in nibbling away at the Norman border in the Vexin for his long-term advantage? – succeeded in taking the vital frontier castle of Gisors. He would have stood a far better chance if Philip had managed to persuade the Emperor to hand over Richard to him, as he endeavoured to do in June 1193. Philip's long-term grudges towards Richard meant that he was unlikely to release him quickly, if at all, and Richard's vassals would realize that and could waver in their allegiance. What was the point of fighting for a lost cause? Luckily, Richard managed to talk Henry out of that and lure him into accepting a lucrative if humiliating ransom, which in political terms required Richard to abandon Tancred's cause and swear fealty to the Emperor.[53] The apparent humbling of the English King by the German Emperor was a major blow to Richard's prestige, but it should be recalled that doing homage to a more powerful ruler was a two-way process. It also obliged the recipient to back their vassal, so Henry had no grounds for supporting Philip against Richard unless Richard broke his word – and in 1213 the equally hard-pressed John was to declare himself a vassal of Pope Innocent to win the latter's backing against Philip and rebel barons.

What if the English State administrative machine had not produced the ransom efficiently and Richard had not been freed so quickly? Or Philip had taken Richard into custody and the disheartened Ricardians had wavered? If John had secured the English crown by military force based on his estates and relied on Philip to win him Normandy in 1193–4, did he think that this new arrangement would last? Would an eventually freed Richard – a better commander than either of them – put up with losing the heart of his dominions? John may have counted on Philip's current marriage to Princess Ingeborg of (the navally powerful) Denmark to bring in King Cnut VI and his fleet, but if so the immediate failure of the marriage ruined that gamble. Even if it took several years to raise the ransom, Richard's long rule of and personal following in Aquitaine (aided by his mother's role there) would make it likely that once he was freed he would be able to secure that duchy. He would then use its resources against John and Philip.

The gamble that John took on the extent of his defiance of Richard in 1193–4 showed that he was prepared to defy the probabilities of military reality in the long term, rather than seeking to win Richard's goodwill by showing his loyalty. The latter might not persuade the King to make him his heir, but an adult – and well-regarded – John was more likely to win the adherence of most of the magnates over a young and foreign-resident Arthur if Richard died childless in some skirmish. John had the precedent of Henry I's position in 1100 to show how a king's intentions for the succession could be permanently set aside if the magnates rallied to a rival claimant. In the event, despite his treachery in 1192–4 his role as the adult claimant and possible antipathy to Arthur as a Breton won him the immediate backing of the Norman magnates in April 1199, and the English leadership followed suit. Arthur's lack of personal contacts with great nobles and clerics in London and Rouen doubtless acted to his detriment; John was known if not trusted, and was married to the co-heiress of the Welsh Marcher lordship of Gloucester/Glamorgan.

The problem with John as a ruler – from contemporary evidence

But have John's modern supporters missed one important factor in the question of an 'inevitable' collapse of Angevin power in 1203–1204? Leadership of a medieval state was an intensely personal matter, based on senior nobles trusting and/or fearing their ruler, and after 1199 the Angevin state had a far different man in charge. It is significant that time after time in John's career he appears to have inspired dislike and distrust from his leading subjects. This cannot be put down to the bias of extant Church-based chroniclers who disliked his religious policies and challenge to the Pope; even those such as Giraldus Cambrensis who personally knew the royal family concurred.[54] It is open to question whether Richard was regarded as untrustworthy, and if the 'yea and nay' characterization means that he changed his mind often or if he was unable to dissemble. ('Yea' meant 'yea' and 'nay' meant 'nay', with no equivocation?) But he was an inspiring leader, and John was not despite his occasional flashes of military acumen such as his dash to the relief of Mirabeau when Arthur was besieging Queen Eleanor there during the 1202 rebellion. He could not secure much loyalty during the 1193 rebellion despite his brother being abroad and possibly imprisoned for life, although his naked ambition and the lack of decorum in attacking a Crusader did not help his cause. He claimed Richard was dead before this could be checked, giving observers grounds to call him an opportunist. He was not much of a strategist in 1200, when he abandoned his right to ally with other 'vassals' of Philip – Richard's vital allies – and paid a feudal 'relief' as Philip's vassal in the treaty of Le Goulet. (His defenders argue that he had to neutralize Philip by concessions, but if so did he give too much ground?) Nor was he a competent general, which could have made up for lack of personal 'elan'. His ability to drive Llywelyn ap Iorweth of Gwynedd into the Arfon mountains and force his submission in 1210 – when he had weight of numbers and equipment on his side – is less important than his later failures. His military strategy during the major rebellion of 1215–16 showed signs of energy but incoherence; he may have been induced to caution by not trusting his vassals but he ended up darting across the country looting and burning at random rather than tackling his foes 'head-on'. His campaign then showed no sign of a coherent strategy, merely of a desire to terrorize any of his opponents who had lands within his reach. The famous story of the itinerant king losing his Crown Jewels in the Wash during this final campaign in 1216 obscures the fact that at the time he was engaged in a series of manoeuvres of no obvious tactical import, rather than securing his loyal areas and preparing to advance on rebel London.[55] So was he deficient as a general compared to Richard? The lack of a vigorous attempt to defend Normandy in 1203 (e.g. relieving Chateau Gaillard) is less damning despite his mysterious period of inaction at Rouen during the siege, as he may have lacked reliable local support thanks to rumours that he had murdered Arthur. But in his place Richard would have been engaged in all sorts of ingenious plans or quick feints to lure Philip away from the siege; the chronicles imply that John was content to relax and indulge in another of his bouts of gluttony.[56] It is possible that he was suffering from depression (at the lack of local support?) and had given up hope of success so he was taking refuge in over-eating – there have been suggestions that he suffered from 'bi-polar disorder' and that this explains his alternation between energy and lethargy.

John's well-known lust for his barons' womenfolk must have made for resentment, although the best-known case of his intemperate and 'inappropriate' womanizing has been misrepresented.[57] His abandonment of his engagement to a Portuguese princess in 1200 to marry the under-age Isabella of Angouleme, aged fifteen at most and possibly under twelve, had a valid political motive. She was heiress to her father Ademar, whose crucial lands would pass to her husband – and she was currently engaged to one of the politically dubious Lusignan family, who were among the principal landowners in Poitou and had a reputation for arrogant disloyalty to their resented overlords the Dukes of Aquitaine. Isabella's fiancé Hugh's uncle Guy had attempted to kidnap Queen Eleanor in 1168, gone out to Jerusalem to marry its heiress, become king and lost his kingdom to Saladin, and been granted Cyprus by Richard in 1192; his brother Amalric was now King of Cyprus and Jerusalem. If the Angouleme lands passed to the Lusignans they could do even more damage and hand both families' lands over to Philip in a rebellion; John secured them for himself by marrying Isabella, though this alienated the Lusignans anyway.[58] His impetuous marriage had its bonuses as well as its problems, and the reputed infidelity of both parties later was of little political import. But his energy in military campaigning was only sporadic, unlike Henry II's and Richard's; his wayward concentration and occasional pointless savagery were reminiscent of the 'Young King'.

His father had also had an obsession with movement from site to site with his court, constantly on the move, resembling a huge camp.[59] Like Richard, John used Philip against his sovereign – but he attracted more opprobrium for it. Like Richard, John could muster an international coalition to take Philip in the rear (in 1214) and it was not his fault that his Flemish allies were routed by the French at Bouvines. But was 'war-weariness' the only reason for the lack of support his planned expeditions to the Loire secured in England after 1204? His streak of violence and vindictiveness surely played a part in people being unable to trust him, unlike his similarly bad-tempered father who was not deserted by most of his English vassals when they had a rival (the 'Young King') to hand in 1173. Henry had spoken the rash words that led to an Archbishop being slaughtered in his own cathedral in the recent past and his wife and older sons were in revolt, but most of his vassals backed him; by contrast in 1216 the similarly revolt-hit John faced a coalition of barons across south-eastern England backing his French foe. The royalist cause did not achieve a decisive advantage until the controversial King was dead, when sentiment could rally round his nine-year-old son and the 'Regent' William Marshal. Neither of these new leaders had a reputation for turning on people without warning that John did, and young Henry III was a useful 'blank slate' on whom to build aspirations for a future monarchy loyal to the Magna Carta and governing justly.

John's making of 'examples' by calculated savagery ranged from his Marcher challengers (starving the de Braose family to death) to Welsh hostages (hanged),[60] though executing hostages for breach of faith was a more common procedure than John's deliberate and calculated punishment of male and female prisoners from the magnate class. His holding potential rivals and their allies for decades without ransom or release, e.g. Arthur's sister Eleanor of Brittany, was not that unusual as William I had held prominent Anglo-Saxon leaders (Earl Morcar and Wulfnoth Godwinson) and Henry I had held his elder brother Robert 'Curthose'. The use of Corfe Castle as a virtual internment-camp for prominent hostages was less unusual than the violent (and secret) punishments that John sporadically inflicted, though Henry II had mutilated and killed (Welsh) hostages too. Whether or not his lack of Richard's military skills and charisma encouraged local barons in his French dominions to resume plotting after his seizure of the Crown and initial victory over Arthur, his turbulent rule soon led to new revolts with Arthur's fate handing Philip an excuse to act as the shocked avenger and confiscate his murderous vassal's Continental domains. Within four years of John's accession the French King was embarked on a successful war to overrun Normandy, Maine, and Anjou and permanently overturn the balance of power between Capetians and Angevins in the former's favour, at last making the kings of France the strongest power in their kingdom. The French King's military power and the lack of John's ability to bring an equivalent force to Normandy to defeat him in 1203–1204 would have encouraged waverers seeking to protect their lands to defect, but the fact of Arthur's disappearance must have had some effect in preventing serious local resistance to a French invasion. The local nobles usually rallied to their Duke even if he could not be present in person, as they had shown in defeating Philip's incursions in Richard's absence in prison (when they could not have been sure that Richard would win).

From the debacle of 1203–1204 the power of the English Crown was substantially reduced, even if the dynasty's forced concentration on affairs in Britain rather than France was to the island's benefit. Having failed to force his barons to accompany him for more futile expeditions to Poitou, John perforce exercised his military machine against the Welsh and Irish, and succeeded in reducing Llywelyn ap Iorweth from domination of all the South Welsh princes to a humbled vassal-prince of Arfon (as any competent English king with the manpower could do). Neither John nor his son Henry III wholly abandoned attempts to regain their lost dominions in northern France, but all these were unsuccessful and in 1259 England finally recognized the loss of all France except a reduced state in Aquitaine and agreed to continue to hold that as a vassal. From now on, all kings would spend far more time in England than across the Channel, with consequently more effort put into campaigning in Wales (and later Scotland), and those lords with lands in both England and Northern France had to make a choice of basing themselves in one or other area. The English barons soon showed that they were unwilling to spend time and resources reconquering the lost lands for John with unprecedented mutinies against his demands for military aid, and his endeavours to rebuild a powerful financial and administrative/ military apparatus in England in 1205–13 increased the latent local resentment of royal demands to the point of revolt. Where Henry II had raised eight 'scutages' in thirty-four years, John raised eleven in sixteen; and his use of fines for offences against the peace ('amercements') amounted to systematic and often arbitrary blackmail. Worse, his principal financial officers were often from overseas, e.g. the Poitevin bishop Peter des Roches. The major royal tenants-in-chief were to prove equally dismissive of their overlord's tax demands and continental ambitions in their angry reaction to John's son Henry III in the 1250s, as the latter endeavoured to acquire the Crown of Sicily from the Pope for his younger son Edmund at the cost of high taxes and a military campaign.

There had been rebellions against the demands of the Angevin Crown in England before, in 1173–4 and 1192–4. But even this can be partially explicable as opportunism by personally ambitious men ready to back a hopefully munificent pretender (the 'Young King' and John) against the King, not principled opposition to financial extortion. There were grumbles about excessive financial demands during Henry's reign, but people paid up and there was no obvious ideological element to the rebellion in 1173–4. When faced with the justiciars' and Queen's orders to pay huge sums to ransom Richard in 1193, there was similar acquiescence not a flood of volunteers to join the rebel John.[61] John's increased requirements of men and money after 1204 were a result of the humiliating loss of Normandy and

Anjou, which he sought to reverse, not a straightforward continuation of a level of military and fiscal demands constant since the 1170s. He had either to raise his own subjects as a new army or require them to pay for mercenaries (an increasing element of the army even under Richard), and his Continental allies had to be bought before they would attack Philip. There followed a 'strike' by his tenants-in-chief against a Continental campaign in 1205, and the major revolt of 1215 that was to lead to the compilation of the 'Magna Carta' and a permanent shift in the relationship between Crown and leading subjects. None of this would have been likely without the events of 1199–1204, which introduced both a controversial new King and special demands on his subjects for Continental wars. Even then, greater loyalty would have been probable without the disturbing instances of John's arbitrary vengefulness, with contemporary evidence indicating that the de Braose incident made a great impact. And even in 1215 only 39 out of 197 baronies were implicated in the Magna Carta rising – with nearly thrice as many in the 1216 revolt.

There has been an argument that the balance of resources between the Angevins and Philip was shifting in the latter's favour around 1200. Thus, Philip would have had the money to recruit mercenaries and bribe restive barons in the Angevins' French dominions to join his cause with Richard or John as his opponent. The Angevin 'empire' in France was thus inevitably crumbling, with its revenues in decline and the local nobility restive at the financial and judicial demands of the rulers. The minor successes that Philip enjoyed on the Norman border in the 1190s could be cited as evidence that the balance of power was changing in his favour, with Richard's huge new castle at Les Andelys (Chateau Gaillard) seen as a 'panic' defensive reaction that was doomed to failure. In fact, it seems that the financial figures upon which this case is based refer to the situation in 1202 rather than at Richard's death in 1199.[62] By this point John's character and actions had already sparked off the first defections, led by Arthur. Richard's biographer John Gillingham concludes that in 1199 Richard still held the initiative, having won over a number of Philip's Northern French vassals and secured the election of his nephew Otto as 'King of the Romans' in Germany, and that it was the King's death and John's accession that altered matters.[63] Indeed, it is arguable that if the pro-English Otto had not been distracted by a struggle over the German throne with Henry VI's brother Philip of Swabia until the latter's death in 1208 Otto could have attacked Philip in the rear in 1204 and saved Normandy from conquest. Similarly, a German-Flemish victory over Philip at Bouvines in 1214 would have prevented Philip from having the time or resources free to assist the English rebels by lending them his son Louis as their leader in 1215–16. John's triumph might well have prevented the discontented barons from daring to revolt openly in 1215. But John's character makes it likely that if Bouvines had vindicated his strategy he would have been pressing to attack Normandy in 1215 – sparking another 'strike'?

Was John unlucky in his timing or demonstrably a worse leader than Richard? The examples of 1199–1203 and the post-1207 clash with the Church

John was certainly unlucky in his Continental alliances, as seen above. His German ally Otto was distracted from helping him by an attack on France in the crucial years of 1203–1205 when Normandy and Anjou were being lost or had just been lost, and the 1214 coalition invasion collapsed. Had Richard's ally Count Baldwin VIII of Flanders – a capable general, as shown by his actions as 'Latin Emperor of Constantinople' in 1204–1205 – not gone off on the Fourth Crusade in 1203 he would have been a formidable Angevin ally and could have come to Normandy's aid. It is not clear if it was Richard's death and his lack of a similar personal relationship with John that made him abandon his English alliance and go off on Crusade; would he have gone had Richard been alive? (Instead of fighting for John against Philip, he won an unexpected throne in Constantinople but ended up dead or captured by the Bulgarians as they attacked his new Empire in 1205.) The Albigensian Crusade also fundamentally altered current papal-French hostility over Philip's illegal divorce from Ingeborg of Denmark, with the King of France a crucial ally in the Pope's religious and later military campaign in Languedoc. After the murder of the anti-Cathar papal legate Peter of Castelnau by a Toulousan agent in 1208 Pope Innocent needed Northern French military aid to overthrow Count Raymond VI of Toulouse and the Cathars, and so had to back Philip – overlord of his potential commanders – in any dispute with John. Philip never obeyed papal requests to lead the 'Crusade' himself, but he lent it valuable aid and as the local lords resisted their Northern French attackers Philip's son Louis twice led a royal army into the Languedoc to try to take Toulouse. Thus John was at a treble disadvantage – in Flanders from 1202–1203, in Germany until Otto's rival Philip of Hohenstaufen's death in 1208, and in France from 1208 – in tackling Philip.

But the depth of John's dispute with the papacy after 1207 owed much to his stubbornness and refusal to compromise. In this his savage temper and violent threats were not unusual for the Angevin dynasty, the so-called 'Devil's Brood' who imaginative contemporaries alleged owed their rages and blasphemies to being descended from Melusine, an evil fairy wife of an earlier Count of Anjou. Henry II as well as John supposedly threw himself on the floor when in a rage and bit the rush-'carpeting', and his occasional outbursts are well-documented. The most famous, of course, was his threat to be rid of Thomas Becket shortly before the latter's murder – whose wording is unclear though it evidently amounted to incitement to violence.[64] John's tempers and occasional savage punishments were not unusual, and probably indicate a degree of psychological disturbance shared with his father – as his restless journeying was shared too. The concept of blatant money-making extortion by a resented Angevin government was not new either – indeed Richard's choice as Archbishop of Canterbury, Hubert Walter, was as harsh and successful an exploiter of royal financial powers as John's choice, de Grey.[65] But this was his role as the King's right-hand man in lay government (as chief justiciar) and the Church, meeting the King's needs efficiently – the role that Henry II had intended for a compliant Becket. Walter was a highly competent and multi-talented administrator, and Richard should receive due recognition for using him as John had done for his personal bureaucratic 'input'. The 'overspill' from royal behaviour into long-term politics was worse in John's case; Henry showed far more political skill in managing to limit the results from his part in Becket's murder than John did in solving his impasse with Pope Innocent, for example, and Richard could be generous as well as vindictive. Henry was able to demonstrate his personal piety and imaginatively show remorse like a lay offender by (probably) having himself flogged at Becket's shrine – and then 'spun' the lucky capture of the rebel King William of Scots in a skirmish in the mist in Northumberland to show that the Saint had forgiven him for his murder.[66] He cunningly withdrew to Ireland during the immediate aftermath of the murder so that no outraged papal envoy could visit him to complain, giving the crisis time to cool off. But John showed no such skill, and his personal contempt for religious practice was well-known though attempts have been made to defend him. Bishop (and soon Saint) Hugh of Lincoln's biographer wrote that he was never seen at Communion after his accession, and his acting as a pall-bearer at Hugh's funeral was a rare act of piety that probably owed more to personal respect than religion.[67] John's real attitude towards religion is seen in his apparent threat to turn Moslem during his confrontation with the Pope[68] – even if it was a barbed joke, it was a poor one that no Crusader king such as Richard would have made. John seemed to have no respect for God or man; Henry's and Richard's faults of temper were more easily forgiven by their contemporaries.

The course of the crisis with the papacy shows that John was far more stubborn than his relations, to the point of political myopia – and he either did not realize or (more likely) care that he was dealing with an opponent as stubborn and determined as himself, one of the most capable and far-sighted of the medieval popes. Innocent had a firm opinion of the place of his office as the superior of all secular rulers, with the spiritual arm of Christendom superior to the secular one and delegated imperial powers by the 'Donation of Constantine', and he was backed up by a mixture of expanding canon law jurisdiction to justify interference and bureaucrats to enforce it. Unlike any pope since Alexander III in 1159–80, he had a long reign so there was continuity in papal policy under one able administrator, not a series of short-term elderly occupants who could be bent to a king's will by bribes or threats. John's quarrel with him over the appointment of a new Archbishop of Canterbury in 1207 was not a unique example of defiance, however. Philip defied the papacy too, over his repudiation of Ingeborg of Denmark, in the 1190s and was threatened with an Interdict – but by 1208 the Pope needed him as an ally to supply troops for the 'Albigenisan Crusade', the reconquest of Languedoc from the Cathars. By contrast the papacy had no need of John as a political ally, and could afford to play a waiting game until he surrendered on its terms. English kings had driven obstructive archbishops into fleeing or withdrawing abroad before (Anselm and Becket), and confrontation over who should determine an election was nothing new. It was, however, unprecedented for both the king (or the bishops acting with him) and the monks of a cathedral chapter to have their nominees superseded by a papal choice of candidate, and the fact that it was an archiepiscopal election made it more politically crucial to select an acceptable and competent choice.

The antagonism between the monks of Canterbury cathedral monastery (who technically had the right to elect) and the other interested parties – King and bishops – was a regular potential 'flashpoint', but was usually resolved either amicably or at least with mutual restraint. The election of two rival candidates by different factions of monks at a cathedral monastery was not unprecedented either. But the Pope naming his choice for a vital archbishopric without prior consultation with the King was provocative. On this occasion the stakes were higher than for a normal episcopal election, as it involved the country's leading Archbishopric and the occupant was bound to become a major political and administrative figure; the previous Archbishop, Hubert Walter, had been effectively chief minister to Richard and John and had been more of a bureaucrat than a holy man. John, in turn, expected to promote a similar figure with known loyalty and administrative ability – John de Grey, Bishop of Norwich. The choice of a governmental 'trusty' and proven bureaucrat who would carry out the King's will was nothing new; this is what Henry II had intended to do by promoting his Chancellor, Becket (not even a clergyman), as Archbishop. At the time the choice of Becket was as controversial a case of royal mistreatment of the Church as a 'department of State', in modern terms, as John's excesses – with Becket being expected to do the King's will and to bring the clergy into the state's judicial system not defy this.

John's choice of de Grey need not have led to the Pope vetoing it and imposing his own choice but for bad luck, and the choice of Langton was not a deliberate snub to royal power or an attack by super-national authority on English independence (as implied by both John and his later post-Reformation Protestant apologists). It appears that Innocent had been annoyed by John's 'strong-armed' lobbying on de Grey's behalf in Rome, and that similarly the election by 'hard-liners' among the Canterbury monks of their prior, Reginald, as a rival candidate was due to anger at royal bullying. Reginald, in turn, over-stated the level of his support in Canterbury to impress the Pope; and John in a rage forced the monks to withdraw their recognition of Reginald, elect de Grey instead, and sent a delegation with this news to Rome. Reginald could now claim that the second election had been due to illegal royal pressure and was void. When Innocent called on the rival delegations of 'de Grey' and 'Reginald' partisan monks in Rome to stage a new election the result was a tie; he then imposed Langton. Had the vote not been equal he could not have done this, although a vote for Reginald would undoubtedly not have been recognized by John either. It seems probable that John's crude attempts to buy or bully the Pope made it more likely that the latter would seek to remind him about the plenitude of papal power by exercising his self-proclaimed judicial right to nominate an archbishop, and the tone of Innocent's subsequent letters to John indeed resembles that of an exasperated headmaster rebuking a truculent pupil.[69]

The outcome of the election in Rome was thus due to factors beyond John's control; but his (customary) bullying attitude to the Canterbury monks in 1205–1206 enhanced the crisis and now his refusal to compromise led to prolonged stalemate. John's refusal to accept Langton – a distinguished academic from Paris university and not just a papal 'yes-man' – was not just a spirited nationalist response to foreign interference (as it appeared to post-Reformation Protestant commentators). These conflicts were usually resolved by diplomacy and compromise, and John's enraged refusal to move his position one inch was politically unwise. His extortionate seizures of Church property and contempt for the clergy had already earned serious rebukes from the Angevin loyalist Archbishop Geoffrey of York, his own half-brother, who now left England in disgust;[70] and the vast majority of bishops followed suit, except those too elderly or ill to be expected to make the journey. Only the secular-minded Peter des Roches, Bishop of

Winchester, obeyed the King. They cannot be written off as disloyal or too timid to risk papal censure, and their agreement in denouncing John is in stark contrast to the way in which the defiance of Henry II by Becket over the question of 'criminous clergy' evading secular legal processes – also backed by papal canon law – had split the English bishops in the 1160s. Nor did John make any attempt to seek a compromise, employing fraudulent claims that the Pope and Langton were requiring his complete surrender, making and then withdrawing concessions in an obvious bid to buy time, and meanwhile confiscating clerical property for his treasury. He made as much money out of the confiscations as the government had had to pay for Richard's ransom in 1193-4,[71] and by doing this (with blatant intimidation to add to the illegal embezzlement) hardened the 'opposition'. His extortion enabled him to pay for his Welsh, Scottish, and Irish campaigns in 1210–1212 without excessive domestic taxation, and thus decreased the risk of revolt – but the gains were short term. Once Innocent lost patience with the played-out talks and excommunicated him – which clearly genuine negotiations could have avoided – he resorted to melting down Church plate and intimidating monks into paying him what amounted to 'protection money'. With a sense of black humour, he made money by rounding up priests' concubines for ransom.[72] His final submission in 1212 only came when he faced invasion from Philip and a papal decree of deposition, and was a sign of weakness in that he had taken so long to accept the inevitable. The tactic of playing for time for years and when he had to submit doing so with a dramatic gesture resembled that of Henry II after Becket's murder; but at least Henry had had most of the bishops on his side at the time. Becket had been deliberately seeking confrontation and avoiding any compromise during his dispute with Henry II over the legal rights of the clergy to separate judicial tribunals in 1162–4, infuriating most of the other bishops, and on his return home had started excommunicating his enemies in defiance of any need to win support. There were no such personal reasons for the English bishops to back the King against an archbishop who represented 'Roman interference' in the established order in 1207–1212; John was in a weaker position but acted even more obstinately than his father had.

The main goal John sought in surrendering appears to have been the gaining of papal support against potential rebels and invaders, both of whom a papal decree of deposition would have inspired. His 'volte-face' duly won him Innocent's backing during the rebellion and French invasion of 1215–16 and, ironically, even papal support against Langton when the latter chose to back the rebels and Magna Carta (which the Pope obligingly denounced).[73] But this major gain was hardly an example of John's superior political skills, as it was his behaviour towards his leading nobles that had caused the rebellion in the first place. Despite the cost and administrative interference in the localities by any Angevin government, Henry II in 1173–4 and Richard's regency government in 1191–3 faced far fewer rebels than John did in 1215–16. That cannot be written off as being due to circumstances beyond John's control, which Richard would have faced too. Notably, once the rebellion had broken out it was marked by bad faith and trickery on John's part, which went beyond an understandable fight for survival. Having sealed (not signed) the Charter when forced to accept military reality by a superior rebel army, he could hardly wait before securing a papal decree invalidating it (writing to ask for one the day after sealing it)[74] and resuming the struggle. Luckily for him Innocent obligingly saw the barons' resistance as an impious attempt to hold up his Crusading plans. The extent of desertions from John's cause in spring 1215 should have given him greater caution had he been ruled by political skill rather than by pique at being defeated.

It was a sign of the alienation that he had caused that the rebels were prepared to call on Prince Louis to France to be their candidate for the throne. This choice – the son of the King of France, a foreign potentate and the man who had overrun Normandy, Anjou, and Maine – seems worse in modern terminology than it would have done in 1215, when concepts of nationhood were more fluid. Other new rulers had been in possession of French lands, if not the heir to the French Crown. Stephen, for instance, had been the second son of the Count of Blois and husband of the Countess of Boulogne, and Henry II had been Count of Anjou and husband of the Duchess of Aquitaine. Most of the English baronage were French by paternal descent, many had family members owning French lands as vassals of the French Crown, and they had the same culture as Philip's subjects and spoke French. In strict dynastic terms Louis did have a valid claim as the husband of John's sister's daughter, Blanche of Castile. (The alternative Angevin claimant was another sister's son, Otto of Germany.) A nephew of the former King had seized power from the King's offspring in 1135, though the latter – Matilda – had been a woman so an unusual heir and the replacement usurper had been the direct heir (Stephen) not the female direct heir's husband. The more obvious candidate to use against John would have been his own eldest son, Prince Henry, as the eldest son of Henry II had been the rebel candidate to replace his father in 1173–4; but Prince Henry was only eight as of 1215 so he suffered from the same disadvantage as Arthur of Brittany had done in 1199.

The only factor that would have affected Richard as badly as John in attempting to defend his realm in 1202–1204 would have been the departure of some of his Continental allies (e.g. Baldwin of Flanders) on Crusade, which reduced the pressure on Philip and gave him more freedom to attack Normandy.

The situation if Richard had lived into the 1200s: Radically different in France, to Philip Augustus' detriment?

Philip might well have preferred to wait until Richard's death before a major war on account of Richard's superiority as a general and in resources. He was a cautious man, unskilled in combat and never known for tackling Richard directly; he had seen him in action in close quarters many times in Palestine and it cannot be assumed that he would have invaded Normandy to confront him with as much confidence as he did in facing John in 1203–1204. The English ruler's personal relations with the major baronial families of the Angevin Continental dominions and the neighbouring autonomous dukes and counts were crucial, and Richard was a proven war-leader and renowned for his generosity and knightly qualities. Men keen to back the winning side would hardly support Philip, an inferior commander as seen in Palestine in 1191 and never victor in a major battle with the Angevins, against Richard.

John had no record of military success, unlike his brother, and had been undistinguished in action ever since his failure in Ireland in 1185. He was widely distrusted as a man who had betrayed his father in 1189, betrayed his brother while absent on Crusade and attempted to prevent him being ransomed from Germany, and then betrayed his new ally Philip by returning to Richard's side in 1194. Richard treated him with patronizing contempt – in public – when he surrendered, saying that he was a boy who had been misled by his elders. These incidents mattered in an era dominated by personal 'image', even if the uncharismatic Philip was the eventual victor in the long struggles over the Angevin state. Philip could expect some support from Norman and Angevin lords in 1202–1204 if he backed Richard's nephew Arthur, born 1187, who arguably had a stronger hereditary claim and had been named by Richard as heir in Sicily in 1190.

Arthur was only fifteen or sixteen when he challenged John in real life, and his inexperience was soon shown up as John caught him unawares besieging his grandmother Eleanor at Mirebeau. He would have been adult if Richard died after c. 1204; would this have made a difference? Or would Richard even have preferred him as heir once he was adult and so abler at defending his lands against Philip than he was in 1199? He would have done his best to win more than the hereditary lands of his mother Constance, Brittany, out of the succession. As with other challengers to the Angevin 'status quo', the 'Young King' in 1173–4 and 1183 and Richard in 1187–9, the nature of the Angevin political structure meant that an aggrieved pretender would seek the support of their ultimate overlord, the King of France. This would not come cheap at any date, and from 1203 the political situation in France would have been complicated by the Fourth Crusade. Assorted pro-Ricardian North French lords such as Count Baldwin of Flanders (who ended up chosen as the Crusaders' new 'Emperor' in Constantinople) would have been absent in the East and so not available to support John against Arthur or either against Philip. Thus Philip could get a share of the Angevin 'empire' from Arthur in return for his backing – the Vexin and part of Maine or Anjou? – or else seize it from a victorious John while the latter was fighting Arthur. Arthur, based in Brittany, was in a good position to seize and then hold nearby Anjou with Philip's support unless John inflicted a major defeat leading to his death or capture, and if Arthur continued at large John would find it difficult to keep hold of distant Anjou – either by land- reinforcements from Normandy or Aquitaine or by sea from England.

The proximity of Arthur and Philip to Anjou meant that self- preservation would encourage the local magnates to back their cause in the long term – John could not afford to leave England for years on end to maintain his military position in the area, and the English barons' resistance to serving overseas in the 1200s indicates that they had no stomach for the sort of major war that John would have had to pursue to protect Anjou. The alternative – deposing Arthur from Brittany – would have involved a long and costly campaign and a possible civil war in Brittany, as occurred between pro-English and pro-French candidates in real life after 1341. (John was lucky in that he was able to capture Arthur at Mirebeau in real life and so prevent the need for a long war with him in 1202–1203.) Revolt by Arthur against John's succession would have followed, not preceded, Richard's death. As long as Richard did not name John as his heir Arthur had no reason to revolt against him, at least as long as he kept his health and appeared a formidable warrior. But here the issue of Richard's failure to have a son by Berengaria of Navarre arises. If Richard had had a son by Berengaria or by a second wife after divorcing her the boy was at risk of being overthrown by Arthur if he succeeded as a minor; and a son of Richard by a second marriage would probably have been under-age until around 1218–20.

Richard's survival: Effects on the 'Albigensian Crusade'
The Albigensian Crusade from 1209 was to bring the French Crown real rather than nominal control over Southern France, a distinct cultural zone with its own language – the 'Langue D'Oc' – for the first time. The Northern French army of 'holy' freebooters employed by the papacy to deal with the 'heretic' Cathars in the region and their aristocratic sponsors,

headed by Count Raymond VI of Toulouse, gained control over much of the large County of Toulouse and numerous smaller lordships together with large amounts of loot. The French King duly lent the papacy his assistance in order to extend French royal power in the region as the Pope's loyal lieutenant – and to improve his reputation with the imperious Pope Innocent III after scandalously divorcing his wife Ingeborg of Denmark and marrying his mistress, Agnes of Meran. (As of the 1190s it was Philip, not the Angevin kings, being threatened with an Interdict for defying the papacy.) Imposing Northern French vassals of Philip's as the new, religiously orthodox lords of lands confiscated from Count Raymond and the other sponsors of Cathar 'heretics' extended the French King's power throughout the 'Langue D'Oc', and brought his political 'reach' to the Mediterranean for the first time, together with distracting such ambitious warlords from using their military 'muscle' in wars in Northern France to his detriment. But his attempt to secure Toulouse for a cadet of the royal line failed due to local resistance, even when his son Prince Louis intervened in person. (The distance from Paris meant that the royal feudal levy, whose term of service was limited, could not be used for the length of time required to subdue it even if the numbers of troops were adequate.). Although Raymond VI's son saved his main domains, the power of his St Gilles dynasty was broken and the King of France now had to be reckoned with in Languedoc affairs. Supported by the papacy as the Church's instrument in destroying heresy, the French Crown thus now had the resources in men and money to deploy against the Angevins and was able to repair the damage that Philip had done to his reputation in Rome in the 1190s over his defiance of the Church concerning his divorce. But would Philip have been able to do all this had the English King still held all of Aquitaine – adjacent to Toulouse to the west – as of 1209–1223 rather than being on the defensive back in England?

Philip's success in Southern France: A matter of timing: This windfall gave the French Crown a vital advantage of resources

But, given the time it took to establish order in the ravaged lands of Languedoc and the physical absence of many Northern French lords there during the fighting, Philip would not have had the men or the money at hand to take on the Angevin rulers in a conflict over Normandy until the Languedoc war was over. Had the English King still held Normandy and Anjou as of 1209, Philip would have had to make a choice of target for his military power between a war in the north and a war in the south – and the timing of the crisis that preceded the southern war was out of his hands as it relied on the timing of the locals' violent reaction to the papal missionaries sent to Languedoc to confront the Cathars. The mission's leader, Peter of

Castelnau, was assassinated near Arles in January 1208, and this was what precipitated Innocent's decision to arrange a major military expedition granted the status of a 'Crusade' – and until a campaign was given full papal legal support Philip had shown no interest in it.[75] Incidentally, the most determined and effective (and brutal) commander of the expedition, the socially obscure Count Simon de Montfort, had been on the Fourth Crusade in 1203 and left it in disgust when it headed for Constantinople not Palestine. Had Richard been alive and taken part in the expedition – or sent an English contingent, possibly headed by John – de Montfort might well have been in English not French royal employ as of 1209, and so not been available to lead the campaign. Even if he had been involved, would Philip have trusted an ally of the Angevins as his new lieutenant in the Languedoc?

With Richard alive and ruling Aquitaine or de Montfort not available as the expedition's leader, the 'Crusade' would have been in even worse difficulties and quite possibly a local, Angevin-backed force would have been on hand to keep Toulouse out of the hands of any French royal nominee. Once the French royal troops had gone home at the expiry of their legal contract for campaigning away from home, the remaining 'incomers' in Toulouse and Carcasonne could easily have faced Angevin-backed revolt ('deniable' and unofficial so as not to arouse papal anger). As it was, the 'Crusaders' control of Southern France was not secure until they had defeated the local resistance's Aragonese allies at Muret in 1213, killing King Peter of Aragon, and even then Toulouse was only temporarily subdued. Philip would have had difficulty in calling in troops from the North to match a rebel army stiffened by Angevin allies – and these French vassal lords would have been unwilling to come to his aid if they faced invasion from Anjou or Normandy at home. Richard was the hereditary foe of Raymond VI whose family had resisted Aquitaine's pretensions to dominate Toulouse, but political necessity would have dictated a 'rapprochement' with him or his son Raymond VII to thwart Philip's plans to control Toulouse. (Henry II had confronted Philip's father over the city back in 1159.)

Philip's real-life military strength in challenging John in 1214–16 was based on his seizure of Normandy, Maine, and Anjou – and if Richard had been alive these would still have been in Angevin hands at this date. Lacking these resources, Philip would have needed all the knights that he could lure from the south to take on the Angevins on equal terms in Normandy. Most of the 'Crusaders' he had sent south would have preferred to stay in their newly won lands to protect them from revolt or an incursion from the evicted St Gilles dynasty's Aragonese allies, at least until King Peter of Aragon was killed at Muret in 1213. The combination of Peter (co-victor of the battle of Las Nuevas de Tolosa over the Spanish/MoroccanMoslems in

1212) and Richard in 1213 was likely to have defeated the invading 'Crusaders' or their 'rescuer' King Philip.

What if Richard had still been alive at the time of the Albigensian Crusade in 1209? Was he capable of risking Church wrath by opposing the French nobility's wholesale attack on the County of Toulouse, his late brother-in-law Raymond V's state? Philip and the French nobles, with land and loot at stake and the Church in Rome supporting them against heretics, were not likely to have let fear of Richard's reprisal put them off the campaign – if he attacked Crusaders or their French royal sponsor he would be excommunicated. But the large number of Northern French nobles, e.g. the de Montforts who went south to join in the Albigensian war would not have been available to fight for Philip if Richard died and an Angevin civil war broke out during the Crusade, i.e. during c. 1209–1213. Philip's aid to Arthur at this point would have been smaller – but if the crisis had come later in the 1210s, when Philip had gained resources in the south and Aragon was no longer a threat, he could have used those to aid his 'push' in the north against the Angevin dynasty.

Richard's taxes and demands were as onerous as John's, e.g. for the Crusade and the ransom. But the latter was a 'one-off' and out of his control; John's taxes were for avoidable Continental wars. Not having lost his French lands, Richard would have been able to spread the burden more equally. Critically for elite reaction, he was not so personally vindictive or 'unreadable'. He was a formidable warrior and more risky to revolt against than John, but over-taxed and judicially-repressed barons could still have been discontented enough to revolt at some point. They rose against the formidable Henry II on behalf of his eldest son the 'Young King' in 1173, and clearly took advantage of inter-family Angevin squabbles to try to replace a strong king with a weaker one. Could they have risen anyway in the 1200s, perhaps after another round of unpopular taxes by the Crusader enthusiast Richard for the Fourth Crusade c. 1203? Or would Arthur, if he was only supposed to be heir to his mother Constance in Brittany not to Richard, have angled for more if it was apparent that Richard's wife Berengaria was barren and tried to insist that Richard named him not John as heir? John might have fed off baronial discontent if Richard did favour Arthur as his heir in the 1200s, presenting himself as the 'English' candidate for the heirship against the foreign-raised, alien Arthur. He had had a body of support against Richard's oppressive and unpopular regency government by Longchamp during the Third Crusade – could he have revived this coalition if Richard had allowed him back into England and relied on harsh administrators? These could have included John's real-life extortionist, Bishop des Roches. Richard might have been over-taxing and recruiting English soldiers to fight yet another faraway war in France – e.g. against the

Albigensian Crusaders over Toulouse. As the English nobles were reluctant to fight in France for John in 1205–1206, they might have been equally reluctant for a faraway war in Languedoc around 1209. The mutinies of tenants-in-chief in the 1200s against John's levies for an overseas war might have broken out against Richard, with John encouraging them.

Richard and the Fourth Crusade: If he had joined it, no sack of Constantinople?

Would Richard have gone on the Fourth Crusade, given his fondness for warfare, Christian zeal, and regret at having left the Third Crusade unfinished with the Moslems still controlling Jerusalem? Despite the chaos that resulted at home, he was quite capable of putting his international Christian duty first – but with Queen Eleanor nearly eighty in 1202/3, Arthur an adolescent with ties to Richard's arch-enemy Philip, and John a proven traitor from the 1190–1194 period, who could he trust to rule the country? He could not trust Philip not to support a revolt by Arthur in his absence despite Church reaction – Philip defied the Church blatantly over his treatment of his wife Ingebiorg of Denmark – and Arthur would have been safer if forced to accompany Richard on Crusade. But could he have insisted on John coming too to stop him allying with Philip again, and left a non-royal regent in control at home? William Marshal, Geoffrey de Mandeville, or Archbishop Hubert Walter were all capable and available at the time. There were also Richard's two illegitimate half-brothers, Earl William of Salisbury and Archbishop Geoffrey of York.

Richard could also have had a major impact on the Fourth Crusade, given that it was the first such expedition not to sail to Palestine and engaged in one of the most shockingly cynical expeditions of the medieval period. Its initiator and planned leader, Theobald of Champagne, had died before it set out in 1203 and there was no clear leader, particularly one able to stand up to the idea 'floated' by the Venetians that it should pay for its loan of Venetian shipping by aiding Venice first. The subsequent attack on Zara in Dalmatia had no Crusading context, and was rightly condemned by Pope Innocent III. Then Venice's Doge Enrico Dandolo adopted the plan that the Crusade should sail to Constantinople to aid a refugee pretender, Emperor Alexius III's nephew Alexius, which would supposedly assist the Christian cause by ending the 'Schism' with the Orthodox Church and enabling the restored Emperors Alexius IV and his father Isaac II to aid them with men and money.

If Richard had been on the Crusade, he would have insisted that it sail to Palestine from Venice not go off to Constantinople to 'restore' the rightful Byzantine rulers, despite all the arguments of the resources that the latter's rich Empire could then give the Crusade. He had no reason to favour the cause of the deposed Isaac II, having illegally refused to return the conquered rebel Byzantine province of Cyprus (which he had seized in 1191) to Isaac's government and handed it on to his Lusignan allies. Alexius IV's brother-in-law and sponsor Philip of Swabia was the brother of Richard's arch-enemy Henry VI, an ally of Philip, and was fighting Richard's nephew Otto IV over the German throne; he was not a natural ally for Richard. An important Crusader and the eventual choice as 'Latin Emperor' in Constantinople, Baldwin of Flanders, was Richard's 1197–9 ally. Venice insisted that the Crusaders go to Constantinople using their power over their loans of money and ships to the Crusaders to win the argument. If Richard's immense prestige from 1190–92 failed to get Baldwin of Flanders and Boniface of Montferrat to support his argument to go to Palestine, he would have been likely to insist on going straight to Palestine anyway. The English contingent would have followed him, and possibly his influence would have won Baldwin over.

Probably far fewer lords and knights would have gone to Constantinople with the Venetians – if the expedition went ahead – due to defections to Richard's cause making the Byzantine gamble now more risky. Without Baldwin, the Crusaders – if successful – would have had to choose another magnate as their 'Latin Emperor' in April 1204 – probably Boniface of Montferrat, in real life the new ruler of Thessalonica. Boniface had a claim on the Empire, or at least on part of it; his elder brother Renier had been married to the late Emperor Manuel I Comnenus' daughter Maria, who might be regarded as the Empire's legitimate heiress after her brother Alexius II's deposition and murder in 1183. (She and Renier had disappeared after arrest by Alexius' killer, the usurper Andronicus I, and were probably poisoned by him.) Boniface might have avoided Baldwin's fate of being defeated and captured by the Bulgarians in 1205 and survived as ruler of the Latin state of Thessalonica or of Constantinople itself for longer; in real life he was killed in a skirmish in 1207. But if Baldwin had not been on the Crusade against Constantinople his brother Henry is unlikely to have been available to rally the Latins after their defeat by Bulgaria in 1205 and save the new 'Latin Empire'. Henry, the most able of the Latin Emperors, saved the infant state from collapse by taking the throne in 1206 and kept its Byzantine rivals in Epirus and Nicaea at bay. With him as well as Baldwin following Richard to Palestine, the Latin Empire could have collapsed in 1205–6 or at best survived as a city-state protected from the sea by the Venetian navy, with Theodore Lascaris of Nicaea ruling all western Asia Minor and 'Czar' Joannitsa of Bulgaria ruling all Thrace. By proxy, Richard could have had a major effect on the history of Asia Minor and the Balkans after 1204 – even arguably saving the Eastern Roman ('Byzantine') Empire from collapsing as soon as it did in real life.

The alternative is that Richard's English fleet would have sailed direct via Sicily to the East, not even called in at Venice. Richard would possibly have trouble with the Kingdom of Naples/Sicily en route due to the late ruler Emperor Henry having been his captor and enemy and his own support for his nephew Otto IV's claims to the German throne against the claims of the new, under-age Sicilian ruler Frederick II and his uncle Philip of Swabia. The regency for Frederick would have been suspicious of Richard's intentions, and possibly refused him landing-rights. Richard would have arrived in Cyprus or Palestine in 1203 to find most of his expected European aid having gone off to Constantinople instead, and unless he had angrily sailed there to demand that they do their Christian duty and come to Palestine instead he would have had to fight the Moslems with only his English/Angevin/Aquitaine contingents.

The Ayyubid realm was now reunited under Saladin's brother Al-Adil, but Richard could still have been able to fight the latter – an old adversary and ultimately on good terms with him in 1190–92 – with a chance of securing at least Christian 'access' to a demilitarized Jerusalem. The Ayyubid realm was no stronger than it was when facing Frederick II in 1228 when those terms were agreed, and Richard was a feared general unlike Frederick even if the English/Angevin/Aquitaine army may have been smaller than Frederick's German/Sicilian expedition. But Richard may have had only a small force if he could not inspire enthusiasm for the Crusade in England, with many North French vassals preferring to stay at home in case Philip invaded or Arthur/John revolted in Richard's absence. Even if Richard had been able to march inland from Jaffa to Jerusalem and the prudent Ayyubids had withdrawn sooner than fight him, he could not hold Jerusalem in 1204/5 any better than he could in 1192. Even if he had been able to bring siege-engines – which he had lacked in 1192 so he could have had the foresight to bring the basic structures needed all the way from England – and the city had surrendered he would have realized it could not be held indefinitely. His army would have been at risk of being starved out, lacking the network of protective castles that Jerusalem had held before 1187, and the Ayyubids would only have to wait and harass his supply-columns to put him in a dangerous military position.

A realist who had not run risks of being caught in an isolated position in or near Jerusalem by Saladin in 1192, he would have had to come to terms – from a weak position of time being on his enemies' side. At best, the Christians would have had to accept a treaty allowing access and a small, nominal Crusader presence under a local lord acceptable to Al-Adil. The latter would know that Richard could not risk waiting for better terms in the hostile climate with his supplies low or to march on towards Damascus to force a battle. Richard may have had the sense to insist that John and Arthur accompany him to the East so he would not face revolt at home, but he still could not prolong his campaign or force the Moslems to battle. But if he had accepted a treaty that gave the Christians limited control of an unfortified Jerusalem he would not have faced the same barrage of papal criticism that Frederick II did for these terms in 1228–9, as Frederick was both an excommunicate and the local Italian foe of the papal states (being lord of Naples and Sicily and in control of the North of Italy as Emperor). The prestige of regaining Jerusalem would have added to Richard's diplomatic leverage had he sought to oppose the 'Albigensian Crusade' in 1209–1213, with Pope Innocent III being in need of his goodwill for its success and Philip of France having his own problems with the papacy over his marriages.

Richard in the later 1200s and 1210s – the same problems as John faced?

Returning to England with the prestige of 'Holy Land' success, Richard would then have faced the same baronial resentment at extortionate Angevin government demands as John did in the 1200s. As he lacked John's genius for offending people, e.g. by his demands on his nobles' womenfolk, this would have taken longer to turn to outright defiance. But mutinies against overseas service were possible if there was a round of fighting on the chaotic Aquitaine/Toulouse border after 1209. Whether Richard had intervened in the Albigensian War on the side of the victims or of the invaders, seeking extra lands to add to his domains in either case, he would have been lucky to have English military support year after year.

The situation in south-western France as of c. 1209–14

The Albigensian Crusade is crucial to consideration of the level of demands on its subjects to be expected of Richard's government in the late 1200s. English politics cannot be considered in isolation – and Richard regarded himself as a Continental dynast first, with Aquitaine as his favourite part of the 'empire'. He had devoted years of his youth to it as his Aquitaine mother's heir and favourite, and had refused to hand these lands over to John after 1183. Philip controlling Toulouse would have meant a new French 'front' for staging cross-border attacks and encouraging local rebels, and as early as 1159 Henry II had marched on Toulouse to attempt to preserve his influence there against Louis VII's claims. Richard could have ended up making a claim to the County of Toulouse as a dependable Catholic ruler to oppose the French royal family's claim, for a relative such as John (to get him out of claims to England/Anjou?) if Richard had had sons by this date. His sister the Countess of Toulouse was dead (1199) so he had no dynastic claim, but neither did Philip.

Philip's own blatant insertion of his son Prince Louis into the County of Toulouse had no accepted dynastic basis, and was only plausible out of a mixture of his rights of confiscation of his vassal fief (for heresy) and Church backing. If Richard had been alive, and in good favour with the Church as a Crusader, Pope Innocent might have preferred to back a claim by him for a close ally or relative as the new Count of Toulouse in the 1210s. Importantly, the papacy was usually in alliance with Richard's nephew Otto IV as claimant to the Empire against the Hohenstaufen until 1218. Richard's arch-enemy Henry VI's son Frederick II had inherited Sicily and Naples from him in 1197, but the papacy resisted a union of this kingdom with the Empire under Frederick (or even giving the Empire to Frederick's uncle Philip of Swabia, murdered in 1208). Innocent III therefore had as much reason to win Richard's goodwill over Toulouse as to back Philip.

Unlike Philip, Richard had a family link (a sister's marriage) to the neighbouring Spanish state of Castile. Had Richard chosen to oppose the French expedition's depredations and confiscations, he had the capacity to rally the Spanish rulers against it – or at least to threaten to do so unless the grants of Languedoc fiefs to Philip's men were restricted. Richard, his brother-in-law Alfonso VIII of Castile and nephew Prince Henry, and the Aragonese could have united to keep French royal control out of Toulouse around 1212–13, even if Pope Innocent risked losing Richard's backing for Otto IV in Italy and imposed sanctions on them. Richard's 'irreligion' has been exaggerated, and he was a conventional Catholic; but he was determined on insisting on his legal 'rights' and could have cited Henry II's agreement with Toulouse in 1159 as giving him the right to intervene. Unless an English/Castile/Aragon alliance had prudently imposed a firm Catholic as the new Count of Toulouse to satisfy the Pope that they opposed heresy, England could have suffered a temporary 'Interdict'.

The Church and the papacy

Would Richard have been as obstructive towards the papacy's candidate for the Archbishopric of Canterbury as John was in 1205–1206, thus arousing papal ire? Had he been at home in the West not still campaigning in Palestine at the time, he was capable of being as unbending as John towards perceived interference. Had he been in Palestine the regency government in England were more likely to have persuaded Innocent to wait for Richard's return before a decision was finalized or have sent an enquiry to their King in

Palestine for his decision. With other priorities at the time, Richard might have accepted Stephen Langton to secure papal diplomatic support as he endeavoured to assist the Kingdom of Jerusalem to restore its military position. Like Louis IX when he was in Acre after his Egyptian disaster in the early1250s, Richard would have been aware of the precarious position of the Kingdom and been responsible enough to endeavour to assist its survival in his absence before returning to Europe – and for that papal aid was essential. Crucially, Richard had been able to bring in his nephew Henry of Champagne as the new King of Jerusalem in 1192, to marry Queen Isabella and to take over military leadership once he went home. (Unfortunately, Henry had fallen out of a window five years later.) This time, in 1205–1206, there would have been another young Queen in need of a consort – Isabella's daughter Marie. Had he been in Palestine Richard might well have needed papal diplomatic backing too much to stand on his rights about the nature of the election to the see of Canterbury. But once he was home in the West, the Albigensian crisis would have required him to seek to ameliorate the danger of Philip imposing his own vassals on Languedoc – if only to prevent a French royal attack (by de Montfort or Prince Louis as the new Count of Toulouse?) up the Garonne on Bordeaux.

An Anglo-French dispute over the rule of Toulouse in 1209–1213 might have come to a military clash with the French royal forces under de Montfort. The local lords might well have preferred an Angevin to a Capetian ruler, given Richard's sister's earlier marriage into the comital House of Toulouse. If Richard had regained a foothold in Jerusalem, he might then have been acceptable to Pope Innocent as the new lord or overlord of Toulouse to restore order after all the massacres – or at least to nominate one of his chosen vassals as the new lord. At best for the kingdom of France, Philip would have gained some extra lands and patronage within Toulouse, possibly dividing up the County with Richard under a papal legate's arbitration to acquire the Rhone valley.

An Angevin civil war if Richard had no son?
Ultimately the danger of 'over-stretch' would have undermined Angevin power in France, even if Richard himself did not face mutiny and revolt due to his excessive financial and military demands and the crisis followed his death. A civil war between John and Arthur was still likely if Richard did not have sons, unless one of them had been put out of the running – and Philip or Louis VIII would have been more likely to back Arthur. The 'backlash' against Angevin government and the usual chaos and civil war/invasion that followed the death of a strong ruler with two rival candidates for the succession, e.g. in 1087, 1100, and 1135, would mean trouble in England as

well as on the Continent and a likelihood that disgruntled barons would insist on a lightening of the burden of government by whichever candidate they supported.

The victor would have had to make a series of promises in their coronation 'charter' and stick to them or face further revolt; the terms would have been fairly similar to those of Magna Carta but without the particular onus on untrustworthy royal legal decisions and favouritism that seem to have afflicted the devious John's rule in the 1200s and 1210s. It is noticeable that many barons were not willing to risk trusting the devious John after he had 'signed' the Charter in 1215 and preferred to bring in his niece's French husband as their new king, although John had already shown his intentions by applying for papal absolution from his legal promises to them. (Richard 'yea and nay' also had a dubious reputation for carrying out his promises, and could have broken his undertakings to subjects which he had glibly made when he needed their support.)

As Richard had not had an heir by his wife, Berengaria, by 1199 she was probably barren, and divorcing her in order to keep the succession among his own children would have risked a diplomatic breach with his crucial neighbour Navarre. An amicable arrangement might have been achieved, but in the difficult circumstances of Anglo-French rivalry for alliances in Spain in the 1200s it was more likely that Richard would not risk Navarre becoming a French ally. Castile, the other most crucial neighbouring state to Aquitaine, was impossible as its royal family were his close kin; the obvious choices of bride there, Alfonso VIII's daughters, were his own nieces. (Ironically, one of them married Philip II's son Louis and thus provided the dynastic claim for that prince as rebel challenger to John in 1215–16.) He could have chosen a daughter of a minor lord in Aquitaine or its small neighbouring counties, strengthening his power on Aquitaine's borders as John's choice of the Angouleme heiress in 1200 was intended to do. John succeeded in alienating his unexpected – and under-age? – fiancée's husband-to-be and his family. John was to be accused of paedophiliac indecency in his haste to marry twelve?-year-old Isabella of Angouleme; Richard had put up with his fiancée Alice being kept from him for years by Henry II and was never accused of such priapic enthusiasms for young heiresses (quite the contrary).

Whether or not Richard had chosen to go on the Fourth Crusade and so postponed a remarriage until his return (c.1206/7?), any son born of this second marriage would be a minor until well into the 1210s and so at a disadvantage in the succession. In that case, either Arthur or John would have remained Richard's heir had he still been alive and militarily active in c.1210–1216. An under-age son of his would have been in a stronger position as the new king of England than as Duke of Normandy and Count of Anjou on his death. The nine-year-old Henry III, John's son, was able to win over more nobles after October 1216 against Prince Louis than his father had done until then, despite his age.

Assuming that Richard had remained childless and the Angevin 'empire' remained intact, the circumstances of Richard's death would have been crucial to the question of who emerged as the new ruler. The reluctance of the English barons to serve with John on his French expeditions, and the stresses in Angevin fiscal and administrative practices apparent in the complaints in Magna Carta, make it probable that any prolonged struggle over the Crown would have led to a 'mutiny' among English tenants-in-chief against endless campaigning in France (or the excessive taxes demanded to pay for mercenaries there). It is probable that Arthur, based in Brittany, would have stood a strong chance of detaching parts of the Continental domains from the Angevin state with Philip's military assistance but would have been weaker in England where he had no connections. Unless John had mounted one of his occasional lightning marches (as in the relief of his grandmother at Mirabeau in real life) and captured or killed Arthur the French King, supported by the resources of the Rhone valley if not Languedoc, was likely to have been able to hold John at bay. Then, as in real life, the English lords' resistance to Continental campaigning and general complaints at the nature of Angevin royal exactions would have hindered John's military effectiveness in the long term.

The most likely military outcome is for Philip and his active son Louis (in real life leading an attempt to take John's throne in England in 1216–17) to have secured the Continental dominions for Arthur, with a weakened John having to abandon even Normandy as his barons resisted a long campaign. If the price of Philip's support was Normandy and/or Aquitaine, Arthur would have been in no position to resist and the Breton-led half of the Angevin 'empire' under Arthur's rule would have been liable to gradual political eclipse by its French overlord. As Count of Anjou and possibly Poitou, Arthur would have been less powerful in military terms than Philip and Louis and would have been lucky to hold onto distant Aquitaine against a resurgent John. Even if Richard had lived long enough to outlive John, perhaps dying around 1220 in his early sixties, that would only have aided the chances of Arthur and Louis of France detaching the Continental half of the Angevin state from the English lands to which John's son (?Henry, born in 1207, as in real life) would have been a more acceptable heir than the distant Duke of Brittany. In that case, as in real life, the mainstays of Henry's cause would have been likely to be the aged chivalric paladin William Marshal and Hubert de Burgh.

Chapter Four

Henry III and Simon de Montfort: The Civil Wars of 1264–7: Personality and Principle in the Clash Between the Two Men

The failings of Henry III as a ruler. Ominous signs of opposition well before Simon became involved so his leadership wasn't the crucial factor in resistance? And were Henry's problems his own fault and avoidable?

The history of Henry III's adult reign has been seen as a continuation of the struggle of the Crown versus an increasingly confident and politicized nobility (or more accurately a section of the latter), continuing the resistance to royal extravagance, impetuosity, capriciousness, and/or misrule commenced under John. This 'resistance', often carried out allegedly for idealistic reasons, is a continuing strand of politics through from the rebellions of Richard Marshal, the second son and eventual heir of the great William Marshal, Earl of Pembroke (and 'Regent' in 1216–19), to the struggle between the King's men and the Montfort faction in 1258–67. A succession of royal chief ministers and personal associates, from Hubert de Burgh in 1230–1232 via Peter des Roches to the King's Lusignan half-brothers and Provencal/Savoyard uncles, faced opposition as monopolizers of influence – often as 'foreigners' – as recounted by contemporary chronicler Matthew Paris. On a longer timescale, baronial resistance to the excessive financial and military exactions of the current King can be traced from the 'strike' that faced John over his demands for service in the Poitevin war of 1205 to resistance to his grandson Edward I's French war in 1294–7.

Attempts to control an untrustworthy and financially oppressive king, a man seen with bitter experience as capable of going back on his word, by a council of powerful barons constraining him and sharing his powers began with the struggle against John in 1214–16. It continued through to the council of 'Lords Ordainers' under Edward II and the revolt of the 'Lords

Appellant' against Richard II in 1387. Arguably the continuous and remorseless royal demands for money and service in foreign war that annoyed the opponents of John, Henry III, and Edward I alike were a result of a king – statesmanlike or vainglorious – seeking to play a major role as an actor on the international stage and his subjects balking at the cost of it all.[1] The cost of this now fell more on England than before, following the loss of Normandy and Anjou, while the resulting accretion of lands, military recruits, and tax revenues to the Crown of France made the English governments more demanding and predatory in seeking resources from their subjects to counter this increased danger. The extra royal demands, and extra resistance to them, thus arose from the geo-political disaster of 1203–1204 and were beyond the control of the English kings, unless the latter had 'given up' on competing with their French counterparts and attempting to regain lost lands and influence. At the same time, after 1215 the fact that a coalition of barons had forced John to 'sign up to' (in fact seal) a document restricting his financial and administrative coercion gave future such coalitions encouragement to repeat this, and a weak king – such as Henry III during his minority – would face demands to confirm the concessions of 1215 by reissuing or extending Magna Carta. The kings were thus in a weaker position relative to their senior nobles at precisely the time that they were making more demands of them – though it should be noted that new kings had already found it prudent on accession to announce their intention to observe just laws and end their predecessors' exactions (e.g. in 1100).

Nor should the apparent extravagance of rulers such as Henry III, who spent fortunes on new building at his palaces (e.g. Westminster and the extant Great Hall at Winchester) and at Westminster Abbey, be regarded as unnecessary folly at a time of 'austerity'. Fiscal prudence was not necessarily a 'given' virtue for medieval kings, and lavish generosity was seen as admirable and a chivalric virtue – though the destination of such generosity, particularly greedy relatives, could be resented. Such building in secular mode reflected the glory and majesty of the king and was thus a valuable element of political propaganda, a visual sign of self-confidence and political stability. In building (or rebuilding) vast churches the king was seeking God's favour and showing his piety, both crucial elements of his role – though Henry's spending undoubtedly added to his problems as he did not have the resources of his equally munificent French rival and inspiration Louis IX. It is notable that Henry's ecclesiastical building and acquisition of relics for Westminster Abbey from 1247 amounted to an open competition with Louis, so if the French King had been less of a builder and religious patron this might well not have occurred.

The financially demanding and judicially intrusive sovereign like John might seem to subsequent historical observers to be thinking with a broader 'world view' of international politics and military strategy than his cost-conscious subjects. Alternatively, his subjects could appear as prototype 'nationalists' conscious of England's real interests not being best served by endless war by a king obsessed with repeating past glories (usually in France). By the latter argument, once the 'Angevin empire' had been lost in 1204 – or at latest when John's grand coalition to attack Philip Augustus on two fronts and reconquer it collapsed after the defeat at Bouvines – the English kings should have given up the struggle with bad or good grace. The attempts Henry III made to regain lands in France from 1225 (when he sent his brother Richard to Aquitaine to reconquer Poitou as its new count) were repeatedly unsuccessful, and the King had two failed personal campaigns there in 1230 and 1242. Was he wasting his time and resources?

The nationalist historians of the nineteenth and early-mid twentieth century were particularly prone to this view, which judged the thirteenth century by their standards. It was geographically 'natural' that the Kingdom of France should expand its control over the territory of Normandy as far as the Channel, and Philip's expansion in 1203–1204 was a 'just' and 'nation-building' exercise in adding to French royal power over an 'over-mighty subject'. Similarly, any English involvement in France was geographically 'illogical' and the sooner the English kings 'inevitably' lost their lands overseas the better. Thus John's wars in Wales and Ireland after his withdrawal from France were proper 'nation-building' exercises and the time he devoted to them showed that he had the 'national interest' more at heart than his father Henry II and (especially) brother Richard I. England's interests were best served by a detached 'insular' approach, which the post-1204 lack of major possessions in France aided. The surviving English portion of Aquitaine – Guienne, around Bordeaux – was thus a historical 'leftover' and the requirement that the English King do homage to the French King for it (formalized when the French King Louis IX finally accepted that Henry III should hold onto Guienne in 1259) was an unnecessary complication to Anglo-French relations. The faded glory of a 'lost empire' was thus seen as dragging Henry III and later Edward I into conflict in France in a futile attempt to resurrect Henry II's multi-state dominions, and all the wars in France after 1204 were against England's 'real' interests. In this determinist view of thirteenth-century politics Henry III's attempts after 1225 to retrieve parts of John's overseas dominions were easy to condemn. His first expedition to France in spring 1230 was a miserable failure, and after landing at St Malo in Brittany he hung around nearby without marching into Normandy and eventually went home. He allegedly listened to the cautious advice of his chief minister Hubert de Burgh, earlier a senior castellan for John in Normandy in the early 1200s and the valiant defender of Dover Castle against the French invasion in 1216. Henry revealed his hopeless over-optimism, timidity in the field (a rebellion was rumoured to be likely in Normandy if he marched there to help dissidents) and lack of adequate planning or support, and he fared no better when he invade Poitou in 1242.

On the second occasion, however, he had every expectation of local support – he had been invited there by his stepfather, Count Hugh of Lusignan, a major local lord who was leading a revolt against Louis IX's imposition of his brother Alphonso as the new count. (It was Alphonso, who had no local connections, not Henry III, descendant of generations of Counts of Poitou, who was the 'outsider'.) Henry's English barons had refused him adequate troops or money so he was not able to rival the French army in size and faced major difficulties – though this does not excuse him from being caught by surprise by the size and nearness of Louis' advancing army at Taillebourg. Henry and his advisers failed to guard a vital bridge that the French seized, and he was trapped with only the River Charente between him and an imminent French attack. Luckily his brother Earl Richard of Cornwall, who had been on Crusade in 1240, had the resulting reputation as a Crusader that enabled him to make a successful 'man to man' personal appeal to the great French lords (taking his pilgrim's staff from his journey with him as a 'prop') to accept a twenty-four-hour truce, enabling Henry to retreat in time.[2] Had the truce not been granted, Henry might well have been overwhelmed and captured. What then? Though Louis was not likely to hold him prisoner long-term as the unscrupulous Emperor Henry VI was prepared to do to Richard I, captive kings taken in battle against their overlord (e.g. William I of Scotland in 1174) could expect to have to pay a stiff ransom and submit to a humiliating peace treaty. It is probable that quite apart from the ransom Louis would have insisted that Henry hand back all of Guienne, ending the English domains in France and so possibly saving England from some of its subsequent French wars over this territory. This would not have stopped Henry's aggressive and ambitious son Edward I from attempting to take them back by invasion, however, given that Guienne was his 'rightful' inheritance. When Guienne was overrun in 1294 Edward drove his over-taxed subjects to mutiny in his efforts to retrieve it.

What of Henry's eagerness to acquire Naples and Sicily for his second son Edmund? (See below.) The notion of a minor prince from North-Western Europe acquiring a major Mediterranean realm by invasion and a papal grant was quite usual for the era, and in 1204 Henry's uncle Richard's ally Baldwin of Flanders had acquired the Eastern Roman ('Byzantine') Empire by conquest. Marquis Boniface of Montferrat, ruler of a state adjacent to Henry's wife Eleanor's mother's Savoyard homeland, had acquired Thessalonica in Greece in the same Crusade and minor barons had acquired Athens and the Peloponnese. Henry's stepfather's Lusignan relatives had acquired Cyprus in 1194 – by grant from his uncle Richard who had overrun it during the Crusade – and Amaury of Lusignan had become King of Jerusalem too, by marriage in 1198. Louis, however, had greater resources than Henry so the financial strain of the war was less for him – and his brother Charles, unlike Edmund in 1254, was adult and so able to lead his own expedition in 1266 and then rule as king without major French support. The real criticism of Henry for taking on this task was that his grandiose visions of international influence outmatched his resources or the willingness of his vassals to pay for such a campaign. Granted that his only adult brother, Richard, was to be the Anglo-papal candidate to replace Conrad as Emperor in Germany he had no other candidate for the Sicilian throne but the under-age Edmund, but the latter's age meant that Henry would presumably have to lead an invasion himself or hire a competent and high-ranking mercenary commander. He was originally meant to be leading a Crusade, along with Louis IX of France, but this plan had been postponed and only Louis went to the East; Henry did not take the Cross until March 1250 when Louis was already in difficulties in Egypt (and had in fact just been defeated and captured). This envisaged him leading a Crusade as late as 1256, possibly due to the time that it would take for the impoverished King to raise the funds necessary[3] – and the Crusade was then turned into the Sicilian expedition. The latter was certainly an unnecessary political complication and a strain on resources for a prodigal ruler already known for his vast expenditure on palaces, churches, and relatives.

So were Henry's European ambitions 'outdated' and hankering back to the days of his grandfather Henry II's cross-Channel 'empire', precipitating long-term resentment from his exasperated barons, which was to feed into the potential support for rebellion in 1258 and 1264? Would a more cautious and realistic strategy on his part have improved his reputation with the political elite and lessened antagonism? His financial prodigality was certainly a major issue, as was his choice of advisers – and the issue of 'royal favourites' abusing power and patronage was a cause of armed resistance from the 1220s onwards. No previous king since 1066 had faced such accusations of being the puppet of a minister or clique; on the contrary, all except possibly Stephen had been headstrong 'warlords' and all except John who faced rebellions did so as a result of rival contenders. John had faced rebellion in 1215 as a result of financial exactions and perceived misgovernment and untrustworthiness, not due to unpopular ministers abusing his trust as des Roches and de Burgh were seen to do in the 1220s and early 1230s. (Both men had been John's 'trusties' in his exactions in the early 1210s, but it had been John who was the focus of resentment then.) Arguably Henry was the first king to be seen as weak-willed and easily manipulated, and to be diverting patronage unwisely to a few monopolists. But his prodigality to resented overseas relatives and diplomatic/military involvement in France and Italy were not necessarily a sign of his lack of concern for 'core English interests'. His incompetence and lack of realism in fiscal matters is unquestionable, given how far his plans outran the funds available, but not his diplomatic versatility. And the readiness with which he ran up debts was not unusual for contemporary rulers, as the supposedly ultra-successful Edward I and Edward III also ended up in difficulty as a result of their Continental campaigns. Edward I resorted to refusing to pay his debts to Jewish money-lenders and targeting them as unholy 'enemies of God' instead, and Edward III refused to pay his debts to Italian bankers in the early 1340s and undermined their institutions' liquidity.

It should be noted here that although the concept of an 'internationalist', cross-Channel baronage with estates and interests on both sides of the sea had suffered a fatal blow with the loss of Normandy this was hardly apparent as of 1204, or even the1230s – contemporaries had no advance knowledge of the fact that the loss of Normandy would not be reversed until 1415–50 (and then temporarily). The reconquest of lost areas of Aquitaine also remained a major objective of English foreign policy, and the situation was stabilized by treaty in 1259 with much of the duchy held by Eleanor of Aquitaine in 1137–1204 still in English hands. There was supposed to be local readiness to revolt in favour of England in Normandy in 1230 and Poitou in 1225 and 1242, though none of this materialized. Contemporary legal attitudes thought of what we call 'states' as the normal hereditary possessions of their rulers, like other legacies, and the English kings were all descendants of a long line of Dukes of Aquitaine (and Dukes of Normandy and Counts of Anjou). It was the French kings' confiscation of rightful inheritances that was illegal and it was the duty of the ousted heirs to strive to reverse this; Henry III was doing no more than any lord would if his father's lands had been unjustly seized. Henry's son Edward I from time to time resided in Bordeaux, as in 1287 – and Henry made a point of calling in at the family mausoleum where his grandfather Henry II, grandmother Eleanor, and uncle Richard I were buried at Fontevrault Abbey in Anjou en route to Paris in 1254 and arranging for his own heart to be buried there too. What seems an 'inevitable' loss of Poitou, Anjou, and Normandy in hindsight was not so to thirteenth-century observers, and changes of political fortune could occur swiftly. The impressive edifice of French 'centralized' royal power might have collapsed given a series of long minorities rather than a line of competent adult male kings, and it was not impossible that Henry might have revived English power in western France had Louis IX died of a fever on Crusade in 1250 (as he did in 1270) and left the kingdom to a regency for his young son Philip III.

Culturally, of course, the English political elite continued to speak French until the mid-late fourteenth century and think of themselves in terms of a universal Western European Christian civilization. The most powerful Anglo-Norman chivalric literary epic on which kings modelled their conduct, that of 'King Arthur', was largely constructed by French writers using French cultural terminology, though with a 'Celtic' undercurrent, and Henry was to rebuild Westminster Abbey on the model of his brother-in-law Louis IX's 'Sainte Chapelle' in Paris. Indeed the key to a proper understanding of much of Henry's seemingly bizarre and unrealistic actions in the field of international diplomacy as an adult ruler is his constant rivalry with Louis, the principal block to rebuilding his position within France. It was this that impelled firstly his marrying off his sister Isabella to Louis' principal Continental rival, Emperor Frederick II, in 1234 and then his own marriage to Louis' wife's younger sister, Eleanor of Provence, in 1236. As of 1234–5 Henry had seemed more likely to marry the heiress Countess Joan of Ponthieu, who owned the lands immediately adjacent to Normandy on its North-East – a useful bridgehead for an invasion? The two went as far as to exchange preliminary vows of marriage, which was normally seen as legally irreversible, but the engagement was abandoned after pressure on Ponthieu by Louis' mother and chief adviser, Blanche of Castile[4] – widow of the man who had attempted to take Henry's throne in 1216–17. As a result Henry, who had also been interested in a Breton bride, settled on Eleanor of Provence in 1235[5] – a move that placed him alongside Louis as an interested party in regional politics and gave him an opening to involvement in northern Italy via the Provencal dynasty's connection with Savoy. But if he had married Joan of Ponthieu instead, would the absence of a 'Queen's party' of ambitious and grant-seeking 'in-laws' seen as leeching off the King have drastically improved his reputation in the 1240s and 1250s? Given his reliance on men such as de Burgh rather than carefully balancing factions at court earlier, it is likely that Henry would have been prone to some other 'favourites'.

The contentious development of what we might call a 'nationalist' and exclusively 'English' outlook by the English kings and political elite was slow and haphazard. Henry III, after all, thought of himself as much as the rightful Duke of Normandy and Count of Anjou as being the King of England, and had a vested interest in the politics of Aquitaine as the son of the heiress Isabella of Angouleme (born c. 1187), who had married King John in 1200 and lived until 1246. This connection via his mother was limited in practical terms as she had remarried soon after John's death and lived in Poitou with her second husband Hugh of Lusignan – son of the fiancé from whom John had taken her in 1200 – and only rarely saw her son or came to England.[6] However, Henry made much of his four half-brothers, who came to England in 1247 after their mother died; the most prominent, William of Valence, acquired the co-heiress and title of the Earldom of Pembroke, which the unexpected deaths of William Marshal's five sons without male heirs had left vacant. He also favoured his Provençal wife's maternal connections from Savoy, who he loaded with court honours, financial grants, and offices (including the Archbishopric of Canterbury for one uncle, Boniface, and the land in London where the eponymous Savoy Palace was to be built for another, Peter).

This long-term aspect of Henry's governance was not necessarily just weak-willed 'favouritism' for friends and relations, as the Lusignans presented Henry with a useful link to Poitou, which helped in the defence of Guienne from French royal attack and could swing local barons in Henry's favour should he attempt to retake the region (as he had done in 1242). The resented Savoyard connection via his wife's uncles was also useful in the arena of international politics, given the crucial location of Savoy on the Franco-Italian border. Henry's actions thus represented an ambitious international strategy to rebuild the dynasty's international prestige after the disasters of 1204–1217 rather than mere over-generosity – though it can be severely criticized for lacking realism given his reduced resources and the unwillingness that his vassals repeatedly showed to paying for his diplomatic plans. Major recipients of his favour included both the technically 'foreign' Bishop of Winchester, Peter des Roches, and his kinsman Peter de Rivalis in 1232–4 and the English (Norfolk landowner) 'new man' Hubert de Burgh in 1227–32, both long-term administrators for Henry's father, John. They were thus trusted and competent royal henchmen and major figures from Henry's boyhood – des Roches had been his guardian – albeit acquisitive and possibly venal ones. Their chief 'sins' in the eyes of the nobles excluded from court favour in the late 1220s and early 1230s appear to have been the way they piled up grants of land and offices for themselves and their relatives, de Burgh acquiring an earldom, blocs of land across England, and assorted wardships of under-age tenants-in-chief and des Roches and de Rivallis court offices and a collection of sheriffdoms. Their success was resisted by those nobles who were thus denied these grants of land and titles and who saw the King's bounty being exploited by an 'exclusive' clique, but the phenomenon of an acquisitive treasurer like des Roches was not new as

Ranulf Flambard (also a cleric) had faced similar fury over his extortion in the reign of William II and Richard I's favoured administrator Bishop William Longchamp had been driven out of his regency by rebellion in the King's absence in 1191. All had been regarded as jumped-up, low-born royal flatterers, and de Burgh's role as a 'new man' collecting titles and estates for himself was no more blatant than that of arch-'opposition' figure Richard Marshal's own father William Marshal, another 'self-made' knight and Court favourite. Where Henry III can be criticized is for the scale of his generosity – the extent of offices given to des Roches and de Rivallis (over twenty sheriffdoms), for instance, went beyond normal royal favour and was bound to attract a backlash. De Burgh was more unfortunate than these predatory clerics, as a long-term loyal 'royalist' who had helped to save the kingdom in 1216–17 (and was famously supposed to have refused to blind the captive Prince Arthur as John demanded in 1203), and his enemies' vociferousness was probably connected to the fact that Henry sought to impose him as a new 'strongman' in the south-central Welsh Marches. The established local Marcher lords, led by the Marshal family, duly resisted this intrusion and were determined to destroy their rival.

In the meetings of the increasingly important 'great councils' and proto-'Parliaments' of the King's vassals the 'middling sort ' of minor landowners and town representatives attacked the monopoly of influence by these royal favourites, and also resisted the scale of the King's financial demands for his overseas plans. Indeed the opposition to royal advisers was – for the first time in such a case – couched in 'nationalist' terms with the courtiers abused on the grounds of being foreigners; this charge was made against des Roches and de Rivallis as 'Poitevins' in 1232–4.[7] But the fact that this argument was used does not mean that it was more than a convenient 'stick' with which to beat the unpopular clique. Resistance to a monopolistic clique of courtiers who were seen as receiving an unfair share of patronage was a common problem in the cases of various medieval rulers who were accused of this favouritism – for example, Edward II, Richard II, and Henry VI. (All of these were to end up deposed.) It should be pointed out that Richard Marshal, leader of the opposition to des Roches in 1232–4, had been living on the Marshal estates in Normandy as the French King's vassal to safeguard this part of the family inheritance until his elder brother William died in 1231 and he inherited their estates and title in the Marches. He was as much 'foreign' as his target, and indeed Henry at first refused him access to England in 1231 as he had not renounced his oath of fealty to the French King.

The lack of wisdom of the King's use of patronage and the lack of support for the King's priorities in diplomacy were the main issue in all these cases, and it was merely the nationality of the beneficiaries – his mother's and his wife's kin – that was different with Henry III after the 1230s. The issue of rule by an unpopular clique dominating an 'ill-advised' King indeed followed up similar resistance to earlier royal ministers, in this case firstly Peter des Roches, Bishop of Winchester, in the early 1220s and then 'Justiciar' Hubert de Burgh in 1230–32. Both ended up dismissed after ferocious opposition, with the King being seen as weak-willed and easily dominated by an unscrupulous monopoliser of power and patronage. Magna Carta gave legal sanction to demands for a curb on royal powers and exactions; did Henry, like John, regard this as a temporary embarrassment that should be reversed and try to ignore it as far as practicable? The King's obstinacy concerning making or keeping to concessions to his critics was a 'constant' from the 1220s to 1264, whether on personal or legal matters; he was very unwilling to sacrifice his wife's unpopular relatives and send them home to Savoy though this would have improved his reputation for accepting advice. (This was partly blamed on the acquisitive Eleanor having a stronger will than he did, and she was notoriously pelted with refuse by the citizens of London at London Bridge during one political crisis.[8]) It led to his being coerced by armed force in 1258 and 1264 – which suggests determination to defend his prerogatives as well as natural obstinacy.

Henry and Simon de Montfort

Simon's presence in England: Unlikely?
Henry III was repeatedly as careless of the likely jealousy and hatred of the beneficiaries of his grants – or the developing threat to his own freedom to issue such patronage to whom he pleased – as his successors. His over-confidence of military success in his expedition to Poitou in 1242 and of his planned expedition to assist the Pope in Sicily in 1254 were combined with bland dismissal of the likelihood of his magnates resisting the vast cost of these plans or sending troops to them. The King's lack of realism and understanding of his vassals' priorities were the main issues rather than resistance to his advisers because they were 'foreign'. Also, the notion of a blanket 'national, English' baronial objection to the monopoly of the King's patronage by 'foreigners' falls down on account of the leader of this developing resistance to the 'Poitevins' in the 1250s. Simon de Montfort (born c. 1208), son of the leader of the 'Albigensian Crusade', was after all the younger son of a minor lord from the Isle de France, his mother (a Montmorency) being French too, and did not come to England until he was in his early twenties. His English earldom, of Leicester, derived from his father's mother, Amicia de Beaumont, being sister and heiress of the

childless Robert de Beaumont, third Earl of Leicester (d. 1204) – and this earldom had been kept from the de Montforts after 1204 due to the war between John and Philip meaning that French subjects were banned from inheriting or holding lands in England unless they gave up all their French estates.[9] But this was not an 'anti-French' and thus 'nationalist' action as such, though it might appear to be so to later historians. Lords with lands in both countries were required to choose which they would live in and own lands in, so that nobody had divided allegiances and was a potential 'security risk' to the King of England due to the danger of the French King blackmailing them into aiding him by threatening to confiscate their French lands. Simon's father chose to stay in France and serve Philip in the 'Albigensian Crusade' rather than claiming the earldom of Leicester in England – and Simon only came to England in 1230 to take up the estates when Henry III chose to invite a de Montfort to take up the estates.[10] (He formally received the earldom in 1239.) As we have seen, his action followed the precedent of previous 'opposition leader' Richard Marshal in living on the family estates in France until he inherited an English domain and title in 1231. This division of a major dynasty's landholdings in different countries among different heirs was normal procedure once the English law demanded that landholders in England could not be vassals of the French King.

Even so, Simon was not the oldest de Montfort son – his two elder brothers preferred to stay in France, his eldest brother, Amaury, as its Constable. His arrival in England was thus due to a family decision not to him inheriting lands as of right, as would have been the case if he was the oldest son. If Amaury or his next brother, Guy, had come to England instead Simon would have presumably ended up as a typical younger son of a minor French lordship, seeking out a rich heiress to marry and probably (given his pedigree and religiosity) fighting in Palestine. The resistance to Henry's 'favouritism' to a group of foreign relatives was thus led by a 'Frenchman', for the second time. Importantly, the irony of this was not seen as unusual or prohibitive of his role as spokesman for the King's opponents.

From royal favourite to critic: Unlikely? Or a disaster waiting to happen? How near did he come to losing any influence in England and moving back to France before 1258?
Simon's first years in England saw him an another of the King's overseas connections, criticized as the recipient of prodigal royal bounty like the Lusignans and Savoyards. He first appeared as a major councillor at the time (1235–7) when Henry's own marriage to Eleanor and his sister's marriage to Frederick had led to new financial exactions to pay for these arrangements,

some of the fiscal demands being contrary to Magna Carta, which had to be reissued to appease critics.[11] The prominence of the new Queen's acquisitive uncle Bishop William of Valence at court was also resented, and the chronicler Matthew Paris names Simon as one of the circle around Henry who were believed to be behind the unpopular summoning of the papal legate Ottobuono in 1237.[12] They were believed to be exploiting their position unfairly and using their influence to settle old grudges, particularly against magnates who had attacked the King's favourites in the 1220s (as in Simon's role in the arrest of Richard Siward in 1236).[13] Simon's clandestine marriage to the King's sister Eleanor in January 1238 was a major factor in the revolt – or more accurately armed protest – against the power of unwelcome aliens at court launched by the King's brother Richard and by Gilbert Marshal, Earl of Pembroke and brother of the late rebel Richard Marshal.[14] Quite apart from Eleanor being the widow of Gilbert's late brother William Marshal – which meant that if William had not died young Simon would not have ended up as Henry III's brother-in-law – and so a Marshal connection, a royal marriage was normally arranged or approved by a lengthy meeting of the King's council. Eleanor had taken a vow of chastity after William Marshal died,[15] so this could be cited as invalidating her second marriage had the Church backed the aggrieved peers and Henry given way. It would be much more normal for the King's sister to be given in marriage to a useful and high-ranking foreign prince, as Isabella had been given to Emperor Frederick, and Simon's role as Henry's brother-in-law – a crucial element in the strength of his links to and alienation from the King – could thus have been stymied in 1236–7. Possibly the cost of Isabella's large dowry in 1235 meant that Henry had not had the time or inclination to find his widowed sister a new husband in 1236–8, thus leaving her at large for Simon to pursue. The fact that the marriage was planned and held in secret was unusual and open to legal challenge, as will be seen below. Given the ambitions and ruthlessness of the de Montfort dynasty, it is logical that Simon deliberately 'targeted' the King's sister as an invaluable 'catch' for himself – even breaching convention by having sexual relations with her before betrothal to induce her brother to accept that the marriage was necessary to save her reputation.

On this occasion, Henry's obstinacy saved Simon rather than alienating him. He could easily have ended up with his marriage annulled and banished to his Leicester estates as a political 'has-been' and an ally of the King's loathed relatives. The King, however, preferred to avoid exposing his sister to the shame of having her marriage annulled (which, perhaps, could have been on the grounds of her misconduct). The crisis passed, and William of Savoy left England, which diminished tensions among the nobility. But a second political crisis nearly finished Simon's career in 1239, when complex problems over his mounting debts led to him naming Henry as his 'security' – without telling him – for sums that he owed Thomas of Savoy, another uncle of the Queen. When Henry found out (due to Simon's ill-wishers) at the festivities for the Queen's 'churching' following the birth of her son Prince Edward, he flew into a rage, banned Simon and his wife from the ceremony, and shouted at Simon that he had seduced Princess Eleanor and forced Henry to let him marry her to avoid scandal. They had to leave hastily and flee down the Thames on a barge to take ship for France, and once again Henry could have broken with Simon permanently even if he did not ask the Church to cancel the marriage. Instead he forgave the de Montforts – though he distrained Simon's lands to pay for a lawsuit that Thomas of Savoy brought against Simon at the papal law courts in Rome for the debt.[16]

Following this, Simon found it prudent to depart from England for several years on Crusade to the Holy Land, where he had family connections among the nobility and earned such a good reputation that he was reportedly asked for by the populace of Jerusalem (regained for its Kingdom by negotiation rather than conquest by Emperor Frederick in 1228 but scarcely defensible) as their governor.[17] Had he accepted, he would have had to come home in 1244 when the city fell to an invading 'Khwarizmian' Turkish army. He returned to France in 1242 in time to answer Henry's appeal for help during the unsuccessful English expedition into Poitou, put up a good showing there, and as a result was recalled to England and the court without any obvious resentment by the nobility. He apparently showed bravery in the English 'rearguard' action at Saintes, which kept Louis IX's army from overrunning the retreating English. But even so his combination of military expertise, self-confidence, impatience, and apparent arrogance reportedly led him to telling the King in an unguarded moment of hot-tempered candour during the retreat across Poitou that he ought to be locked up for the near-disaster at Taillebourg, citing the example of the incompetent French King Charles 'the Simple' (deposed 923).[18] In military terms, he had a point – it was the English barons who had failed to finance a large enough army to take on Louis, but Henry was taken by surprise by the size of the French army at Taillebourg, had to send his brother Richard to their camp to arrange a truce, and had to retreat in a hurry. A more realistic general would not have exposed his smaller army in this way, and it is possible that Simon had had experience as a teenager of fighting in the 'Albigensian Crusade' (this is unclear), as well as having learnt from veteran warriors at his parents' estates and in Palestine. Henry did not bear enough of a grudge for this reproach to lose Simon royal favour, although the opportunity for him to dismiss Simon was there – apparently Simon's father's ex-victim in

Languedoc, Count Raymond VII of Toulouse, was at Henry's court in Bordeaux spreading ill-will.[19] Once again Simon survived as a royal courtier. But the rough manner with which Simon treated his sovereign was the 'down-side' of his abilities and honesty. Both Simon and his sons would end up alienating valuable allies in the English elite in this manner, and thus probably weakened their ability to hold onto power in 1264–5. What if Simon had had a more diplomatic manner of treating his king and his own peers and had learnt from his early clashes? Or Henry had taken enough offence in 1239 or 1242 to banish him?

As of the mid-late 1240s Simon was second only to Richard of Cornwall in the number of court charters that he witnessed, a reliable guide to who was attending and thus in favour with the King.[20] The King's expensive Poitou (1242) and Welsh (1245) campaigns increased his financial problems, as did his building projects and lavish lifestyle, but within manageable limits. Worryingly, however, direct taxation was refused by the emerging forum of the 'political nation' in Parliament again in 1244 and 1248, and the assembly also requested control of the chancellorship and justiciarship – the two senior offices of state – for their approved nominees on both occasions. A request for the appointment of four elected 'conservators of liberties' to assist the King's ministers (who were to be subject to Parliamentary veto) was also made;[21] the notion of controlling the King's spending and potentially unwise appointments by a committee was thus not an innovation of the 'opposition' in 1258. As far as can be seen – our only source, Matthew Paris, does not name names – none of the greater nobility were involved with the demands, and probably lesser tenants-in-chief and the untitled 'gentry' of the middling sort were behind it. Simon certainly was not involved at this stage, though he was not a target of criticism as in the 1230s, and in the later 1240s his witnessing of charters sharply declined, which suggests that he had left the King's political 'inner circle' of trusted magnates centred around Earl Richard of Cornwall and the earls of Gloucester, Norfolk and Hereford.[22]

The question of how Simon drifted from the position of a comparative 'insider' at court to a sharp critic and would-be coercer of Henry III is linked to events of the early- mid 1250s rather than to his earlier clashes with the King, though he was clearly capable of impolitic exasperation as early as 1242 and was no respecter of royal mystique. Both King and Earl were men prone to grudges and standing on their dignity. Henry could not be relied upon, as shown by his sudden reversals of attitude towards his ex-mentor Hubert de Burgh who he backed consistently through the 1220s and then suddenly dismissed, arrested, and implausibly accused of treason in 1232 (and was to arrest again in 1237). The way that de Burgh had ended up hiding in sanctuary from his sovereign's men and was sent off to Devizes Castle as a prisoner was a warning of Henry's capriciousness. Ironically, he had owed his partial rehabilitation to his enemy Richard Marshal having him rescued from prison so he could flee to safety and negotiate a pardon. The context of Simon's reproach of Henry in Poitou in 1242 indicates a potential long-term problem with the way that Henry acted in high politics, mixing bold schemes with impracticality in carrying them out. No recent English king had been so lacking in military competence, always a problem for a medieval ruler – and the equally unlucky or impractical Edward II, Richard II, and Henry VI all ended up deposed. Simon's irritation at Henry's incompetence and disastrous optimism about a risky foreign campaign implies a probability of this recurring over other imprudent royal actions such as the Sicilian imbroglio; Simon was the sort of honest but intemperate adviser likely to speak out and receive the royal 'cold shoulder' for some act of 'lèse-majesté'. His abrasive and confrontational character was an example of what his episcopal mentor Robert Grosseteste saw as the prevailing 'sin' of the arrogant nobility, with the addition of the ruthlessness of his father. (Grosseteste indeed rebuked him for his greed over money and his harshness on occasion.)

There was also potential for Simon to take a stand on an issue of principle over perceived misgovernment, though assessments of his character and ideology are more difficult. But heredity and upbringing alike suggest a probable degree of religious zealotry, with his father a fervent and uncompromising 'hard-line' Catholic, a disciple of the Crusading preacher Fulk of Neuilly who cold-bloodedly perpetrated assorted massacres of 'heretics' (civilians included) during the Albigensian campaigns and his mother a patroness of the Dominican Order of Friars, at the 'cutting edge' of contemporary Christian evangelism and spirituality. Simon's piety was also well-known to contemporary and later chroniclers and was shown by his relations with leading theologians like Grosseteste,[23] and would have served to add to his sense of being in the right when he confronted an incompetent or unjust sovereign. Importantly, he associated himself with some of the age's most noted Christian theologians, most notably Grosseteste (d. 1253), who was Bishop of Lincoln and archdeacon of Leicester in his 'home area' as Earl of Leicester and who acted as his spiritual mentor and epistolary confidante.[24] The two men collaborated in the expulsion of the Jews from the town, at the time seen as an act of piety ridding the place of God's enemies, and more charitably Grosseteste persuaded Simon to return good for evil and not to retaliate after Henry unjustly dismissed him from the governorship of Gascony in 1252.[25] Two more associates of Simon's were the leading Franciscan theologian Adam Marsh, resident at Oxford,[26] and the 'reformist' Bishop of Worcester, Walter de Cantelupe, who served on the 'Montfortian' councils constraining the King and acted as chaplain to Simons' forces in battle with the King's armies in 1264 and 1265 – actions of a man who put principle above his career.[27] These men had in common not only active spirituality and respect for Christian learning but enthusiasm for the notion of a true Christian taking an active and sincere part in the rite of confession and acting according to his conscience, putting God's needs above worldly motives.[28] Simon apparently had a sense of guilt about his marriage having breached Eleanor's vow of chastity, which caused him to abstain from marital relations for a time and later to repeat his vow to go on Crusade – even though no less an authority than the Pope had declared his marriage legitimate at the time.[29]

Specifically, Matthew Paris records an exchange between Henry and Simon in 1252 when the vociferous local complaints about Simon's strict and supposedly unjust governance of Gascony had led Henry to agree to put him on trial as requested. Simon defended his actions as carrying out his legal contract with the King as governor, and implied that Henry had broken his part of the contract with him by prosecuting not supporting him. Henry shouted that he would not keep his word to a traitor, and Simon retorted with words that if they were accurately recorded suggest that he accused the King of not understanding what confession and penitence involved and not being a proper Christian. Whether or not he was calling the King a liar or fool, the issue of Christian repentance clearly mattered to him and he was prepared to argue with his sovereign about it.[30] All this suggests that Simon repeatedly followed what he saw as his Christian duty and was no respecter of his brother-in-law's alleged unreliability. This was an explosive cocktail, and made the chances of a breach between the two men stronger.

But this did not mean that Simon would take an active role in coercing the King rather than withdrawing to his estates – or to Palestine as a godly Crusader? – in a huff in the 1250s. Once he had taken the Cross again in 1247 the latter was a real possibility. Indeed, his mentor Grosseteste appears to have suggested that Simon join him for missionary work, possibly in the Middle East or among the Christians of central Asia threatened by the Moslems and Mongols.[31] This was the era of friars like William of Rysbruck journeying to the court of the Great Khans in Karakorum to encourage them to attack Islam in the rear, which could have appealed to Simon's idealism. Grosseteste was over seventy at the time and unlikely to have acted on his missionary plan or to have survived long on a voyage to these distant regions, but that does not rule out Simon going off with some band of friars in disillusion at his failure at Court. Alternatively he could have turned actively to the religious life and renounced his worldly goods to become a friar himself, though this was rare among the nobility. Contemporary sources, such as the 'Opusculum de nobili Simone de Montforti' (written around 1285), state that Simon lived a devout and holy life, desiring to be associated as a lay follower with the religious orders, eating sparingly, following the daily religious services in his primer, and taking part in vigils at night, and wearing a hairshirt. If this is based on accurate memories rather than speculation, then his taking up life as an ascetic friar (founding and joining monasteries was less popular than a century earlier) was a possibility. But many devout lay supporters of the most charismatic religious leaders of the era remained active in secular life and sought to do 'holy' works there instead, such as Louis IX of France. Indeed, the 'Opusculum' dates Simon's enthusiasm to the period of Louis' most fervent enthusiasm, after he returned from the Holy Land in 1254, and says that it was inspired by Louis – and that Simon began following a daily religious routine after his first political confrontation with Henry in 1258.[32] By this point Simon, like Louis, had too pressing a secular 'mission' to withdraw from the world. Also, the roles of men like his wife's ex-brother-in-law Richard Marshal and his early patron Earl Ranulf of Chester as leaders of armed 'opposition' blocs of peers in the recent past implied that active resistance was always a viable and traditional way of fighting back for 'justice' in England against a King perceived as being unjust and wilfully incapable of good rule. Marshal, coincidentally or not, had also been a protégé of Grosseteste. In terms of his character and upbringing, he could combine his father's Crusading zeal with his experience of Henry's incompetence and his own sense of grievance to psychologically justify his role in assuming command of the opposition to the King.

As of 1247–8 his likely future would have seemed to be as a participant in the Crusade called after a horde of Central Asian 'Khwarizmian' Moslem Turks, fleeing from the Mongols, reconquered Jerusalem from the Crusading Kingdom in 1244. Other leading English nobles such as the Earl of Salisbury took the Cross and departed for the East, where the Crusade's eventual leader, Louis IX of France, ended up attacking not Palestine but Egypt in a repeat of the failed attempt of 1218–20 to seize that rich centre of the Ayyubid Sultanate and force its exchange for Palestine. As such, Simon would have been able to participate in Louis' conquest of the port of Damietta, precarious advance up the Nile Delta towards Cairo, and eventual defeat and surrender at Mansurah. But instead Henry III chose him for his new governor of Gascony in May 1248, with a seven-year term[33] that ruled out his participation in any stage of Louis' Egyptian expedition or resulting sojourn in the Christian state surviving in coastal Palestine. Simon apparently demanded and received – in writing – the full powers of a royal lieutenant rather than a more junior, removable official, with control over the civil governance and military command of the duchy, which was threatened by a combination of the usual turbulent nobles, autonomous towns, resistance to any form of centralised control, and French attack plus the ambitions of the neighbouring kings of Aragon and Castile.[34] In taking this task on the King chose a tough and persistent politico–military operator who would not be intimidated by local baronial disobedience or by invasion, though Simon's exact military experience is unclear, but he also chose someone already known for his abrasiveness and lack of tact. Was this sensible in such a complex political situation?

Gascony was a problematic choice for Simon to serve as governor, though its political volatility and strong-minded barons made the choice of a ruthless and confrontational royal 'trusty' logical provided that the latter had the money and troops to enforce his will. Simon did not, thanks in part to the King's problems with balancing his books and prodigality – what was needed was for the King to have a capable and honest treasurer who assessed how much money would be needed for troops before and if it was impossible to find it warned Henry of this problem. In that case, Simon would have to be told to be more conciliatory; his way of raising the extra money was to be to arrest refractory barons and hold them for ransom, which was partially effective but led to complaints. Henry and his advisers at court did not have the foresight to ask Simon beforehand about his tactics and then either give him precise and definitive 'carte blanche' to do what was necessary or else rein him in by precise legal prohibitions – instead he was given vague orders and the complaints about his 'misrule' were then taken seriously and investigated in detail. The local barons were used to semi-autonomy, particularly in the case of the viscounts of Bearn, and were more than ready to be offended and to take up arms or launch legal cases in the King's courts. They had a history of refractory behaviour as was apparent from their 1170s–1180s resistance to the vigorous rule of new Duke Richard (later King Richard of England). A close royal 'trusty' had not been in charge of the province at all, let alone for a long-term governorship, since Richard's time. Any 'centralizer' was bound to arouse resistance, let alone a governor who tactlessly rode roughshod over local customs and imposed harsh punishments for the endemic local disorder without consultation.

Simon's rule of Gascony was thus a potential disaster waiting to happen, though some degree of reining in the local disorder was necessary and he was seen by the nepotistic Henry as reliable as a close royal kinsman. Finding a 'balance' between the permanently feuding nobles without offending many of them was next to impossible and some antagonism from those the King's representative punished was normal. Simon soon aroused an avalanche of complaints for his firm rule and was perceived to be advancing his own as well as the King's interests by holding malefactors to ransom to fill his own coffers and confiscating estates for himself – though in this era it was difficult to distinguish between any great lord's 'public' and 'private' financial interests. Filling his own treasury and confiscating lands was plausibly only on the King's behalf as his governor – as Simon was to insist. The main criticism of the King's actions should be for the lack of any plans to ward off the expected local complaints, either by backing up Simon fully (as the latter expected and argued he was entitled to) or by sending orders to halt specific 'abuses' once the first complaints reached the King. He was meant to be recovering the King's 'rights' without a precise definition of these and acquiring personal gain in the process or pursuing vendettas against his detractors was not exceptional, but arguably a less abrasive or acquisitive governor would have produced less problems albeit been less energetic or persistent. In any event, the King was alarmed enough to listen to his critics and free some of his victims – one of them Gaston of Bearn, not coincidentally his wife's cousin.[35] As a more realistic ruler would have expected, the latter did not show him any thanks for it by staying loyal.

The money Simon had been granted by the King as his revenues proved inadequate. Eventually in 1252 the complaints made to Henry's commissioners led to Simon being recalled for a judicial investigation where he and his accusers could put their cases to the King and his judges, usually seen as a 'trial' of Simon. This was clearly felt by him as a stab in the back, but was a perfectly proper procedure. As a conscientious lord it was the King's duty to listen to his vassals' complaints and do justice, and the complainants could produce a well-argued dossier of cases of arbitrary arrests (defying grants of safe conduct), imprisonment, and extortion. Simon's defence, as agreed by the two accounts by Matthew Paris and Adam Marsh, was that he had acted under the King's orders to regain royal rights and had had to be severe in his repression of gross and treasonous rebellion against royal authority.[36] Almost all the peers and ecclesiastics present backed Simon – as did the King's brother and the Queen's uncle, probably on account of Gascony having been granted to the King's son Edward (born 1239)[37] and needing to be pacified before the Prince took it over himself.

The formal judgement was made in Simon's favour, but the King undermined this by imposing a truce between Simon and his enemies, which implied that 'loyal governor' and 'rebels' were being regarded as on equal legal footing. As Henry did not have the troops to impose peace by force, an even-handed appeal to both parties to obey their King's wishes was politically logical but added to Simon's resentment. Henry seemed to be accepting that the complainants might have a case and that there had been abuses of authority, and he refused Simon's request to accept his resignation but in return pay his expenses and exonerate his innocence.[38] A new war between Simon and assorted rebels broke out as the Earl returned to Gascony, whereupon the King accused him of breaking the truce and deprived him of the governorship without waiting to find out the truth.[39] As another example of Henry's over-optimism on financial matters the King was then unable to raise the money to hire troops for his own projected expedition. Simon hung on in Gascony until Henry bought him out and paid his debts; Gascony was handed over to the rule of Prince Edward.[40]

After 1252: The Sicilian imbroglio and the pursuit of the Imperial title. Unnecessary complications that pushed containable anti-royal feeling over the brink?

But rebellion against English rule continued, spearheaded by Gaston of Bearn who Simon had arrested but Henry had released, and the royal expedition there in 1253 – with money somehow scraped together in England – was bogged down until Henry persuaded Simon to end his self-imposed boycott of the campaign and assist him. Simon had reputedly recently refused an offer of the stewardship of France and effective leadership of the regency for the absent King Louis when the latter's mother Blanche of Castle died,[41] another crucial choice, which if implemented would have set him on a career in Louis' service and probably ended his availability for political action in England. Instead, his abruptly curtailed governorship of Gascony added to his distrust of Henry – and provided more examples of his ability to make enemies by his abrasive manner of proceeding when set in authority. The stage was set for further confrontation – but the resulting crisis was not entirely due to events or personal choices made in England. If Henry had carried out his pledge to go on Crusade in 1256, made in 1250, the English political crisis of the late 1250s would have been delayed – and any financial exactions the King made to pay for his expedition would have been backed by the Church as necessary for his 'godly' duty to Christendom. He would have gained in prestige as a warrior for the Faith as his contemporary and rival Louis IX did in 1249-53 – and his lack of military experience or competence would not have been crucial as (St) Louis was fought to a standstill in the Nile delta by the Egyptians, forced to surrender, and humiliatingly ransomed but was still eulogized. Renown did not have to depend on military success, and it was the 'taking part' as a warrior of the Faith that counted; Henry's brother Richard had done little effective campaigning in his time in Palestine in 1240 and lack of men compared to the Moslem Sultanate of Egypt would have made Henry's campaign ineffective but won him praise regardless. The hard work of risking reputation and life in a gamble to overrun Egypt and confront Islam 'head-on' had been done by Louis in 1249–50 – and had failed miserably. There was no point in a further attack on the Nile delta as this had now become bogged down (literally) twice, in 1220 and 1250; Henry would have had to do what he could in the coastal strip of fortresses remaining to Christendom in Palestine as his son was to do in 1271. Luckily, the coherent and reasonably stable Ayyubid state (Egypt/Palestine/Syria) founded by Saladin had been overthrown by the murder of Sultan Turan Shah in an 'officer's coup' by his generals in 1250 and the new regime was a precarious junta of senior Turkic commanders without dynastic legitimacy, vulnerable to more coups. As of 1256–8, the likeliest time of Henry's Crusade had he gone ahead with this, this 'Mameluke' regime was not firmly established and lacked the dynamic aggressiveness it was to take on in the 1260s under Sultan Baybars, Edward I's opponent of 1271.

But the Crusade was called off, with the troops and money involved being pledged instead to the planned expedition to conquer Naples/Sicily for the Pope (technically its legal overlord since 1053 so entitled to confiscate it) from King Manfred. This was controversial to the English political elite,[42] and was open to vociferous challenge in a way that a Crusade to Palestine could not be – though both were technically 'Crusades' provided that the Pope sanctioned them as such. Quite apart from the usefulness of winning papal favour and countering French influence, it is likely that Queen Eleanor's Savoyard uncles added to pressure on Henry to accept the Sicilian offer as it would benefit Savoy to extend English, not French, influence in Italy. Three of the King's committee set up to negotiate with the papal envoy offering Sicily in 1253 were the Queen's Savoyard uncles and a fourth was their clerical countryman and protégé, Peter d'Aigueblanche; and the Queen's uncle Thomas of Savoy was lined up to provide troops for the expedition and once it succeeded take over the principality of Capua. Significantly, Thomas was married to the niece of Pope Innocent IV (born a Dei Fieschi) who was to offer Sicily to Henry.[43]

The 'King of Sicily' traditionally had a major military role as protector (or oppressor) of the smaller, adjacent papal state and Frederick II had built up a large mercenary army (including a fearsome Moslem regiment based at Lucera). Accordingly the papacy was desperate to end the resultant military threat and turn the kingdom into a pliant vassal. The crucial factor in timing in this distraction for Henry and addition to his financial woes was European politics not English statesmen's mistakes. Pope Innocent IV detested the entire Hohenstaufen dynasty and had excommunicated and technically deposed Emperor Frederick II, trying to replace him with a rebel German prince (William of Holland) as Emperor and starting a German civil war.

This long-term struggle of the 1240s ended in the Pope's favour with Frederick's death on 13 December 1250, aged fifty-six, but the Emperor's eldest surviving son, Conrad (IV of Germany and I of Sicily), was able to succeed him. Seeking to split up the Hohenstaufens' realms, Innocent proposed to depose Conrad from Sicily and sent his envoy Albert of Parma to offer it to Henry III or the latter's nominee late in 1252.[44] The following negotiations led to Henry's brother Richard declining the chance to rule Sicily, allegedly scoffing that he might as well be offered the moon,[45] but Innocent's alternative offer of the kingdom to Louis IX (in Palestine) for his brother Charles of Anjou was turned down too thanks to the brothers' mother Queen Blanche. Henry accepted a second offer on his second son Edmund's behalf when Albert returned to England in 1254 – while Conrad was still alive and so envisaging war against an adult and competent male Hohenstaufen ruler with a large German army behind him, another example of Henry's lack of realism.[46] But what if Henry had followed the scrupulous Queen Blanche in protesting that if Conrad was to be removed his infant son, Conradin, was the correct heir to Sicily and should not be replaced by an outsider? This appeal to normal legal practice was a logical and acceptable excuse for non-intervention.

Luckily Conrad died a few months later; this left the Hohenstaufen realms of the 'Holy Roman' Empire (basically Germany and northern Italy) and Naples/Sicily leaderless and made overrunning Sicily more practicable with Conrad's only son, Conradin, a baby. A further reversal of fortune saw the offer of Sicily 'on hold' in autumn 1254 as Innocent initially came to an agreement with Frederick's illegitimate son Manfred, 'vicar' (governor) of the kingdom for the infant Conradin as of Conrad's death, for Conradin to remain king and was allowed by him to enter the Campagna with an army en route to Naples. Manfred even met Innocent at the frontier and took the bridle of his horse as a loyal vassal of the papacy. But Innocent's presumptuous granting away some of Manfred's lands to papal favourites and rumours that he would arrest Manfred led the latter to flee to the regiment of Moslem troops at Lucera and lead them in rebellion. Innocent entered Naples regardless but then died too (December 1254), giving a chance for the next pope to abandon the invasion and accept Manfred as ruler of the kingdom – which would have left Henry and Edmund out of the agreement despite the earlier offers to them. But the new pope, Alexander IV, was equally determined to seize the 'Regno' (southern Italy and Sicily) for his own, non-Hohenstaufen candidate and resumed the negotiations with England.

The 'Regno' was now overrun in a military coup by Manfred, and his attempt to win Alexander's acquiescence failed. The Pope, who regarded the kingdom as his vassal and so his to bestow on an ally, refused to accept another Hohenstaufen as its ruler, and continued the offer to Edmund. Henry agreed and prepared to divert his Crusade there in 1256, and even to pay a total of 135, 541 'marks' to pay off the papacy's debts incurred so far in the war. The prospect of French acquiescence – vital for his troops to cross France, and possibly to avoid an attack on Aquitaine while many of its lords and their tenants were in Italy – was raised by his successful 'State visit' to Chartres and Paris en route home from his stay in Gascony in autumn 1254. Apart from sightseeing in the cathedrals he held successful meetings with Louis and his advisers, with his wife's sister Queen Margaret of France and her mother, Countess Beatrice of Provence, acting as 'middlemen'. The Provencal/Savoyard link was vital to the Anglo-French rapprochement and also served to encourage Henry to act in Savoyard interests in taking over Sicily. His potential rival for the throne of Sicily, Louis' brother Charles of Anjou, appears to have been sidelined – though Louis apparently could not persuade his nobles to agree to return any of confiscated Poitou, Anjou, or Normandy to Henry as requested. (This was his excuse, anyway.) An Anglo-French treaty ending the hostilities over Angevin lands was now in the offing. As of October 1255, when Edmund was invested as King of Sicily at Westminster by papal legate Roland Masson,[47] Henry had reason to think that Louis would not stand in his way and the only person his generals would have to fight was Manfred – who was to be overthrown and killed in one battle by Charles of Anjou in 1266. The expedition to take the Sicilian throne thus seemed a viable gamble in terms of international diplomatic reactions in 1255–6[48] and the cost of it was to be met by taxation of the English Church not the barons (to decrease the risk of problems as well as due to it being a papal cause?). This was assisted by harsh financial demands of all the nation's monasteries, with threats of excommunication for anyone who did not pay up and seizure of their property.[49] However, this was too optimistic financially, and the collection was too slow to enable troops to be hired for any expedition in 1256. When Masson returned to England to collect the substantial amount of money still owing in 1257 the bishops claimed that the taxes required were impossible to meet. They could offer £52,000 instead, but only if the junior clergy were able to approve it at an assembly first – evidently they feared a 'tax strike' and could not enforce papal demands on their juniors.[50]

Nor did the plan take account of the difficulties of a long march/voyage to Italy and adequate command, manning, and supplies; if the expedition was to set out from England or from Gascony it would have had to march across southern France and then probably sail from the French Crusading port of Aigues-Mortes (first used by Louis in 1249) to the Papal States or else cross Provence and the southern Alpine passes to the Po valley. (Luckily, the Queen's uncle Thomas of Savoy was guardian to the Marquis of Montferrat so they could have used the passes in that principality.) The latter was the route that the eventual invader of the 'Regno', Charles of Anjou – by now ruler of Provence in right of his wife, Queen Eleanor's youngest sister Beatrice – used in 1266. It is possible that Henry meant to use the money to hire mainly Italian troops (via his Savoyard relatives?) rather than try to dragoon many of his countrymen into fighting, as the latter would have met with as much resistance as had his earlier attempts to raise troops for a Poitou campaign in 1242. But in that case he would have needed much more money than he was able to raise in 1255–7, and in 1266 Charles was to rely heavily on funds raised from Italian bankers in the Papal States.[51] The army that Charles was to use to destroy Manfred's was allegedly around 6000 cavalry, 6000 mounted infantry (half of them archers), and 20,000 infantry according to contemporary sources, which probably exaggerated;[52] as of 1258 the Pope was demanding that Henry bring an army of 8500 men to Italy by 1 March 1259 or be excommunicated.[53] Either way, the numbers required were beyond the resources that Henry's administrative machine could collect and once again he was hopelessly over-confident. Moreover Henry had accepted the offer of the 'Regno' for his dynasty when adult, legitimate and capable foe Conrad was still alive so he had not waited until he had a weaker opponent in Manfred. But had Frederick not died in 1250 would Henry have become involved in Mediterranean politics at all? And without the additional problems caused by the papal demands on the Church in 1255–8 would opposition to his fiscal imprudence and rash overseas ventures have crystallized into coercion?

The death of Conrad IV also left the Imperial throne vacant, and in 1256 Henry's brother Richard – who had turned down the offer of Sicily for himself as impractical to conquer – launched a plan to be elected the next 'King of the Romans', i.e. 'Emperor'-in-waiting (the actual title of emperor was received at coronation by the Pope). As a result he was to spend large amounts of money and diplomatic efforts in trying to win over the seven 'Electors' who chose the next emperor, rather than playing a potentially mediating role in English politics or – more vitally? – using his financial resources to prop up Henry's tottering financial position as he had done in the 1240s and early 1250s. In 1256 he left England for the Rhineland to start canvassing opinion and exerting diplomatic and financial pressure ahead of the next Imperial election at Aachen, and the following January he was to be elected by a majority (four) of the seven Electors as 'King of the Romans' with the minority backing his rival, King Alfonso X of Castile (unlike him descended, in the female line, from the Hohenstaufen dynasty). Luckily, for once Henry's ambitious diplomacy had succeeded in keeping one threat at bay rather than exacerbating it as Alfonso, neighbour and potential invader of Gascony, had been bought off from attacking it by Henry in 1254 – his half-sister Eleanor was married to the King's son Prince Edward in the treaty of Burgos.[54] As a result Gascony was safe from invasion from Castile as well as from France during the crises in England in 1258–64. But did Richard's absence from England and inability to lend money to Henry in the crucial years 1256–8 make the King's financial position worse and lose him an important voice of moderation in dealing with the barons' complaints? Or was his marriage to the Queen's sister, Sancia of Provence, an indication that he too would have been liable to back the unpopular Savoyards against baronial demands for their dismissal from court and administration had he been in England?

The struggle for power, 1258–65

Political confrontation and coercion, 1258: Inevitable given the King's failings?

As of 1255–7 Simon was back in royal favour, though continuing mistrust on his part is clear in his hard-headed insistence on his long-standing debts due from the King being resolved as comprehensively as possible in enforceable legal documentation.[55] He was chosen to be the King's ambassador to Scotland, where Henry's sister was married to the under-age Alexander III and rival factions were fighting over the regency, in autumn 1254[56] and to France for extension of the current truce in January 1256 and again in February.[57] His major role in diplomacy with France reflected his lands and personal connections in both countries, although his desire to be on good terms with Louis IX was also connected to his legal claims for repossessing lands and that which his father had acquired in the County of Toulouse during the 'Albigensian Crusade' via the French courts.[58]

Henry and Simon were both seeking 'justice' for lands lost to the French monarchy in past decades and a settlement could have been included in the Anglo-French treaty that was eventually signed in 1259, with the belligerent French nobility rather than the penitentially minded ex-Crusader French King the main obstacle.[59] Simon also managed to achieve a titular grant of the county of Bigorre in Gascony, which he had been seeking while governor of Gascony, from its current holders in 1256 – their need for help against their foe Gaston of Bearn was the reason and it was not implemented but it implies that he still sought a Continental as well as English role. But in practical terms Henry's new financial embarrassments meant that he would have difficulties paying what he owed the demanding Simon, particularly dower payments due to Simon's wife, and Simon was certainly at odds with the King's acquisitive uncles-in-law and half-brothers. He was supposed to have said in 1252 that if the King confiscated his lands as a result of the Gascons' lawsuit against him some Savoyard or Poitevin would receive his earldom of Leicester, indicating who he saw as out to ruin him.[60] In May 1257 Simon and William of Valence had a furious quarrel that nearly ended in a fight at the King's Council over William's men allegedly raiding Simon's lands and then having their loot recovered by Simon's steward, and at the time of the crisis in spring 1258 William was accusing Simon of putting his enemy Llywelyn of Gwynedd up to raiding the earldom of Pembroke.[61] Such personal clashes made it more likely that Simon would gravitate towards any factional 'stand' against the King that required Henry to remove his kinsmen from power and the country, for reasons of self-preservation as much as idealism. In practical terms, removing them would also open more chances for Simon's own poorly endowed sons (who were after all the King's nephews but had not been given any heiresses to marry unlike the Lusignans and Savoyards).

The lawsuit over Simon's governorship of Gascony in 1252 had been pivotal, both in giving him a grudge against Henry for 'bad faith' over the terms of his contract as governor and in winning him the backing of leading magnates. One chronicler reckoned this as the main reason for Simon gravitating to the 'opposition' in 1258.[62] But his long-term grudges seem to have been personal ones rather than of principle concerning the conduct of government, as he did not take part in demands in 1253 and 1255 for the full observance of the past Charters or demands in 1248 for control of the appointment of the chancellor, treasurer and justiciar (though in all these cases he was abroad when the crises came to a head).[63] In fact, hardly any of the higher nobility were involved in these, and they appear to have been late converts to the cause of legally constraining the King – unlike in 1215 when they had taken the lead. Probably they had not yet despaired of persuading the King to alter his patronage in their favour of his own accord, and they did not bear the brunt of his taxation anyway. The favours in legal and land-grants and donations of money to alien courtiers, biased patronage to the benefit of a small clique, rapacious local officials, high taxation, financial exploitation of the Church, and breaches of Magna Carta cited as Henry's worst sins in the reformers' appeal to Louis IX in 1264 – along with the idea of a so-called 'Crusade' against fellow-Christians in Sicily[64] – reflected the complaints of all classes. But the worst financial oppression and injustice were suffered by the Church and the 'middling sort' rather than by great magnates, and the latter would appear to have been most incensed at the monopoly of patronage by the King's chosen few. Nor would the idealistic complaint against the idea of a Crusade being used against the Sicilians rather than the 'Infidel' have mattered to many people apart from personally devout and 'questioning' Christian enthusiasts. The taxes that had to pay for it were aimed at the Church, where most of these 'intellectuals' were employed – would the Sicilian candidature have met this intellectual challenge had the Pope not ordered taxation to pay for it but raised the funds from Italian bankers instead? This suggests strongly that more judicious distribution of favours by Henry at court and avoidance of the mid-1250s clerical taxes would have meant that latent criticism of his partiality and finances – as we have seen, a factor in politics since the early 1230s – did not come to a head in 1258.

As events turned out, it was personal disputes among the great magnates that brought a substantial faction of them into the 'opposition' ranks in spring 1258. A split in the ranks at court and a fear among those opposed to the King's favourites that they would not secure justice from their sovereign occurred, always a danger for a narrowly based regime. Already even two of the Queen's uncles, Peter of Savoy and Archbishop Boniface, had been in dispute with the King's half-brothers, and on 1 April 1258 a dispute between the ex-Justiciar of Ireland, John FitzGeoffrey, and the King's half-brother Aymer de Valence (Bishop-elect of Winchester) over the advowson of the church of Shere in Surrey led to their retinues brawling. Aymer's men were the aggressors, but when John complained to the King he was ignored.[65] This latest example of royal partiality sparked off demands for widespread reform at the Parliament, which met at Westminster around 9 April, with the threat of excommunications and an Interdict if the money for the Sicilian expedition was not found hanging over the realm. On 22 April seven leading magnates – Simon de Montfort, the Earl of Norfolk (Roger Bigod) and his brother, the Earl of Gloucester (Richard de Clare), Peter of Savoy, John FitzGeoffrey, and Peter de Montfort (Simon's retainer and Warwickshire neighbour but no relation) – committed themselves to a sworn oath of confederation. They then confronted the King, weapons in hand, to demand that he expel the alien courtiers and accept reform of the realm by a committee of twenty-four; Henry had no loyal magnates with troops to hand to defy them and had to agree to this.[66] It was significant that Norfolk, who had been involved in the Parliamentary demands for a reformed constitution in 1244 and led a delegation to the Church Council of Lyons in 1245 to complain at papal taxation of the clergy, and Gloucester (who had personal experience of the abuses of royal patronage and fiscal extortion as an unwilling ward of Hubert de Burgh on royal orders after his father died in 1230), were cousins and were the sons of 1230s rebel Richard Marshal's sisters. Norfolk, son of the eldest daughter of William Marshal, had inherited the role of 'Marshal of England' after his brothers-in-law and had also fought briefly in Richard's rebellion. He had violently quarrelled with the King and been threatened with the ruinous demand to pay all his debts at once in retaliation (1255) and had since been in dispute with Aymer de Lusignan. Norfolk thus had experience of royal capriciousness and unreliability, like Simon, and had reason to fear the Lusignans' malevolence and to want them expelled. Both these senior Earls were dynastic rivals of William de Valence to lands which the latter had acquired by his marriage to a Marshal co-heiress; they as well as Simon had practical reasons to turn to the opposition cause rather than continue to rely on the King. As heirs to long-established regional dynasties, the de Clares (Southern Marches) and Bigods (East Anglia), they had family pride to consider and would have regarded their families' role as senior advisers to the King as being usurped by greedy 'parvenus' – and the future course of their loyalties was to show that Norfolk at least was prepared to swing back to the King's side once the initial tranche of reforms had been achieved. Peter of Savoy was an 'alien' and Savoyard himself, and owed his position to his niece the Queen; but he was at odds with the Lusignans over patronage. The motives of most of these figures were thus personal as much as ideological, and Simon was not the only leader of the 'reformists' whose reasons for backing coercion of Henry in 1258 were mixed. But did the dispute concerning the Shere case finally push them over the brink, usefully at a time when most magnates were at court?

The committee of twenty-four consisted of twelve men nominated by the King and twelve by the confederate magnates, and prepared measures to be brought before a Parliament at Oxford in June. In the meantime Simon had another personal confrontation with William de Valence, over the latter's accusations that he had encouraged Llywelyn of Gwynedd to attack the earldom of Pembroke's lands, was called a liar and a traitor, and had to be restrained from assaulting him in public.[67] Typically, Simon made sure as the committee began its work that Henry promised to act on the latter's recommendations concerning the payment of money that the King owed Simon – as usual, he was quick to advance his own financial agenda.[68] It is also possible, though unproven, that Simon used his part in the ongoing Anglo-French peace negotiations (as Henry alleged in 1260) to ask Louis to demand that one article of the treaty required not only Henry and his brother but their sister Eleanor, Simon's wife, to renounce her claims on the Angevin lands in France which had been lost in 1204. Eleanor's agreement was thus essential if the treaty was to proceed, and she showed no hurry to agree – was Simon using this as a threat to force Henry to agree to pay him and Eleanor all the debts from her dowry that the King owed them?[69]

Sharp practice and personal financial gain by Simon apart, the committee's proceedings led to the gathering of a much wider and more representative meeting of the nation's 'political classes' at Oxford on 9 June 1258. This duly provided the opportunity for a much wider airing of grievances and demands that these be met in a legislative framework, extending the April 1258 confederates' demands into a broader move for 'reform' of decades of complex abuses. Parliament was already accustomed to debate such issues as a prelude to granting the King taxation for war – and not to grant him taxes or a muster of troops if the delegates were not satisfied. The procedure of 1258 thus followed naturally on from demands made of the King in 1244, 1248, 1253 and 1255, and the calling of a Parliament was to be expected – but it still seems to have resulted in a degree of momentum in areas not anticipated by the magnates who coerced the King in April. Only Norfolk – and certainly not Simon – had shown any interest in legislative constitutional reform and controlling the King's appointments before. The military factor in calling a Parliament should not be forgotten, as it followed alarming advances made against the embattled Marcher lords in South Wales by Llywelyn of Gwynedd, who had evicted his older brother and co-ruler Owain from his lands in Gwynedd in 1255 and was aggressively expanding his principality into territories to the south, which were either ruled by minor local Welsh princes or by English barons (including the reformers' target William de Valence in Pembrokeshire). The expanded but precarious 'super-state' of Gwynedd set up by Llywelyn's grandfather Llywelyn 'Fawr' ('the Great'), with areas to its south as far as Carmarthenshire under his control or titular overlordship, had briefly created a tentative 'Principality of Wales' from 1216 to 1240, with Llywelyn using that title, but had been driven back into a smaller state consisting of Western Gwynedd alone by Henry in 1240–41 after he died. His grandson Llywelyn of Gwynedd was now resuming his work, overthrowing some of the princelings of mid- and South Wales and reducing others to vassalage and evicting English settlers from disputed lands; a repeat of Henry's large-scale campaigns of the 1240s to keep Gwynedd in check was urgent. Thus the June 1258 Parliament was supposed to provide a muster for a new Welsh campaign, with the King concentrating on his 'backyard' rather than Italy for a change and helping out his embattled Marcher barons – was there to be a wider than usual gathering of minor gentry at Oxford partly as they could be asked to approve and join a campaign? The meeting at Oxford was meant to precede a muster at Chester on 17 June for the war, with a larger than usual complement of landowners called up for the latter.[70] The fact that the bulk of the de Clares' lands lay in Glamorgan, in the path of Llywelyn's expansion, is an important factor in explaining why the Earl of

Gloucester was keen to see Henry diverted from Italy to Wales in his military interests.

The gathering at Oxford took the opportunity to draw up what was known as the 'Petition of the Barons', a collection of grievances variously attributed to the earls and barons (major landowners) or knights and freeholders (lesser landowners). This showed demands for controls on the Crown's intrusive and oppressive local agents, a less dilatory and biased judicial system, and an end to extortion by assorted leading beneficiaries of royal patronage on their estates.[71] The committee of twenty-four, or parts of it, drew up the 'Provisions of Oxford', probably a series of 'working draft' memoranda of their plans rather than definitive published proposals. This envisaged systematic and permanent control of the royal government by people other than the King and his nominees, a 'first' for English government (the controlling committees of barons set up in 1215 had been temporary, to achieve specific objectives in a fixed period). The committee of twenty-four would be superseded during this Parliament by a committee of fifteen, chosen by a complicated electoral system and crucially including seven of the twelve 'reformist' baronial nominees of the 'twenty-four' and only three of the King's twelve. It was thus meant to give the 'reformers' a permanent majority and end the current veto that the King' twelve could impose on progress (and apparently were doing). It would oversee all the royal officials and appoint the leading ones – an advance from the measure proposed in Parliament in 1244, which had only the leading ministers to be subject to Parliamentary choice and veto. It would have to approve all non-routine royal writs, thus controlling grants of money, offices, and other favours, and it was to remain in being for an indefinite number of years (perhaps twelve). It would co-operate with Parliament, which was now to meet regularly at prescribed times thrice yearly, with the council meeting there with a board of twelve elected representatives of the 'estate' of landowners holding baronial rank. The justiciarship, the chief judicial/administrative office held by the King's most powerful ministers in the twelfth century and last used as the basis of Hubert de Burgh's power, was to be revived in favour of Hugh Bigod, Norfolk's brother.[72]

This plan in effect institutionalized politico-administrative control of the Crown's powers by the senior landowners, with a mechanism for making it semi-permanent and for over-riding royal objections and controlling all the King's grants of office and wealth – in a form that was still to be contentious and hotly resisted when something similar was attempted by Parliament in 1641 and was to be reversed in 1660. It was a stark comment on the political nation's lack of trust in Henry III and his chosen intimates and the agreement by at least a majority of the 'reformist' half of the committee of twenty-four that the King had to be controlled and his alien favourites and corrupt officials checkmated permanently. Possibly the extent of the anger and demands for judicial and administrative reform of abuses revealed in the 'Petition of the Barons' gave the leadership an opportunity they had not expected to extend a planned purge of royal officials into a permanent mechanism for governance. Equally, the desire of men like Simon de Montfort and the Earls of Gloucester and Norfolk to secure control of patronage for men they could trust rather than their personal enemies – thus securing their own estates from confiscation at a later date by a vengeful King and his Lusignan kinsfolk – came together with idealistic demands for justice and even-handed, Christian government by Bishop Cantelupe and thinkers such as Adam Marsh, influencing the increasingly devout and zealous Simon in particular. Personal interest in preventing a revival of royal capriciousness and inconstancy (as experienced by Simon and Norfolk in person) and a wave of revenge dismissals thus coincided with the petitions for structural reform submitted to the meeting at Oxford. It is logical that Henry's mixture of openness to unscrupulous relatives demanding special favours plus unreliability at keeping his word would suggest an institutional answer – controlling his power permanently.

There had clearly been a flood of grievances building up for years – but would this have reached the point of magnate leadership and a structured plan to remedy it but for the Sicilian crisis or the personal disputes between leading 'opposition' peers and the de Valence brothers? Would Simon have joined the protest but for the threat of William de Valence to his future as a royal adviser and senior magnate? In personal terms, the accusations of treason made by de Valence against Simon at the height of the crisis were a sound reason to curtail the danger that the King would listen to his half-brother – or be able to act on any accusations. And if Simon had not taken a leading role or been absent in France negotiating again in spring 1258, it seems likeliest that Norfolk – already involved in constitutional demands as of 1244 and another personal enemy of the Lusignans – would have taken on his role.

The attendees at the Oxford Parliament proceeded to take an oath to observe the Provisions before they dispersed, in accordance with the precedents of 1215 and serving to affirm the religious nature of their action but also a means of 'smoking out' objectors and prosecuting those who agreed to this but subsequently defected. The Lusignan brothers refused to take the oath to a plan that would undoubtedly deprive them of their ill-gotten gains, and were duly deprived by a second Parliament that met within weeks at Winchester, and fled overseas.[73] This decapitated the King's faction, and the council of fifteen and a subsidiary committee that was set up to negotiate a financial 'package' for the King were dominated by reformists and their allies. This was to be expected in order to prevent obstruction and get things agreed quickly, but there was a notable presence of Simon's friends and retainers on these bodies and among the castellans appointed to take over the King's castles.[74] Having had little to do with the 'reform movement' in the 1240s and early 1250s and been overseas as a negotiator in France until just before the Oxford Parliament, Simon was clearly moving 'centre stage' and seeking a leadership role. The presence of Bishop Cantelupe on the council and financial negotiating committee was more certainly idealistic, and it is more likely that he rather than Simon provided the religious atmosphere of a 'crusade' for justice seen in the reformists' procedures and language. Simon's personal air of religious zeal for reform was only noted after, not before, Oxford, according to the Melrose chronicle – and possibly the religious atmosphere of the oath-taking, at the Dominican Friars church, added to his sense of religious commitment to the cause.[75] If there had not been an oath to observe the Provisions in 1258, would he have been more flexible in pulling back from confrontation with the King in 1260–64 in order to safeguard his own estates – as Norfolk appears to have been?

Simon's hesitation to take on a leading role in a movement against royal powers that could get out of control was a possibility in 1258, given the apparent 'grass-roots' nature of the crucial 'Barons' Petition' and lack of connection between many of the reformist demands and the personal interests of him and other great magnates. His absence from criticism of the King's misjudgements or from demands for institutional reform in 1244–58 indicates this; his disagreements with and feelings of betrayal by Henry were more personal. But if he had been more hesitant in 1258 it would have been unlikely to alter the outcome – at this juncture the chroniclers identify Gloucester and FitzGeoffrey as well as Simon as the reformist leadership,[76] and Cantelupe's participation in the vital council and committee suggests that he was the Church representative. The possibility indeed remains that despite Simon's disquiet at and vocal disapproval of royal blunders he was a late convert to the concept of wholesale reform and committee control of the King's government, and elbowed his way to the forefront of it partly to preserve his own interests – with ideological commitment only emerging gradually. Indeed, some evidence exists that he may have been hesitant about taking an oath to observe the Provisions, which would indicate that he did not want the reformers to be committed by an irrevocable action to go too far. Allegedly he complained that the English were well-known for being inconstant and the reformers could easily change their minds later so it was necessary to accommodate this possibility. (If this was his terminology, he still saw himself as a French 'outsider'.[77]) The possibility also remains that if the 1258 Parliament had not coincided with a need for widespread participation in order to arrange a military muster the membership would not have been so extensive, and the demands for action drawn up – and acted upon – would not have been as extensive.

From reform to military confrontation, 1258–63: Was a clash inevitable given the King's truculence and the factionalism within the opposition?

The main danger of the administrative coercion of the King in June 1258 was that it would turn the latter irrevocably against the reformers and cause him to seek to restore his freedom of action by any means necessary – encouraged by greedy courtiers who had lost their ability to loot the nation's resources due to the reformers. This was a problem for any coercive reform of the royal administration, and was to overthrow the initial achievements of 'reformist' barons in Edward II's and Richard II's reigns – and was to present a (literally) fatal threat to the chance of compromise between Charles I and his Parliamentary defeaters after 1646. Could the King be trusted to abide long-term by any agreement that was forced out of him by military defeat, and if not what was to be done to save the victors from a royalist counter-coup? Henry's father John had not stood by the concessions forced out of him at Runnymede in June 1215, and had indeed secured a papal decision that the oath he had taken to observe the Magna Carta was invalid. This route might well be taken by Henry, not least as the reformist coup had prevented him from fulfilling his plan to overthrow Manfred of Sicily on the Pope's behalf and the reformers' targets had included the papal taxation to pay for that campaign. As of 1258, Henry already had a reputation for capriciousness and untrustworthiness; the fate of ex-justiciar and royal mentor Hubert de Burgh (sacked and forced to flee to sanctuary, then imprisoned) was a warning to the King's potential foes.[78] The reformers sought to prevent any papal intervention on Henry's behalf by sending a mission to Rome asking for approval of their actions, the appointment of a papal legate to bring 'on-the-spot' papal legal backing to their work, the cancellation of the grant of the 'Regno' to Edmund, and the dismissal of Aymer de Valence from the bishopric of Winchester. The only one of these requests granted was the cancellation of the Sicilian grant, which events in England had now made impossible to fulfil anyway.[79] In the meantime the new 'Justiciar' Hugh Bigod undertook an 'eyre' across England to listen to and act on judicial complaints, and a panel of knights in each county collected complaints to be acted on by the next Parliament, in London in October – practical, ''grass-roots', countrywide action.[80] Notably the reformist measures enacted by the council and Parliaments included judicial action to remedy abuses of office by officials on the barons' own estates. Gloucester was to resist this early in 1259 – and Simon was to insist on it and quarrel with him over it, showing his idealism (and probably a religious element of virtuous self-denial).[81] The systematic reining in of corrupt and abusive royal officials also may have had an influence from Louis IX's zealously Christian 'purge' of corrupt officials and issuing of ordinances for just governance after his return from Crusade in 1253. Given Simon's frequent negotiating visits to Paris in the mid-1250s, his biographer J.R. Maddicott believes that Simon was also the likeliest conduit for these ideas.[82]

The finalization of Anglo-French negotiations with a treaty in winter 1258–9 had been meant to be done with another visit to Paris by Henry III. But the reformers were unwilling to let him leave the country lest he turn on them, so a committee including Simon, Norfolk, and Bishop Cantelupe went instead. This duly finalized the Treaty of Paris, confirming the continuing English control of Gascony – but as a vassal of the Kingdom of France – and abandonment of claims to the rest of the Angevin 'empire' South of the Channel. It also achieved some personal gains for Simon, such as his acquisition of the county of Bigorre.[83] The slow progress of practical arrangements for reformist legislation by the council in his absence was seen as connected to the latter by one chronicle indicating that he was the most committed or energetic of them, and the death of FitzGeoffrey and judicial work across the country by 'Justiciar' Bigod left Gloucester as the most determined reformist magnate.[84] When the next Parliament met in February 1259 the 'Ordinance of the Magnates' that was issued envisaged the magnates and other baronial holders of manors allowing complaints against their judicial malpractice. The judicial rights of the baronage were laid out and regulated in the 'Provisions of the Barons' – and published so the wider political 'public' would be aware of them.[85] At one level this was morally approvable, Christian self-denial and putting the barons under the same restraint as the King – no doubt under pressure of potential demands for this action in Parliament. On another, it separated the more altruistic (or ultimately realistic) leadership from those who preferred to act for their own self-interest and would be scared off by this act into preferring a royalist 'revanche'. The initial planned text was altered to the barons' interests, and allegedly helped to cause a quarrel between Simon and the less generous Gloucester about the reformers becoming self-serving – though Matthew Paris is incorrect to state that Simon's subsequent journey to Paris (April 1259) was a withdrawal from England out of pique rather than a planned embassy concerning the Treaty.[86] A rift between 'moderates' – self-serving or not – who could drift back to the King's side and Simon's zealots was possible once the initial reform-measures needed to be backed up by action that would affect the barons' own judicial position. This problem was inevitable if the reforms were to be comprehensive – and if the barons had not included their own judicial powers demands for this would have surfaced in a subsequent Parliament. Thus those lords unwilling to go this far would be a potential reinforcement for a revanchist King and the Lusignans, with Queen Eleanor and Earl Richard always ready to push Henry into confrontation. As the hot-headed Prince Edward (aged twenty-one in 1260) emerged into political maturity he could be expected to join this faction too, to regain his 'lost rights' and prevent himself from being held in tutelage by a baronial committee once he was King.

The loss of reformist unanimity, a split between its leadership, and a political chance of a 'comeback' for the King was thus not the exclusive fault of an 'impatient' or 'over- idealistic' Simon that a more hesitant or judicious alternative leader – Gloucester or Norfolk – would have avoided. At the most, a degree of personal resentment between the King and Simon was revived by the large extent of dower payments due to Eleanor (that is, Montfort's wife) set out by the legal arbitrators of her claims in 1259, namely 2000 'marks' per year plus huge 'back-dated' sums still owing from past non-payment. Paying this was beyond Henry's current means, but was essential in order to secure Eleanor's abandonment of her claims on the lost Angevin domains as an integral part of the Treaty of Paris.[87] It thus amounted to blackmail by the de Montforts, holding the vital Treaty's ratification up for them to be paid the sums they believed the King owed them – though this 'hard bargaining' was par for the course among litigiously belligerent medieval magnates concerned for their 'rights'. Simon was supposed to be behind Louis' delay in ratifying the Treaty too, or so Henry later claimed.[88] In the event, the Treaty clause concerning Eleanor's rights and renunciation of her claims was left out of the final document agreed later in 1259 and Louis did not hold up the Treaty. But Simon had clearly put his personal interest above the nation's, and he made matters worse by formally demanding Eleanor's share in her father King John's lost territories.[89] Gloucester took the lead instead in subsequent council business.[90] Simon's conduct in autumn 1259 thus did not show whole-hearted personal commitment to implementing reform or mitigating his own interests. But did his dispute with Henry over his wife's dowry rights point out that he was personally less likely to pursue reconciliation than the future 'royalists' Gloucester and Norfolk? Or that the King would be more vindictive?

The peace-treaty with France created two new problems for the crucial personal relationship between Henry and Simon. In the first place, its conclusion ended his period of political usefulness as an Anglo-French 'middle-man' with friends in both kingdoms and an invaluable role as negotiator. In the second place, the issue of his financial claims against Henry was still not settled and the new arbitration committee on the money was not well-disposed to his demands. Their conclusions would take another two years to finalize. Worse, the possibility of bad faith on the Provisions by a temporarily checked but grudging King appeared, as Henry demanded that the Parliament due at Candlemass (2 February) 1260 be postponed as he could not be there. He had business in France and Wales so this was a reasonable demand, but it was also a test of his strength to breach the terms – like the Stuart monarch Charles II's similar breach of the requirement under the Triennial Act that he summon a Parliament every three years in 1684. In both cases, could the 'opposition' summon a Parliament if the King breached his legal duty? Simon thought they should and arrived in London on 2 February to call a Parliament, but was overridden by 'Justiciar' Bigod.[91] At the time the most politically 'moderate' councillors – that is, those more cautious of alienating the King – such as Gloucester and Peter of Savoy had stayed in France with Henry after the recent signing of the peace-treaty in Paris. Simon's men who backed him at Candlemass 1260, e.g. Peter Montfort and Bishop Cantelupe, appear to have returned home with Simon; the two groups were physically separate.[92] In the middle between them stood Norfolk, his brother the 'Justiciar', and Philip Basset. But at this point Simon had the adherence of Henry's son the 'Lord' Edward, albeit partly out of the latter's discontent with the French treaty (as selling out part of his inheritance) and enmity towards Gloucester. This 'reversionary interest' antagonism between ageing father and impatient son was a long-term English political problem, and in practical terms gave Simon the adherence of Edward's landed interest and its landholding knights (including the Earldom of Chester) plus Edward's entourage. Possibly Edward also had genuine idealistic interest in Simon's concept of just and competent Christian government, a concern of his throughout his long career – and he was to be a Crusader too.[93]

The uneasy admiration of Edward for Simon was a factor in politics in 1258–65, and the two vigorous and ruthless warriors and political operators had attitudes in common (including their mixture of self-serving greed, piety, and abrasiveness). Was it possible for Simon to have won him over long term? But in a crisis Edward was always to put his family first so it was unlikely that Simon could ever have winkled the Prince away from primary loyalty to his father and so won him as a military ally rather than foe in the confrontations of 1264–5 (unless Edward had felt threatened by his father's partiality for a rival protégé, logically his younger brother Edmund, which did not happen). As of spring 1260, however, Edward's support for Simon led to someone spreading rumours that he was planning to depose his father in a revolt, presumably as Simon's ally[94] – possibly a malicious plan by Gloucester to discredit both men and make himself indispensable to the alarmed King.

Henry now returned to England with a force of mercenaries to add to his military power, and left Simon and several of his allies off the list of tenants-in-chief who were summoned to bring their troops to London for a meeting in late April.[95] Simon managed to arrange the meeting of a Parliament at Westminster despite the King banning it, but Earl Richard of Cornwall held the City militarily for the King and when the latter and his troops arrived an uneasy reconciliation was arranged between Henry, Edward, and Gloucester. Having failed to get 'Justiciar' Bigod to ban the King from returning or bringing mercenaries, Simon – who had thus shown his lack of conciliatory intent – faced the King putting him on trial. The investigatory panel consisted of two bishops allied to the King, two to Simon, and two 'neutrals' with Simon's request to have five unnamed lay 'enemies' of his excluded from the list granted. The trial, during the July Parliament, saw Simon accused of obstructing both the French treaty and Henry's return, attempting to do the latter by armed force, and denying it all boldly and making sarcastic comments that testified to his lack of fear or desire to be submissive.[96] The need for adjournment for another campaign against Llywelyn of Gwynedd, who was attacking Builth in Mid Wales, held up a resolution, and the trial was abandoned. Both Simon and Henry appear to have drawn back from confrontation after failure of their bolder plans – Simon to keep Henry out of England and Henry to put Simon on trial – and the autumn 1260 Parliament saw Simon back witnessing charters and taking a leading role in Council administration. The senior ministers were changed, Bigod (who had crucially denied Simon any legal support for coercing Henry earlier) being replaced as 'Justiciar' by Hugh Despenser. Henry was to complain at these changes being forced on him and to sack the new officials when he had the chance in 1263, so presumably Simon and Edward were their backers.[97] But the autumn Parliament now gave the power to remedy the misdeeds of lords' own officials to the lords themselves, a setback to the 'grass-roots' demands of the new general 'eyre' (i.e. a touring legal investigation into abuses), which also lacked the powers to correct these misdeeds and enforce the Provisions by its own 'fiat'.[98] In political terms, this watered down the achievements of 1258 and reasserted the lords' own rights. It was a betrayal of what had been achieved or a practical acceptance of the need to satisfy alarmed nobles, depending on the viewer's standpoint.

Both Simon and Gloucester ceased to attend the Council in midwinter 1260–61, and royalist adherents purged in 1258 returned unchallenged to court. The initiative may have been Henry's or his relatives', and it had the political skill to keep on 'moderate' Montfort allies Bigod, Hugh Basset, and Despenser in office. Simon returned to France and apparently appealed to Louis for help in his and his wife's legal claims against Henry. After Louis wrote to the latter Henry agreed to abide by the arbitration of Louis, his wife Margaret of Provence, and French minister Peter de Chamberlain.[99]

The King forces confrontation

Henry now sent an envoy to Rome to seek papal absolution from the Provisions of Oxford, using his father's tactic against Magna Carta in 1215 – a move attributed by the chroniclers to Earl Richard, the Queen, or the Queen's kinsmen. Summoning armed assistance from loyal barons to the February 1261 Parliament, he addressed the latter in tones of virtuous indignation to complain that the post-1258 regime had failed to reform his finances, had enriched itself, and had treated him as its minister not its lord. The King (or his prompters) did not attack the Provisions head on but made accusations of misrule and personal gain that were less easy to brush off as arbitrary royal 'special pleading', and the Council were unable to deny specific charges of going beyond the Provisions' rules on occasion in ignoring or meeting without Henry or vetoing his appointments. Wholesale grants of land and money were made to royalist barons and mercenaries to buy their military backing, and once Henry was ready in May he marched into Kent and Sussex to take over strategic castles (especially Dover) and the Cinque Ports, receive oaths of fealty from the locals, and secure the region for his army and potential foreign aid. Returning to London at the head of his vassals, he ousted the 'opposition' governor of the Tower in favour of John Mansel, father of his current envoy to the Pope – whose return with the papal bull of absolution from Henry's oath to the Provisions (June) enabled him to declare the latter invalid.[100] The bull also enabled him to absolve others from their oaths to the Provisions, an invitation to the scrupulous to desert the reformers with clear consciences. As in 1215, the Pope backed the King against barons. In effect it was a mixture of military coup and a successful display of royal duplicity, in a manner similar to the late activities of the equally determined and untrustworthy Charles I in the 1640s.

Given Simon's and Edward's absence in France and the probable 'buying off' or disillusionment of their most crucial potential ally Gloucester, there was little chance of a concerted stand against the King by an effective force of armed magnates in April–June 1261. Simon was once again pursuing his legal and financial claims overseas, though this did gain him the relatively even-handed aid of Louis IX, and Henry was thus able to take the initiative. Had either Simon or Edward been in London and been prepared to defy

Henry this would not have happened, and possibly the King would not have taken the risk that he did. But the revelation of Henry's duplicity, as with John's in 1215, meant that the 'gloves were off' and as Simon returned to England Gloucester, Earl Warenne (principal magnate in Surrey), ex-'Justiciar' Hugh Bigod, Norfolk, and Despenser headed a baronial assembly denouncing the papal bulls of absolution. The possibility arose of a march on London, and Henry took refuge in the Tower. He confidently proceeded to dismiss twenty-two of the sheriffs appointed under the Provisions in one fell swoop in July, installing hard-line royal allies instead and giving these men custody of his local castles as if to ward off any resulting revolts.[101] In an ominous sign of probably spontaneous 'grass-roots' reaction, local opponents of these men installed baronial 'keepers of the counties' in office instead in defiance. Clearly the 'Montfortian party', as they may now be called, were able to organize or assist local challenges to the King's actions. Appeals for support against the King's violation of his oaths were also made to Louis IX and to the papal court following Henry's ally Alexander IV's death; could a new Pope reverse the Bulls as a favour to an ally of Louis?[102] But neither party had the military strength to attack the other yet, and the King (based in London) opened negotiations.

A mixture of promises and bribery, plus probably the desire to avoid a risky war, led to Gloucester and other 'opposition' magnates drifting back to the King. Simon summoned three knights from each county to his headquarters in St Albans to discuss the situation, a reaction to the local initiatives in his favour and a possible move for a 'Parliament' free of royal leadership, but the King summoned a rival meeting and had more attendees. As a result Henry had the military 'muscle' to be able to impose terms on the 'opposition' in the resulting talks held at Kingston-on-Thames, and a treaty on 2 November 1261 agreed that three representatives of each faction would negotiate on the future of the Provisions and the disputed sheriffdoms. If they failed to agree, firstly Richard of Cornwall and then Louis IX were to arbitrate. The 'opposition' leadership duly accepted this and took part in the resulting arbitration processes, except for Simon who refused and left for France again – apparently saying that he would rather be landless than perjured.[103] His estimate of how far Henry could be trusted was more realistic, and the new Pope duly upheld the King's absolution from the Provisions while the baronial Council lapsed and the Lusignans were allowed to return to court. But events through 1261 had shown that Simon lacked the military backing yet for outright civil war, from the majority of the landed magnates if not from local initiative lower down the social scale. His angry departure for France – if the sources are correct, presenting himself as the 'betrayed' idealistic man of honour let down by his colleagues

– seemed to leave him isolated and potentially an exile. And if the arbitration by Louis IX between him and Henry went against him, confiscation of his English lands and permanent exile was probable. The fact that Henry was prepared to go to France himself in summer 1262 to canvass legal support at the University of Paris and try to win over Louis shows how much importance the King put on winning the case.

How did the seeming triumph of the King's faction and frustration of the reformists in 1261 come unstuck and give Simon an opportunity to rebuild his position? And was this inevitable given the personal quarrels between Henry's disparate allies? Arguably the King overplayed his hand, as he had done already by recalling firstly de Valence and later the Lusignans in a blatant sign that he would take who he liked as his advisers and give them more honours whatever his subjects had wanted (and he had agreed) in 1258. Henry, like Charles I, clearly believed that questioning or vetoing the sovereign's decisions was impertinent and treasonable and the King was justified – as God's chosen representative – in wriggling out of extorted promises. In tandem with the blatant recall of unpopular relatives, in 1261–2 Henry gradually 'targeted' figures of the recent 'opposition', including men more associated with Edward than with Simon such as the Prince's steward, Roger Leyburn, who was found guilty of peculation and stripped of many of his possessions and lands. Even if he was guilty, trying some targets of the 1258 protesters at the same time rather than giving them new honours would have been more politically wise. Others from the group of Edward's Marcher vassals and friends had their debts called in or were forbidden to go around the country armed and attend tournaments, and the surprise death of Gloucester (barely forty) in July 1262 led to an investigation into his usurpation of royal rights and a legally correct but unwise decision to keep his eighteen-year-old heir Gilbert as a royal ward (for financial exploitation of the family estates) rather than allow him to succeed to his inheritance at once. The hot-headed Gilbert, known as the 'Red Earl' from his hair, was as feisty a character as Simon and just as determined not to be intimidated; in reprisal he refused to do homage to Edward as the King's heir when he was finally allowed to take over the lands.[104] Henry's action temporarily drove him to back any challenge to the royal family and so to provide crucial 'muscle' for his return to active defiance in 1263–4, which might have been absent had Earl Richard of Gloucester, at odds with Simon, still been alive or Gilbert been handled more carefully.

The next outbreak of a successful Welsh revolt in the middle Marches in November–December 1262, which Llywelyn backed, acted as a precipitator for the next round of domestic confrontation in England. As in 1258, Welsh politics – in particular the presence of a united and aggressively expansionist

Gwynedd under Llywelyn – thus indirectly aided Simon and the reformers. Revolt by Welsh tenants against their alien and oppressive lords – in the case of 1262 the Mortimers of Wigmore – was not restricted to times of English weakness and Gwynedd strength, as a large-scale revolt had broken out in 1244 despite current English military strength after Llywelyn's hostage father Gruffydd had fallen to his death in an escape bid while trying to abseil down the wall of the White Tower in London. But revolt was more dangerous with Gwynedd to take advantage of it and aid rebels. Needing military support from reliable royal tenants-in-chief in a new campaign, Henry prudently reissued the Provisions on 22 January 1263 and sent them around the country for publication by his officials with assurances that he was reissuing them out of his altruistic goodwill. The imminent Welsh war then led to Edward's return from France with a large mercenary army of Burgundians, Champenois, and others from central France, whose leaders he promoted over the heads of his aggrieved English tenants (these latter included the men recently targeted by Henry). This army was supposed to be aimed at the baronial opposition as well as at the Welsh, though Edward's interests on the Eastern flanks of Gwynedd make it unlikely that he only used the Welsh war as an excuse. (John had used overseas mercenaries against domestic opponents in 1215–16, as had Henry II in 1173–4.) But the grant of lands and offices within Edward's estates to the newcomers' leaders alarmed the Prince's excluded Marcher allies. Some disgusted English lords from Edward's estates thus linked up with other, more definitely 'Montfortian' objectors to the alleged threat that Edward's troops – who should not have been brought in without Council permission according to the Provisions posed to the King's opponents. A 'leadership group' from these factions, headed by Edward's loyalists, then invited Simon home to assume command.[105]

The Welsh war and Edward's recruitment of mercenaries thus provided the spark to turn discontent into an armed challenge to Henry again, though if this had not occurred there would have been other opportunities – probably an unwise act of blatant royal patronage of one of the Lusignans to an estate, post or heiress coveted by an 'opposition' figure. The timing here is crucial, in that if this had not occurred – and presented Simon with a nucleus of an army – until well after he had lost out in Louis' arbitration between him and Henry in 1264 Simon might well have lacked the means to challenge Henry. Would he have not chosen to return to England at all (particularly with Gloucester still alive and hostile, or his son Gilbert in control of the family manpower but of uncertain allegiances)? Instead, he was able to return with a basis of support for criticism of the King that led some of Edward's close associates, such as John de Warenne and Roger

Clifford, and even Earl Richard of Cornwall to join him for a meeting at Oxford – the emotive site of the Provisions so no doubt chosen as such. They reaffirmed their oath to the Provisions, and sent Henry a letter demanding that he adhere to them too, publicly, and denounce all the enemies of the Provisions as mortal enemies. This was followed by 'direct action' in the Marches, always a region suited for military acts of defiance to a challengeable king as by Richard Marshal in 1234. The 'Montfortian' Marcher barons, including Edward's affinity, proceeded to arrest the unpopular Savoyard 'royal favourite' Peter d'Aigueblanche in his own Hereford cathedral and ravage the local estates of royalist 'hard-liners' such as Robert Walerand. Strategic towns were seized to cut the Marches off from a royalist attack, with sporadic attacks on royalist barons' lands and goods occurring elsewhere. Simon appears to have made approaches to Llywelyn for help, an alliance that coincided with their common interest in military defeat of Prince Edward (Earl of Chester so a local foe of Gwynedd) whose castle at Diserth was attacked by the Welsh. Apart from securing Sussex and Kent – his route for Continental help – the King did nothing to challenge the 'opposition' rampage across the Marches and disorder elsewhere. Instead it was Simon who moved forward once he had secured the Marches, leading his men round to the South of London to take over Guildford and Reigate castles and then to secure the Cinque Ports in July. The proudly semi- autonomous civic authorities at the latter defied the King and declared in favour of the Provisions, and there were hopes that the civic authorities in London would do so too. Once Dover Castle had surrendered Simon could advance on London, and despite Edward's mercenaries (at London and Windsor) Henry preferred to negotiate rather than fight. This time the balance of numbers of armed barons – plus the lack of co-operation for royalist sheriffs from the county elites – was on Simon's side, and the resultant negotiations and settlement (16 July, London) reflected this. All the Provisions were now to be enforced, except those found objectionable by an arbitration panel, but corrections could be made; all aliens were to be excluded from government, which targeted the Savoyards and Lusignans but also Edward's recently rewarded mercenary captains. (Technically, of course, Simon was an alien too as he was born in France.) The role of Bishop Cantelupe and a panel of other bishops in drawing up and sending the basic baronial demands to the King's chancellor with a recommendation that he tell Henry to agree was notable.[106] The targeting of 'aliens' by name and demands that they not only lose offices but leave the kingdom seems to have reflected a degree of popular 'nationalist' hostility to greedy foreigners who could not speak English, according to the Dunstable abbey chronicle.[107]

There was also violent hostility in London to the Prince's alien mercenaries after he broke into the 'bank' of private deposits held at the Temple to pay his men, which seems to have precipitated riots in the City and signified the adherence of the Londoners to the 'opposition' from this time.[108] The riots and the loss of the City may have finally persuaded an unnerved King to negotiate rather than fight. The disturbances in London included the famous occasion when the (French/Savoyard) Queen's barge was pelted with refuse by the City crowds at London Bridge as she attempted to head upriver from the Tower to Windsor, and this and the country-wide attacks on 'alien' clergy who her faction had secured posts in the English Church gave a personal element to her hatred of Simon.[109] How much the 'vigilante' action to evict foreign clerics and seize their property was spontaneous (probably so in origin) and how much engineered as a political weapon is unclear; but if the latter it was a risky tactic. It also annoyed the papacy – a useful mediator and source of authority to be cited as an authority, but usually pro-monarchic. The insult by the 'rabble' to his mother would cause Edward to charge off the battlefield of Lewes after the London contingent of Simon's army in 1264 and so help to lose the battle. The London incidents were thus vital to Simon's success in July 1263 and to his victory in May 1264 – but his association with a wholesale attack on the 'aliens' possibly ended any lingering hope that he and the Queen could achieve a *modus vivendi*. This was dangerous for his long-term ability to coerce her irresolute husband. Nor were the Marcher lords who had deserted Edward in 1263 reliable long-term allies.

The road to Lewes, 1263–4: How and why did the first settlement fail and the political struggle end up on the battlefield?

The collapse of the King's faction's resistance in July 1263 left the reformers in control of the government, with Simon de Montfort now seen as the undoubted leader of this faction and not a 'joint leadership' as in 1258. The death of Richard de Clare, Earl of Gloucester (the only socially comparable magnate reformist) plus his personal leadership of the 1263 campaign made this inevitable, though the reinstitution of the full Provisions meant governance by a ruling council of allegedly equal members. The emergence of Simon as undisputed leader presented one problem that the reformists had avoided in 1258 – the challenge that his acquisitiveness and personal disputes with Henry would lead to *ad hominem* attacks on him by the King's faction, claiming that the 'rebellion' was due to one man's greed and power-seeking not a constitutional 'stand' by a broad-based faction. (Arguably this strengthened Henry's chances of winning when the political and legal issues were submitted to Louis IX's arbitration.) On the 'plus' side, however, it gave the movement a clear and forceful leader – he did not abandon hope in the face of overwhelming force and seek a negotiated 'climb-down' on terms that abandoned the Provisions, as a more cautious leadership would possibly have done after Henry III's most stunning successes in 1263–4 (Louis' judgement of the arbitration in his favour and the fall of Northampton). Like Richard II after 1397 and Henry VI/Queen Margaret in the 1440s and 1450s, Henry III constantly over-played his 'hand' and deliberately failed to show magnanimity to his opponents.

Force of personality and clarity of purpose and vision placed Simon in this eminence rather than any great weight of resources – his earldom's wealth and potential for patronage was less than that of Gloucester or Norfolk and he had a brood of sons to accommodate – though he now seems to have made the most of his role as Steward of England for control and reform of the Royal Household to Henry's complaints.[110] The change of personnel in the great offices of State was in favour of 1258 reformists such as new 'Justiciar' Hugh Despenser – and also of personal loyalists of Simon's such as new Treasurer Henry, prior of St Radegunde's in Bradsole, Kent. The new council included the four from the original reformist one of 1258 who were still alive and loyal to reform – Simon, Peter Montfort, Bishop Cantelupe, and Richard de Grey – plus new members who from the charter-witness list do not seem to have been very active; the 'ruling clique' was smaller than in 1258 and more based on Simon's affinity. The apparent enmity between Simon and the Queen's uncle Peter of Savoy, a 1258 reformist now firmly back on the royalist 'side', was ominous of the narrowing of the reformist 'base' and their alienation from courtiers who had the Queen's ear.

Unlike in 1258, the King's hostility and probable later 'revanche' to punish his coercers was now clear, and Edward had also been a target of the reformists – due to his mercenary army alienating the Marcher lords – so he could not be paraded as a show of the 'reversionary interest' being in favour of reform. It was not a case of the King's heir being available to be put on the throne if the King proved untrustworthy – the course of action taken by the untrustworthy King John's enemies in 1216, with Prince Louis of France being his nearest adult male kinsman. That lack of support from Edward for the 'Montfortians' in 1263 may account for canny, cautious, or cowardly political actors not joining the government – and the lack of senior peers in Simon's army in 1263–4. The Prince's mercenaries were sent home amidst the expelled aliens, and the new regime proceeded to secure the outlying counties against disorder by appointing new knightly 'keepers of the peace' to assist rather than supersede the King's nominees as sheriffs. The illegal deposition of assorted legally appointed foreign churchmen in the 'grass-roots' evictions was remedied by orders to reinstate all those who had been deprived who had been appointed by legally- entitled patrons, provided that they took an oath to the Provisions. But this was not always enforceable and the victims could and did provide ammunition for Henry in his list of complaints about Simon, which Louis IX was still arbitrating; it implied 'bad faith' and so would be useful to Henry in blackening Simon's reputation to the scrupulous French King. Expelling Churchmen – some of them French – by brute force with no legal excuse was hardly likely to appeal to the devout King of France, and 'victimized' Bishop d'Aigueblanche of Hereford (threatened by armed knights in his cathedral so a potential Becket-style 'martyr') and Archbishop Boniface of Canterbury both turned up in France in autumn 1263 to 'lobby' Louis. This propaganda success for Henry – which Simon riskily did nothing to counter – was probably not a crucial factor in his winning Louis' support, however. The fact that the insulted and vengeful English Queen was sister to Louis' wife Margaret of Provence (both women being Savoyard on their mother's side) and it was the two Queens' kinsmen and countrymen who were being targeted as 'aliens' also assisted Henry.

As Henry's feudal lord Louis could summon him before his court in Paris, which he now did – apparently at Henry's request, as a way of getting the King out of England so he could rally support unhindered. Simon's attempts to delay the request being implemented by sending an embassy to excuse Henry's absence were ignored by Louis, an ominous sign.[111] Before the English King was due to leave a Parliament met in early September, where the July treaty was approved, plunder returned to victims, and prominent arrested royalists such as Bishop d'Aigueblanche released. The planned orders to restore plundered property, no doubt unwelcome to the pro-reform plunderers, seem to have been held up by resistance from the victors to such a measure. Then Henry and his wife and sons were allowed to journey to Louis' court at the conveniently close site of Boulogne, but Simon and two minor reformist clerics (one the non-English Bishop of Glasgow) also attended to put their case that the French court had no jurisdiction over English affairs – it should only consider those of Henry as lord of Gascony. This legal argument carried the day. Louis also confirmed the Provisions and the July 1263 treaty, possibly as long as restitution was made to those despoiled, and backed the notion that a kingdom's offices should be staffed by its own nationals.[112] Louis was thus being scrupulously just, which would have encouraged Simon to submit his next dispute with Henry to him too and made the French decision against him that time seem less likely.

The principals in the political struggle now returned to England for the Parliament, but the latter saw the peace-agreement break down over the vital issue of restitution of lands and goods seized from the defeated that summer. Enough 'Montfortians' objected to this to block it,[113] and Simon could or would not do anything to override this (by force of character as he had no right of veto over the council or Parliament). The issue was submitted back to Louis to arbitrate. But more importantly Edward had come to terms with the Marchers who had abandoned him that spring, and after he suddenly rode off from Westminster to Windsor Castle and set up his base there a substantial body of lords, including them, joined him. Henry was not stopped from following[114] – presumably as Simon had no legal warrant to restrain him, but a blow to his legality of authority.

Whether or not Edward offered bribes,[115] the dismissal of his unpopular mercenaries by Simon's regime thus facilitated the reconstruction of his armed 'affinity' of Marcher lords and so aided the King's cause. Without this coherent body of experienced fighters with large bodies of tenants, could the royalists have challenged Simon at all in late 1263 to early 1264?

Henry assured the political public of his goodwill towards the Provisions, and started to build up an army while Richard of Cornwall brokered a temporary truce. He moved to Oxford to summon and resume control of the chancery and appoint new royalist ministers. He then moved forward with an army to regain control of his birthplace, Winchester Castle the gateway to the south-east, and into Kent. The intention was to seize Dover Castle and secure it for armed support from abroad to be brought in by the Queen, but reformist custodian John de la Haye (deputy for the absent governor, Simon's close ally Richard de Grey) refused him entry. The 'Cinque Ports' stood by Simon's government and Henry returned to Windsor.[116] One alarming moment for the reformists saw Simon, who had hurried to London to intercept the returning King en route to Windsor, caught on London Bridge with a small escort as they confronted royalist troops in Southwark. Some Londoners in league with Henry pulled down the Bridge gates behind them, cutting them off, and the royalists moved in for the kill. Tellingly, Simon and his men – faced with being killed in minutes – took communion and crossed themselves like Crusaders facing a horde of infidels and Simon refused to surrender to 'perjurers and apostates'.[117] The gates were broken down in time by a rescue party and they escaped to safety, but what if the trap had worked and Simon been killed? In all probability, the 'rebellion' would have collapsed given that he was its most determined leader and the balance of force would suggest to waverers that Henry, Edward, the Marchers, and other defectors would inevitably prevail.

The letters sent to Louis by both sides in mid-December to formally accept his arbitration show that most of the principal magnates – the men who until now had dominated the Kingdom's affairs – were on his side. The

'Montfortian' party included two bishops (one of them Cantelupe), no earls apart from Simon, his own sons, a few important lords already aligned to him such as Hugh Despenser, Ralph Basset, and Richard de Grey, and a band of 'middle-ranking' landowners from northern and central England who were almost all untitled. Modern analysts have pointed out that many of them were young, and most were personal adherents of the de Montfort family and cause rather than a grouping with 'weighty' and long-established regional political and social standing. (The same geographical and social catalogue of adherents is apparent in 1265, as shown by the location of the estates confiscated from 'rebels' after Simon's defeat.[118]) The most that can be said of the absence of a substantial body of leading magnates from both sides is that temporary vacancies due to minorities or illnesses distorted the figures from what would have been the case in a confrontation in 1258 or 1261–2.

The 'Mise of Amiens', January 1264. Inevitable 'monarchic solidarity' by Louis or a shocked condemnation of reformists' targeting of 'aliens'? A crucial mistake by Simon in any case?

Having appointed royalist barons as 'keepers of the peace' in twenty-two counties to seize command there from Simon's regime's nominees,[119] Henry crossed to France for the announcement of Louis' arbitration. On 23 January 1264 his party and a rival group of reformists led by Peter Montfort attended the French King at Amiens, but due to Simon falling off his horse en route from Kenilworth to take ship and breaking his leg the baronial leader could not be present and his legal case was presented instead by Thomas de Cantelupe, the Bishop's Paris-educated Church lawyer nephew. The most prominent victims of 'Montfortian' despoliation were also present to show their enemies' breach of faith – including the French King's wife's uncle Peter of Savoy, a supporter of reform in 1258. Peter had backed Montfort at the initial clash with the King in 1258 but had defected back to the royal side in the early 1260s, thus weakening the chances of the King (his wife's nephew) listening to any pro-Montfortians within his close circle and so being influenced against violence. Then Louis announced his decision – in Henry's favour. Reversing the earlier decision, Louis' 'Mise of Amiens' declared that Henry should rule without any restriction on his decisions or appointments and that the expulsion of aliens from and banning of grants to foreigners in England were illegal. So were the Provisions of Oxford, despite the baronial arguments that they had only built on Magna Carta – which was accepted in English law and had been used as the basis for Parliamentary legislation – and were intended to remedy Henry's illegal breaches of the latter.[120] The decision was seen as a surprise by chroniclers,[121] and was clearly unexpected or Simon would not have gambled on using Louis' arbitration. Was it a mistake of his party's to include all the aspects of dispute with Henry – including the arcane quarrels over landholdings and the blatantly high-handed seizures of 'alien' property – in the terms of reference, not just submit the Provisions to Louis? (The latter on their own could have stood a better chance of being accepted, as Louis had already indicated his approval of them once.)

Was Simon over-confident that his personal relationship with the French King, another devout enthusiast for Crusades and just rule, would win the day? His own appearance at Amiens was intended and he was a fluent speaker and a friend of the French King so he could have put up a more authoritative case and impressed Louis with his pious belief in the justice of his cause. But would this have mattered if Louis was determined to do 'justice' for his brother-in-law Henry and for the expelled 'aliens', his wife's kin among them? In that case, the failure of Simon's faction to accept the need to reimburse or reinstate some of the expelled clerics was a factor which Simon did not adequately consider and a sour taste may have been left for Louis by the way that some of Simon's family and friends secured confiscated royalist estates. In that case, Simon would have been safer just submitting the Provisions to Louis, not all the post-1258 disputes. The latter could have been left for a subsequent occasion, or given to a panel of French jurists. Or was the complex mixture of disputes so intractable to resolution among English 'vested interests' that he thought that an uncommitted 'outsider' would solve them quicker and gambled that Louis would be won over by his force of argument? Given Louis' earlier 'nod' for the Provisions, he may have been over-confident – and his absence from the meeting at Amiens was unexpected. Should he have trusted Louis to decide against a fellow-king – and if Simon had not had such close ties with France would he have been so trustful? But it is hard to see who else except the new Pope Urban (also likely to back an established sovereign's unfettered power as his predecessor Innocent III had done in 1215) had the reputation and authority to be acceptable as an external arbitrator and have his decisions accepted in England. The learned doctors of law at the University of Paris or the devout and respected Archbishop Eudes Rigaud of Rouen (a personal friend of Simon's) were alternative arbitrators, but all were open to Louis' influence – and as likely as Louis to take a dim view of 'alien' clerics being chased out of their livings and denied justice. Unfortunately Grosseteste was dead (1253) and Adam Marsh had withdrawn from open involvement with the reformists so Simon lacked an internationally respected senior theologian to back him up and impress Louis, and he sent no bishops to Amiens – though the younger Cantelupe had French contacts and was known to Louis in person.

Notably, Simon's team sought to link the validity of the Provisions with that of Magna Carta and tie all the current issues of dispute in with the 'surer grounds' of the 1215 Charter being legal, and Louis 'decoupled' them and refused to accept the link. Showing his hostility to Simon's despoliation of churchmen, Louis had already written to the Pope asking him to send a legate to England to sort out the intractable disputes with a show of papal authority, and the man chosen – Guy Foulques – was a Frenchman and a confidante of Louis'; his orders showed that he was to restore Henry to his full powers.[122] Assuming as is likely that this was done with Louis' support if not at his behest, it means that before the verdict was announced Louis was already looking to reverse the Provisions – and thus Simon's presence in Amiens would have made no difference.

War – and apparent royalist predominance. Would the reformists have given up but for Simon?

The decision at Amiens left Henry with the moral 'high ground' in being able to claim that his power was being illegally fettered and his allies denied justice by a party of factious and self-interested rebels, and to claim French and papal support. The Londoners, the Cinque Ports, and most of the 'middling men of the kingdom' rejected the Mise,[123] and the solid bloc of support for Simon meant that a fight was now probable. Given his character and belief in his Crusade-style mission – as seen by his reaction when trapped on London Bridge – surrender and probable exile was not an option for him. Simon's sons Henry and the younger Simon de Montfort attacked Edward's Marcher allies, particularly Roger Mortimer of Wigmore, to hinder their potential aid to Edward, who returned from France to follow them West and start reprisals. In a confrontation at Gloucester, Edward secured the castle but faced attack by a superior force which Henry de Montfort brought from Worcester; however Bishop Cantelupe called for a truce and Henry accepted and withdrew to Kenilworth. This probably saved Edward from defeat and capture, or at least loss of many of his men; Simon was furious with his naïve son. The King returned from France, was refused entry to Dover but was able to move on to Oxford and have the time to raise an army there unhindered with the support of Edward and of Richard of Cornwall – allegedly for a war with the attacking Llywelyn of Gwynedd, now in alliance with Simon, in the Marches. Ecclesiastical mediation between Henry at Oxford and Simon at Kenilworth failed, and only gave Henry time to add to his strength. Despite the 'rebel' consolidation in and around London the King left the capital alone, and concentrated on the Midlands where he stormed Northampton on 5 April before moving on to Leicester and Nottingham to link up with Northern supporters. The King's unchecked rampage was in Simon's own area of landed estates and influence, and the loss of Northampton was compounded by the capture of Simon's eponymous son, his allies Peter de Montfort and Baldwin Wake, and around eighty barons and knights in the disaster, which Simon – held up by his broken leg – heard about as he arrived at St Albans on his march to relieve the town.[124] He abandoned the march and returned to London, where an ugly pogrom against the capital's Jews – seen as the enemies of Christ by many devout Crusaders and targeted in Palestine – followed and was probably due to seeking popular support as much as a hunt for money.[125] This was all too reminiscent of the brutal way that Simon's father had waged war in Languedoc, and this time there was no excuse of papal sanction. A southern army of royalists under Earl Warenne (lord of much of Surrey and holder of Reigate Castle) and Roger Leyburn had moved into Kent to take Rochester, threatening the Montfortian route to Dover and a crucial strategic point in the 1215–16 civil war with a massive keep. Simon advanced to besiege it, took the town and the castle's outer bailey but not the keep, and had to pull back as the King hurried south from Nottingham to Croydon. Once Simon was back in London the royal army moved across Kent to take Tonbridge, receive the submission of the Cinque Ports, and threaten Dover.[126]

Once the region was overrun Henry would have the option of using the Cinque Ports fleet to blockade London immediately or waiting for reinforcements to arrive from the Continent first, and so it was best for Simon to challenge him before this potentially overwhelming threat developed. Thus the 'rebel' army moved out of London into Sussex, and Henry headed west to the security of Warenne's castle at Lewes. On 12 May Simon and his army – outnumbered by about three to one in cavalry[127] – arrived at Fletching, a Montfort manor, en route to intercept him. The location of the resultant clash, on the Downs immediately north of Lewes, was thus due to the success of the King's unhindered campaign in Kent and the fact that Simon had avoided an earlier clash over the royal threat to relieve Rochester Castle and had not reacted quickly to the attack on Tonbridge. The Montfort army was the smaller, and he was apparently waiting unsuccessfully for the arrival in London of Robert de Ferrers and his Derbyshire allies – who had enough to do that April coping with attacks on their lands by Prince Edward. The failure of Henry de Montfort to capture or rout Edward at Gloucester thus inhibited the full strength of the 'rebels' from collecting in London, and possibly prevented a battle over the royal attacks on Tonbridge and the Cinque Ports. Simon had consulted his episcopal allies in the past few weeks about possible peace-terms. He had agreed to negotiate on the basis of offering the King compensation for his financial losses if Henry would uphold the Provisions,[128] a sign of willingness to compromise absent at Amiens. Would this offer have had any influence on Henry or Louis if offered in autumn 1263? A second attempt to mediate by the Bishop of Chichester and local friars with Henry at Lewes failed, with Simon again requiring the King's adherence to the Provisions and the withdrawal of 'evil counsellors' but prepared to submit all other issues to a panel of learned clerics.

The Battle of Lewes: An unexpected Montfortian victory? Due to royalist blunders?

If Edward had been captured or lost most of his men at Gloucester he would not have been able to 'draw off' the Ferrers contingent of reformists to defend their home territory, and arguably Simon would have had the manpower to challenge Henry earlier – as Henry tried to relieve Rochester Castle or as he was overrunning the Cinque Ports. If Simon had not been forced to use a litter to travel rather than riding in the march to relieve Northampton (or had had a deputy he could send in his place such as Richard de Clare, who had died in 1262) the King's Midlands campaign would probably have led to a battle in that region. The clash at Lewes was thus fortuitous, though the King's strong position meant that after the royalist successes in Kent in April 1264 Henry was unlikely to have accepted the proffered mediation either while Simon was still in London or when he was within a few miles of Lewes at Fletching. In any case Simon still insisted on the King's acceptance of the Provisions as 'non-negotiable', clearly seeing this as a matter of honour and conscience; the 'Song of Lewes' (probably composed by a Franciscan 'cheer-leader' for his cause and highly sympathetic) says that he would only abandon his oath to the Provisions if senior canon lawyers (not the Pope) would absolve him. In terms of personal history, Simon's fanatical and indomitable father had not given up when facing huge odds as his unpopular 'Crusading' army in Languedoc faced attack by a much larger army of Aragonese under the veteran King Peter II in 1213, and had won the resulting battle at Muret; he had let God decide the rightfulness of his cause in battle and had been vindicated. Thus Simon was unlikely to avoid battle at any price, though his second mission on 13 May (Bishop Cantelupe and the Bishop of London) did offer Henry £30,000 for the cost of reformist spoliation of his assets and Earl Richard of Cornwall and Prince Edward advised the wavering King not to accept this.[129] Neither Richard nor Edward had, however, fought in a battle before, unlike Simon.

During the night of 13–14 May Simon moved his army forward from his initial position at or near Offham, in the Weald on the north side of the

Downs, to climb the steep northern slope of the ridge and occupy its summits. He would thus be fighting downhill southwards towards Lewes, giving him the advantage of momentum and cancelling out the royalist advantage of numbers. The King and his men, quartered in and around the town, had to advance uphill – though on a reasonably gentle slope. Simon's address to his men before the battle next morning repeated the aura of moral righteousness seen in his actions on London Bridge; according to the 'Song of Lewes' he said that they were about to fight for the kingdom of England, the honour of God, the Blessed Virgin, and all the saints, and of Holy Church. They then prostrated themselves on the ground, confessed their sins and were absolved by the two bishops, and donned the crosses of Crusaders[130] – which also helped to distinguish them from the foe as both armies would have been wearing similar mailcoats (if they could afford them) or padded jerkins with the higher social classes adding tabards adorned with their heraldic emblems. The battle then commenced, with the Montfortians drawn up neatly in four divisions and fighting with a coherent strategy arranged by an expert leader who retained control of his men. Unlike the inexperienced King, he was able to react to events and keep control of his subordinates – though due to his literally keeping the 'high ground' he could look out over the sloping battlefield easier than the King (on lower ground) could do. (A royal 'grand strategy' could have been co-ordinated better from the high Lewes Castle keep, but this was a mile or so back from the fighting so a relay of riders would have had to be used to transmit orders and the King's senior commanders would have been easy to locate rather than been in the middle of combat.)

The impression of the royalists failing to use their advantage of numbers is reinforced by the crucial muddle on their right wing – the east side of the battlefield. Here, the ground fell away from the hillside into the Ouse valley, and Edward was in command. Already a capable cavalry commander (a likely achievement for a physically active and intelligent young noble used to riding and hunting) and in command of a force including his personal Household intimates, other young aristocrats, plus the hated 'alien' royal kinsmen William de Valence and Guy de Lusignan, he faced the London infantry and broke through their ranks with the force of his charge. This fate was to be expected when relatively inexperienced volunteer infantry without a compact 'hedge' of pikes met a charging force of cavalry, and as yet there was no concept in England of arranging a tightly packed body of infantry with pikes to present a bristling barrier to nervous horses. This was to be first seen a little over thirty years later, an innovation by William Wallace and Andrew Murray as their Scots faced similar aristocratic English chivalric cavalry at Stirling Bridge. (A body of infantry did, however, have to deal with a massed, Turkish cavalry charge from time to time in the Middle East.) Clearly Simon had not trained his infantry to withstand a charge, and regarded this danger as containable – as it turned out, correctly but due to Edward's rashness not his own skill. As a French nobleman used to cavalry fighting, did he disregard the importance of 'lower-class' civilian infantry on the battlefield anyway? The impetuous Prince foreshadowed the tactical incompetence of Prince Rupert in the English Civil War by pursuing the Londoners off the battlefield for miles, keen to avenge the insult they had done his mother (by pelting her barge with refuse) in blood, and chased them for miles across the river and up the Ouse valley. According to local legend he then slaughtered a body of trapped and exhausted Londoners on 'Terrible Down' at Halland, five or six miles up the Roman road. But while he was conducting his private feud the absence of his 'right wing' of cavalry from the battlefield enabled Simon's men to press the royalists back elsewhere, and neither King Henry nor Earl Richard were capable of steadying their 'wings' on the royalist centre and left. Eventually the royalists broke and fled back downhill into Lewes. The King took refuge in the Priory in the town, and Richard of Cornwall was trapped on the battlefield, hid in a nearby windmill, and was mocked by rude opponents as they surrounded him and called for the unlucky 'miller' to surrender. By the time Edward returned it was too late to fling his cavalry into the fight and rescue his allies, and he had to fight his way back into Lewes to join the King at the Priory. But the Priory was on a ridge south of the town and close to the navigable River Ouse, so this raises the question of what would have occurred had some royalist managed to get hold of a trading ship at the town wharf in the retreat and brought it to a suitable landing-place near the buildings. Could Henry – if not the still-absent Edward – have been smuggled aboard and taken to safety before the Montfortians surrounded the Priory? The royalist-held Pevensey Castle was some miles down the coast and could serve as a refuge. Without the King to sign any terms of surrender and acceptance of Simon's political programme, the war could have gone on or if not the new regime would have been even more insecure.

The settlement of 1264: Could it have succeeded and why did it fail?
The King's position as of the night of 14–15 May 1264 was not entirely hopeless, in that he might have lost his army but he was in sanctuary under the protection of the Church. Storming the Priory would lead to bloodshed on the holy premises and probable excommunication for the perpetrator, which might not be lifted for years whatever the political advantage – as befell Robert Bruce for murdering his rival John Comyn in a church in Dumfries in 1306. It would not look good for a self-proclaimed Crusader to

defy the Church, and if the Priory was blockaded to starve the King's party out the royalist garrison at Tonbridge might try to rescue them. As a result Simon needed recognition by the King that he had won and royal orders to demobilize his remaining followers, and Henry was able to negotiate his surrender albeit on weak terms. The resulting 'Mise of Lewes', which can be reconstructed from chronicle accounts, provided for the King to pardon the 'rebels' and assure them of their lands and goods, restoring all goods and hostages seized so far in the war. Henry would uphold the Provisions of Oxford in full and dismiss 'evil counsellors', and one panel of arbitrators (four English bishops or magnates) would consider amendments to the Provisions and if they could not agree hand over arbitration to Henry's (and Louis') brother-in-law Charles of Anjou and the Duke of Burgundy. The other issues outstanding – including the long-running saga of the money owed by Henry to Simon and Eleanor regarding Eleanor's dowry – was to be dealt with by two French arbitrators (named by a panel of six French nobles and prelates free from Louis' veto on their membership) and one English arbitrator. Edward and his cousin Henry 'of Almain', Richard of Cornwall's son but known for his admiration for Simon until he put family loyalty first in 1263, were to be hostages for the implementation of the deal, but those 'Edwardian' Marcher barons captured at Lewes were to be freed. The latter was probably necessary to win the 'clannish' and violent Marchers' goodwill, but events were to show that they could not be trusted.[131]

The 'Stage One' of a settlement thus envisaged put the Provisions back in place and removed those of Henry's advisers who the reformists objected to. But it gave the royalists potential for amending the Provisions or using the second, Anglo-French arbitration panel to achieve other successes. The issues that the panel were to consider included – as far as can be assessed – corrections to the King's mode of ruling, problems in the current governance of England, and various personal/legal disputes between the 'parties'. This would then provide a final, as opposed to the 15 May interim, settlement.[132] The submission of the issues to a partly 'outside' body who would be seen to be free from partisan rulings is not as much of a surprise as allowing Louis IX to have any involvement, given the latter's actions at Amiens, but presumably Simon relied on his own French noble allies (e.g. Charles of Anjou) and sympathetic clerics (e.g. Archbishop Rigaud) being on the panel. Would a reformist leader with less involvement in France have been less confident and so have chosen alternative arbitrators, who would have been more reliable – prestigious university jurists at Paris (or even distant and less risky Bologna)? But in immediate political terms, Simon now had the King in his power and the potential 'resistance leaders' among the royal kin – Edward, Richard of Cornwall, and Henry 'of Almain' – in custody and he could remodel the Royal Household and offices of state as he wished. He also had the prestige in an intensely religious age of having submitted his daring challenge to the 'established order' to the judgement of God and won by right of conquest on the battlefield, and no doubt used what literary and oral propaganda he could arrange (including the 'Song of Lewes') to present a firm 'narrative' of himself and his cause as Divinely favoured.[133]

Militarily, the threat of a royalist 'revanche' was always latent and would probably have been less had the most organized and traditionally defiant batch of dissidents – the Marchers – been held in check by holding some of them as hostages. (Presumably Henry or Edward insisted on their pardon in the Lewes priory negotiations, with an eye to their future use.) Had Simon held them down more firmly, the actual course of revolt in summer 1265 – the Mortimers helping Edward to escape and set up his base at Wigmore Castle – would not have occurred. But there were other unhampered royalists, such as John Balliol and his allies in Durham and Northumberland who in case of attack could call on Balliol's kinsman (and the King's brother-in-law) Alexander III of Scotland. Simon was too preoccupied elsewhere to secure the royalist headquarters at Nottingham Castle until December. Meanwhile Louis IX was a potential source of invasion, Peter of Savoy's castle at Pevensey held out (and was a potential site for an invasion to land), the garrison of Tonbridge fled to join Edward's men at Bristol who held out for months, the Exchequer had ceased to function (for the first time since the 1216–17 civil war) so the administration and its finances were in a poor shape, and a new board of 'keepers of the peace' had to be created to cope with local disorders.[134] None of this was prohibitive for the new regime to function, however, and the situation of a new regime under a 'strongman' having to start afresh in the name of an incapable King after a civil war had been faced before in 1217. Given the recent chaos, a victorious Henry and Edward would also have been in difficulties and needed to compromise with defiant rebels – as they had to do after ending the next civil war in 1267 in real life.

The summoning of a Parliament had been promised in the 'Mise of Lewes', and was also necessary to endorse the initial settlement and present the illusion of a united nation in case the invasion-army that Louis was gathering landed (probably at royalist Pevensey). It would also give a united front to the imminently arriving papal legate, Foulques, if he threatened an Interdict as was likely given the papal stance for Henry's regaining full powers. Accordingly Henry was required to authorize Simon, his young ally Gloucester, and Bishop Berksted of Chichester (Simon's peace-envoy to Henry before the battle of Lewes) to draw up a list of nine councillors to deal with the matters concerning the future of the kingdom. This was endorsed by representatives of the peerage (Norfolk), clergy, and commoners – the 'three estates' of Parliament taking a part in decision-making and no doubt enlisted by Simon to show the unity of the nation in his favour. On 28 June representatives of these three corporate groupings in Parliament witnessed an ordinance in Parliament, which authorized the three representatives mentioned above to nominate nine councillors and, when necessary, replacements. Three of the nine were to be in permanent attendance on the King, who was thus to be placed under tutelage and surveillance – a radical innovation for a sane adult male. The nine were to decide on the affairs of the nation and to sanction appointments (castellans and Royal Household officials as well as ministers) with the King, and in case of disagreement a two-thirds majority of them was to have the casting vote; if they could not arrange this a two-thirds majority of the three representatives was to decide.[135] It thus built on the notion of 'government by committee' in the powerless King's name created in 1258, but now excluding any royalists unless these were admitted to councillorships in future – the fruits of royalist untrustworthiness not merely of rebel victory.

This solution to the endemic political struggles of recent years and to the King's attempts to break free from the Provisions – to perjure himself, as Simon had portrayed it – was logical given the threat of the King or his allies seeking revenge and/or blocking Montfortian measures given any leeway. Something similar was to be considered by the victorious Parliamentarians in the years after Charles I had started to 'wage war on his own people' in 1642 and in the abortive settlement plans of 1646–8. According to the Merton chronicle the appalled Henry had to be threatened with deposition to secure his agreement to the new 'constitution', as it may fairly be described.[136] Had he not given way, would Edward have let ambition outbid family loyalty and accepted the throne or would Simon have moved from elective councillors to an elective monarchy? Could he have secured backing from Churchmen for the idea that Henry was a perjurer who could be deposed, his son Edward (who had not taken any oaths to the Provisions) and warmonger Richard of Cornwall could not be trusted, and so Henry 'of Almain' – a former ally – should be raised to the throne? If that had happened, the Pope could be guaranteed to declare it illegal and Louis IX to invade on behalf of the 'rightful' king, possibly joined by all the opportunist enemies of the Montfort family who were to desert Simon in real-life 1265. Unlike the 1216–17 civil war, resistance to the French would not be able to rally round the cause of an 'innocent' and legitimate new king. As it was, the allegation that Simon had deserted the cause of legality out of ambition could be – and according to the chroniclers was – made *sotto voce* on account of the Ordinance treating the Provisions as a 'given' rather than as something which was open to arbitration, as laid out in the 'Mise of Lewes'.[137]

The failure of the victors to allow any arbitration on aspects of the 'Mise' was perhaps politically inevitable, given the use that such a move would be to complaining royalists. If there was a breach of faith, Louis shared in that by refusing to set up his panel of Frenchmen to select two of the three planned arbitrators on other issues. The creation of a supreme board of only three leading councillors to be supreme over the 'nine – Simon, Gloucester, and Bishop Berksted – cut down on the risk of arguments and delay at a time of disorder and financial collapse plus an invasion-threat. It was not an unnecessary imposition of autocracy by a power-crazed 'rebel' leader, although such 'juntas' have a habit of becoming permanent and a larger membership would have accommodated more interests. The nine included Bishop Sandwich of London, a senior reformist since his appointment in 1263 and as a former junior cleric in Lincolnshire a probable protégé of its late Bishop Grosseteste, and also Peter de Montfort and baronial 'insider' Humphrey de Bohun but not 'Justiciar' Hugh Despenser (possibly due to his workload). The new arrangements were ratified by the representatives of the community of England present in the June Parliament, though we do not know exactly how many representatives appeared for each shire. In a further bid for popularity, the new sheriffs now appointed during the Parliament – which may mean that it helped to choose suitable men in each county – were not given a fixed sum of money to raise and hand over to the King as tax-farmers,[138] which had previously been the case and so encouraged extortion to raise extra funds above this amount for the sheriffs' personal gain.

The invasion threat, autumn 1264

The threat of invasion by Louis and the refugee Queen Eleanor, now joined by the legate, was serious. Eleanor, to whose determination and energy chroniclers paid tribute, assembled a large fleet at Damme in the Low Countries, assisted from her husband's lands in Gascony, and had experienced French and Italian mercenaries plus a capable commander in her refugee uncle, Peter of Savoy (an ex-Montfortian). Her money to pay them seems to have run short, diminishing the threat after a few months, but an invasion of East Anglia, Kent or Sussex was possible that autumn and the fleet's inaction was mostly ascribed by the chroniclers to Divine Providence or contrary winds. The threat was met by raising a larger than usual army from across the nation, and Legate Foulques' demands for Henry to be released and restored to his full powers and the Provisions cancelled were ignored. As in 1213 a 'national' army and an allegedly united nation defied the threat of a King of France invading despite the threat of an Interdict, and the legate was refused entry to England so he could not publish any inflammatory papal calls for rebellion against the new regime. Simon's regime's response to the legate's demands, the so-called 'Peace of Canterbury', indeed envisaged reform of the Church, a ban on all aliens holding office in England in future, and prolonging the King's 'tutelage' by the Council for the rest of Henry's reign and for an unspecified period into Edward's. This was undoubtedly provocative and was possibly a negotiating tactic rather than a *sine qua non* – and it was modified in a subsequent list of terms presented in person to Foulques by Peter de Montfort, Bishop Cantelupe, and other 'high-ranking' envoys. But even this initial 'stand' did not repeat the 1263 demands for all aliens to be banned from living in England and it envisaged compensation for those who had lost property in the disturbances in recent years so this could 'buy off' the Savoyards and Lusignans. Louis and the legate did not agree to this – or to another, more conciliatory plan (probably the work of bishops keen not to be condemned by the legate) to have the Canterbury terms arbitrated by a panel of English and French clergy plus Louis' brother Charles of Anjou. The English negotiators were joined by Henry 'of Almain', possibly at the bishops' request[139] and certainly a useful 'middle-man' who could be used to show that the royal males were not all hostile to Simon. Did this show that despite his internment since the battle of Lewes Simon trusted him more than he did Edward or Richard of Cornwall?

The legate persisted despite his being refused entry to England, and told the Montfortian envoys who met him at Boulogne that Henry must be restored to his full powers or the regime would be placed under an Interdict. The envoys' modified demands on their second mission – a revision of the Canterbury terms – agreed that the legate should have a casting vote in detailed arbitration decisions, the King's councillors (who were still all to be English) need not be able to override his decisions on appointments and the demand for no alien junior officials was dropped. This would save people's faces on both sides, and may represent the bishops forcing Simon to be more flexible; it was still rejected. (The notion of a papal legate heading an interim panel of governance had been seen before, in Henry's minority under legate Guala, so it was not unacceptable.) Foulques used the embarrassed but surprisingly united bishops – who were prepared to negotiate but not to accept his orders unquestioningly and insisted that Henry would have to accept specific men as councillors and take their advice – to take his requirements to Simon's leadership group, in charge of the army assembled in Kent. He endeavoured to have the resolution of all disputes between Henry and Simon and the resolution of the constitutional question placed in his hands, with both parties handing over castles (Simon was to hand over Dover) as pledges of accepting his verdict. There was a high-handed timed ultimatum of excommunication for the baronial leaders and publication of the Interdict if the 'rebels' did not give in and admit him within fifteen days. Was this stand a legalistic adherence to the 'letter' rather than the 'spirit' of the Pope's orders by an arrogant papal official, or did it represent the fact that Foulques was a Frenchman? (He was a native of the county of Toulouse and trusted ex-councillor of Louis IX's brother Alphonso, its count following confiscation from the St Gilles dynasty. Currently Archbishop of Narbonne, he was an intimate of the French royal family.) Was he thus naturally disposed to favour the autocratic rule of an unquestioned king rather than a state with a more flexible constitution, and eager to help Louis' brother-in-law regain power? Would a different, non-French legate have been more flexible, or acceptable to Simon's faction as an arbitrator in England? (As pope a year or two later, Foulques was to bend over backwards to promote French interests; see below.) The bishops' stand in favour of the Montfort regime's right to coerce the King was impressive and showed their independence of spirit – their superior, the Queen's uncle Archbishop Boniface of Canterbury, was an exile currently urging Louis to invade England so they were institutionally leaderless. In 1208–13 the bishops had been in favour of the Pope, not the current English regime, in a confrontation.

When the negotiating group of English bishops arrived back at Dover with his formal letters of excommunication and the Interdict, entrusted with the publication of these if needed the indignant townsmen seized and destroyed the documents. This entailed a delay, and notably the threat of papal displeasure and condemnation did not shake the loyalty of the bishops to the new regime rather than to the Church – a sign of incipient independence from papal orders not seen in the dispute between Pope Innocent III and King John in 1209–13. No risings in the legate's favour were possible in England, the waiting English army held firm, and luckily for the resolution of the impasse Pope Urban now died, which made his legate's authority redundant and meant that Simon's enemies would now have to apply to the next Pope for help – after a lengthy papal election procedure.[140] The royalist tactic of relying on the Pope for aid thus failed, and the solid 'front' presented by the political 'nation' and the senior clergy added to the regime's stability for a few months.

The fall of de Montfort: An international threat fades, a Marcher plot is frustrated, but a second one erupts. Was Simon caught unawares on the second occasion?
The probability of a military challenge to Simon's regime seemed to be more likely from Louis IX, Queen Eleanor's army of mercenaries, and the furious

legate Foulques as of autumn 1264 – with a French invasion probable as in 1216. Once again the south-east would be the likely site, with the army most likely to land at Pevensey Bay in Sussex to use the Queen's uncle Peter of Savoy's castle there and then marching on either the Cinque Ports or London. Would Simon's Cinque Ports fleet play a vital role in intercepting the invaders (or reinforcements) at sea and destroying them to cut off the survivors in England, as had happened to Eustace the Monk's invasion-fleet in 1217? Instead the threat of invasion faded, as the negotiations were spun out into late autumn to make a crossing of the Channel unwise in mid-winter – though an extant rebellion in England could still have enabled the French to take the risk. Then the Pope's death made Foulques' authority void and Louis did not take action on his own. Ironically, the papal electors' choice of candidate to succeed Urban in February 1265 was none other than Foulques – elected *in absentia* en route back to Rome and now taking the name of 'Clement IV'. This represented the influence of French and Francophile cardinals in Rome, and posed a major threat to the English regime – would Clement take revenge for the defiance of his peace-terms and launch a 'Crusade' against them with Simon cast in the role of the defiant 'heretic' and Louis as the holy Crusade leader? This potential threat of Italian politics having a major impact on English affairs and England facing invasion as in 1213 has been downplayed by historians – if papal priorities had been different the Montfort regime could still have faced overthrow in 1265 or 1266 despite a scenario where there were no rebellions at home.

Luckily for Simon, the 'Sicilian Business' came to his rescue as it had done in the 1250s. The previous Pope had agreed to invest Charles of Anjou as the new King of Sicily and give him the right to invade this papal fief and remove the detested Manfred in 1263, insisting that in return he should pay all the papacy's debts from the failed offer to Edmund of England, renounce the Sicilian monarchs' usual control of ecclesiastical appointments in the 'Regno', never unite the kingdom with the Empire as the Hohenstaufen had done, and act as a humble papal vassal who would abdicate if the Pope ordered it. The plan could have been null and void if Manfred's current campaigns in the Abruzzi had gained him control of Rome (always inclined to faction and sedition) and enabled him to prevent the papal-Anjou agreement being implemented by a rigorous control of the region, or even to intimidate the cardinals into electing a pro-Hohenstaufen pope in early 1265. The election of Foulques was by no means easy or assured due to a split in the electoral body, he was not the 'first choice' of many cardinals, and a different pope might have come to an agreement with Manfred or sought Charles' aid and been unable to deliver him Rome as a base for his invasion. In that case, would Charles (ruler of Anjou and Provence) have given up on the 1263 agreement until Manfred's power waned and instead devoted his manpower to assisting Henry III in 1265–6 with an invasion of England? (His wife, Beatrice, was sister to Henry's Queen.) As events turned out, Manfred failed to secure Rome, Clement IV repeated the invitation to Charles to invade the 'Regno', and Charles decided to implement the 1263 agreement despite its 'one-sided' terms and in May 1265 arrived in Rome. Ensconced as 'senator' there, he proceeded to drive the half-hearted Manfred back from Tuscany and had the 'breathing-space' he needed to raise cash from Italian bankers and summon an army to meet at Lyons in October 1265 ready to march on Naples with the status of a 'Crusade'. The overthrow and death in battle of Manfred in February 1266 followed on from this, and Charles thereafter had his hands full as the new King of Sicily.[141] But had the expedition been impractical, would Clement or a different pope have been ordering an expedition to attack England instead? Would it have been Simon not Manfred who fell in battle against a papal champion, with French troops restoring Henry III to untrammelled power?

As events turned out, it was domestic rebellion that gave Simon's enemies their chance. Such a threat was always in the offing, long-term if not immediately, and he could not keep the royal 'hostages' – most dangerously Edward – locked up indefinitely as they were supposed to be released once the 'Mise of Lewes' had been fully implemented. Once that happened, a dispute between Simon and Edward and the latter raising an army was highly likely, with a probable 'flash-point' the need of the de Montfort dynasty to build up an adequate landed inheritance for Simon's four adult, mostly aggressive and arrogant sons (Henry, Simon, Guy, and Aimery). They would want lordships and heiresses, and a quarrel over estates and fiancées – or a personal dispute – with some aggrieved aristocratic member of Edward's entourage was a realistic scenario for the future. The more Simon attempted to build up his sons' power, the harsher the criticism of him for greed and probable alienation from crucial magnates – most probably the young and ambitious Gloucester – would result. The size and magnificence of Simon's personal following (e.g. at his Christmas 1264 celebrations at Kenilworth) and the haughtiness and display of his sons was already attracting adverse comment. By contrast, power and prestige had seeped away from the 'sidelined' King, whose humiliation could be used to earn him sympathy.[142] Both these factors were probably inevitable, and served to increase the chances of rising dissent and assistance for any potentially successful rebellion – with an unpopular chief minister as 'chief executive' of government not having the traditional bonds of feudal deference that would aid an equally unpopular King to escape active resistance for longer. Simon's position was unprecedented and he did not even have a long-established dynastic name and geographically secure region of influence to fall back on as a Marcher baron (e.g. Gloucester or any surviving member of the extinct Marshal dynasty) would have done in his place.

The terms of Simon's settlement with Edward in March 1265 required him to hand over his main source of landed power in the Marches – the Earldom of Chester lands – plus Newcastle-under-Lyme and his Peak District lordship to Simon, in return for lands of an equivalent value elsewhere. The town and castle of Bristol were to be held by Simon as a pledge that Edward would implement the agreement, for five years. Edward was to restrict his household and council to men approved by the King's Council and refrain from bringing any aliens into England, and was to remain in England (not setting foot in the Marches) for three years.[143] This prevented him from seeking Marcher or Louis' support in person, or bringing in another army of mercenaries; if the agreement was kept Edward should be politically 'neutered' and his threat held in check.

The 'wild card' in all these arrangements remained disputes within the baronage over lands, which could easily turn into factional confrontations and provide would-be rebels with an army if not defused. As events turned out, the first open threat to Simon came from the predictable source of the Marchers, who apparently formed a plot to rescue Edward in autumn 1264 with the involvement (or at the instigation of?) the exiled Queen Eleanor. Edward's mother's agents had discovered the layout and defences of Edward's prison at Wallingford Castle, and according to one account a band of rescuers led by one Robert Walerond got as far as breaking into the outer bailey; the defenders rallied, held their prisoner at sword-point, and threatened to throw him over the walls until he called out to the royalists to persuade them to leave. Edward and the other royal hostages were moved to 'top-security' Kenilworth, which indicates how seriously the threat of rescue was taken. The Marchers went ahead and defied the regime in an armed assembly of their tenants; Mortimer, Clifford, and Roger Leyburn were the ringleaders. But if Edward had been rescued, would they have made a stronger 'stand' and refused to negotiate – or would Edward have managed to get away to France and led an invasion in 1265?

Simon ordered a summons of the feudal host for 25 November at Oxford, and after the offenders failed to obey a summons to meet him at Warwick moved into the Severn valley with his forces. The would-be rebels were persuaded to obey a summons to meet him at Worcester, and under an agreement – which they were allowed to discuss with Edward as he was their feudal superior – Simon was to take their lands into custody for a year and a day while they went into temporary exile in Ireland (the usual refuge for

Marcher lords in trouble with the government who had lands there, e.g. de Braose in 1211 and Richard Marshal in 1234). In return, Edward was to be liberated and to settle with the government at the February 1265 Parliament – which was duly carried out, unlike the Marchers' promises to leave England. There are two crucial pointers for future events and 'what ifs' at issue in this incident. Firstly, the armed assembly west of the Severn and plan to rescue Edward directly foreshadowed what happened in May–June 1265; and in this first episode Simon acted with vigour and speed, unlike in 1265, despite it being winter. Llywelyn of Gwynedd aided him by threatening the Marchers' rear. What if Simon had been so forceful six months later? Secondly, if the Marchers had gone into exile the threat of them revolting again and rescuing Edward would have been postponed from 1265 to 1266 at the earliest. It is also possible that if they had managed to hold out west of the Severn over the winter – due to heavy snow or floods? – they would have been available to aid a French invasion in 1265, if the latter had not been called off due to Pope Urban's death and the diversion of French troops to Sicily.

A second challenge came from the Derbyshire magnate Robert Ferrers, Earl of Derby, who was in dispute with Edward (lord of the 'Peak' lands and of Peak Castle) as of 1264 and who had used the civil war as an opportunity to seize Peak Castle and other lands of the Prince's. Simon now took the right to these over in the March 1265 agreement. It apparently added to grievances felt by Gloucester, who had the leading role in pressure on Simon in the February 1265 Parliament to dismiss his own mercenaries (ironically, 'aliens' like Edward's much-criticized army of 1263) and hand over custody of assorted royal castles from his own personal nominees. Both a 'private army' of mercenaries and trusted castellans were militarily useful security-measures for Simon, but could be seen as autocratic and a sign of 'double standards' by the regime's leader. Was he behaving any better than Edward had done in 1263? Gloucester, whether out of ambition or out of principle, was able to seize the moral 'high ground' on the issues, and later that spring he accused Simon openly of failing to observe the Provisions and 'Mise of Lewes'. At the least Simon was becoming politically careless, and after Gloucester's personal dislike of Simon's sons led to a threat of a planned tournament at Dunstable ending in a brawl Simon cancelled it and infuriated him. Gloucester left court for his Marcher estates, where he could plot and collect troops if so inclined.[144] As in the 1250s, the head of court and government had allowed his 'loyalist' entourage to break up into faction – but given the presence of assorted hot-headed young nobles with rival ambitions and sharp tongues (and swords) this was probably inevitable at some point. According to the Guisborough chronicle, when Simon faced destruction by Edward's army at Evesham a few months later he was to tell his eldest son Henry that he and his brothers were to blame for this[145] – but by then it was too late.

Gloucester failed to turn up as expected for a new tournament at Northampton on 20 April, a warning that he expected to be arrested like Ferrers had been. The danger of armed tenants being massed by him and his ally John Giffard in the southern Marches (possibly at St Briavel's Castle in the Forest of Dean) brought Simon's entourage to Gloucester at the end of April. The uneasy mixture of de Montfort household and royal court that accompanied Simon everywhere included both the King and Edward, which was necessary for security – neither could be trusted away from their unwelcome controller – but was yet another breach of the supposedly inviolable peace-settlements. The move to the Marches was to end up with Simon trapped west of the Severn by rebellion, but was logical enough at the time to keep an eye on and possibly confront the Earl of Gloucester; as the regime's leader and best general Simon could not trust the campaign to anyone else and bringing the King along gave it royal authority. Negotiations between Simon and the Earl followed, albeit with Simon's choice of arbitrators (all his close allies) so Gloucester had every reason to distrust the outcome. But now the exiled John de Warenne and William de Valence landed in the latter's Pembroke lordship with troops ready to join a rebellion, presumably with Gloucester's encouragement as he now held the lordship on Simon's behalf, and a plot for rebellion seems to have taken shape at Wigmore Castle, 'caput' of the Mortimer lordship in northern Herefordshire. Simon remained inactive for vital days at Hereford, planning for a new Parliament for June and seemingly unperturbed by the nearness of Gloucester's armed retainers to the town in hostile mode. Gloucester's brother Thomas de Clare, still trusted by Simon, negotiated between the two Earls.

Simon was clearly over-confident at this point, and failed to appreciate that Gloucester's approach was more than a negotiating tactic or what was going on at Wigmore. He was thus wrong-footed by a brilliant rebel 'coup' on 28 May, as Edward was allowed to ride out of Hereford Castle to exercise his horse across the Wye in company with Thomas de Clare, an old friend, and some Montfortian knights. Instead, waiting Marcher rebels arranged for Edward to change to a fresh horse and the Prince made a successful break for freedom, joined by de Clare and outracing their pursuers. He rode to Wigmore for a rendezvous with the Mortimers and then on to join Gloucester (at Ludlow), who insisted that he agree that he would respect the ancient laws and customs of England and that the King would remove all aliens from his council and kingdom and govern through natives once he was restored. This enabled them to present themselves as enemies of the self-seeking and autocratic de Montfort faction, innovators who were constraining the King, rather than of the Provisions and 'just' government and to reassure backers of the 1258 and 1264 reform programmes who might be persuaded to join them.[146]

As a result of this Simon was left without the principal figurehead for potential revolt by his own carelessness, facing a major Marcher revolt, which Warenne and de Valence now reinforced. Edward was a quick learner as a general, and had a reconstituted and aggressive affinity of Marcher lords at his back. In the following ten days or so they proceeded to take Shrewsbury, Bridgnorth, and Worcester, break the bridges over the Severn, and take all the boats, and on 14 June the town of Gloucester fell too (followed by the castle on the 29th). This left Simon and the court cut off in Herefordshire with no easy route back to his headquarters at Kenilworth. It remains a mystery why he did not take the chance to withdraw at least as far as Gloucester while he had the time, in the first or second week of June, but probably he was too busy with the ongoing negotiations with Prince Llywelyn of Gwynedd that were designed to gain him Welsh military aid. The Welsh could then take the Marchers in the rear and attack the rebel lords' lands, preventing them from crossing the Severn and attacking the Montfortian government in its 'home region' until it had had time to raise an army there. Logically Simon needed to negotiate in person and to have Henry handy to sign any agreement as King, but in retrospect it would have been safer to leave the talks to an intermediary and secure his route of retreat by moving back to the Severn within days of Edward's escape. Was Simon's fatal flaw an inability to rely on other people to take on major tasks, and was this why he did not have senior allies such as Peter de Montfort with him in Hereford ready to be sent to Llywelyn instead?

These talks resulted in the 'Treaty of Pipton', a village on the middle Wye near Hay-on-Wye, which Simon, the captive Henry, and Llywelyn signed on 19 June. In return for military aid and a subsidy of 3000 'marks' a year for ten years, Llywelyn had all his gains from his rival Welsh princes and from royal lands since his accession recognized, in effect abandoning all the King's Welsh policy of 'divide and rule' since Llywelyn's grandfather had died in 1240. The native-ruled regions of Wales, considerably expanded into the outer Marches by Llywelyn, now passed under the rule of the Prince of Gwynedd or his vassals, reversing the King's policy of breaking up Gwynedd (and occupying what he could of its eastern lowlands) and making the other Welsh rulers vassals of the English King. Notably the agreement provided for the Welsh subsidy to be paid to Henry and after him to his – unnamed – successor, which implies that at this stage Simon was contemplating replacing Edward as the heir.[147] But having the ability to do this meant defeating the rebellion, and to do that he had to return quickly to the lands east of the Severn to link up with his gathering troops there. Instead, he moved south from Hereford to Monmouth (24 June) and took Usk Castle (2 July) en route to Newport to take ship for Bristol. Had the Montfortian force been evacuated safely by sea from Newport, they would have had the time to regroup east of the Severn and link up with Simon's younger sons at Kenilworth. Instead, Edward and Gloucester moved in undetected, retaking Usk en route, to burn the Montfortian ships in the River Usk at Newport before they could embark. This left them stranded and they had to move back to Hereford on 16 July.

The sight of the Montfortian ships burning in the Usk estuary under the windows of the castle at Newport was a reminder that military expertise in English politics in the 1260s was not restricted to Simon, who had for the second time been caught unawares. Where were his guards on the ships, or had he been too exhausted, short of men, or preoccupied to realize the risk of an attack? There had been a strategic reason to linger in Hereford after the Severn valley towns started falling to Edward, namely securing Llywelyn's aid to take the Marchers from the West and diminish the number of troops that they could send east for Edward's expected attack on the Midlands. Llywelyn had driven a hard bargain, virtually securing recognition of his newly created Welsh overlordship as an autonomous and united state on equal terms with England – as his grandfather had achieved at the time of the civil war in Henry's minority. Had the campaign then gone according to plan, after arriving in Newport Simon's host would have taken ship for Bristol and headed for Kenilworth and safety. Edward would have been left west of the Severn, at the head of a larger and more dangerous Marcher revolt than that which Richard Marshal had raised against his father in 1234 but still at a disadvantage if he moved east to tackle Simon.

However, the Montfort army, arriving in Bristol around 12–15 July, would not have been able to join up with their second main force under Simon's eponymous second son. He had been raising troops in friendly London since news of Edward's escape and the Marcher revolt reached Eastern England. The army had headed not directly for Bristol but south-west on a diversion to Winchester, which he reached and sacked on 18 July; his diversion may have been to deal with rumoured disaffection there as well as to do some looting but it was not militarily useful. He did not head for Bristol, where his father's force should have been arriving by sea before he left Winchester and for all he knew might still arrive – in diminished numbers? – if they found a few ships at a small South Wales port (Cardiff or Swansea?) without being caught up by local lord Gloucester, ruler of Glamorgan. His route looks as if he was keen to reach the safety of the family stronghold at Kenilworth, a meeting-place for their assembling vassals, rather than to hang around the Cotswolds or Avon valley waiting for his father to arrive. He was probably afraid of meeting Edward's army, which could have been anywhere south-east of Worcester if Edward was marching to intercept him. He proceeded at a leisurely pace to Kenilworth, arriving on 31 July, but chose to camp his army outside its walls not within the protection of the outer bailey – allegedly the troops wanted to enjoy the comforts of the town, such as baths. Two nights later Edward mounted his third daring coup of the campaign, marching swiftly east from Worcester to storm the town and take many of the younger Montfort's army's leadership prisoner, killing or dispersing their men. The younger Simon fled into the castle so he was not killed or taken hostage and a substantial body of men joined him, but his army was broken up and he did not dare to risk venturing out with the survivors to try to reach his father before Edward did. He was unable to come to his outnumbered father's aid as the latter finally crossed the Severn at the ford of Kempsey near Worcester on 2 August. Worse, Edward took the 'rebels' banners as he withdrew and was able to parade them before the elder Simon's army when they met at Evesham, fooling them into a false sense of security so they did not have time to prepare a defensive position.[148]

Had the younger Simon had the strength of will and military sense to quarter his men inside the outer bailey at Kenilworth, an elementary precaution, Edward could only have set fire to the town. Could he have fooled the defenders into thinking that he was settling in for a siege by setting up a fake 'siege' with a few men and taking the rest off again? That might still have made the inexperienced younger de Montfort wary of emerging from the castle to tackle the royalists, and so kept him away from the clash at Evesham. But a more experienced commander should have been able to keep his army safe from the humiliating attack on Kenilworth town, or at least set sober guards around the town's perimeter to warn of any royalist approach. Alternatively, a more experienced and competent commander – one of Simon's minor vassals who had had experience of the 1240s or 1250s wars in Gascony? – should not have bothered to swing away south from the route to Bristol to waste time sacking Winchester. The 'relief force' would then have been in position in the Cotswolds around 18–22 July, less exhausted after an easier march, even if it then moved off north to Kenilworth to evade an attack by Edward in open country. Did Simon's unwise reliance on his family for the crucial task of bringing an adequate army from London and keeping it safe ruin his chances at Evesham?

If any of the above suggestions had been the actual course of events, then it can be assumed that an adequate, well-rested, and non-traumatized army would have been stationed at Kenilworth Castle as of 1–2 August and as soon as messengers arrived from the elder Simon saying that he had crossed the Severn they would have marched out down the (Warwickshire) Avon valley to meet him. They rather than Edward – around the same distance from Evesham at Worcester as the Montfortian relief-force was at Kenilworth – should have been intercepting the elder Simon, at or near Evesham, as he arrived early on 4 August. Even if they arrived after Edward had arrived from Worcester to intercept the elder Simon, they would have been marching down the Avon to take Edward's attackers on their left flank and so would have been a serious threat to him. The elder Simon, trapped in the town on the north bank of the river with the Avon to his rear (south), could not retreat over the river as Mortimer's Marchers had seized the bridge. But all he would have to do was to hold out until his son's troops could take Edward in the flank – and it is probable that the two armies would have been fighting with around equal numbers so either could win.

As events occurred, the elder Simon arrived at Evesham early on 4 August, expecting to meet his son's army soon, and was buoyed up by seeing an approaching force bearing the de Montfort banners. Instead this turned out to be Edward's larger army, carrying the banners they had taken at Kenilworth, and it was clear that there would be no rescue. The psychological effect of this was a major boost for Edward, as was the capture of the bridge to the south of the town by Mortimer's men; the 'rebels' had every reason to think themselves doomed. Simon boldly marched out of the town northwards to attack the royalists head-on, but his army was overwhelmed in a fierce hand-to-hand struggle and he was cut down along with his eldest son Henry and many others. The fallen 'rebel' leader's body was hacked to pieces by vengeful royalist knights, probably Marchers with a grudge. This was a sign of the personal nature of the hatred that some felt towards Simon and his arrogant sons and possibly showed belligerent aristocratic contempt for the 'jumped-up' foreign intruder who had amassed a substantial landed endowment to their detriment (though King Harold II had suffered a similar fate at Hastings). The mutilation was seen as shocking by contemporary chroniclers on both 'sides'. The bitterness felt in the civil war was also reflected in the fact that around thirty knights of Simon's entourage were killed in the savage battle[149] – usually men of such rank were carefully taken alive to be held profitably for ransom and a code of ethics inhibited killing people of high rank. Very few knights had fallen in the crucial battles of the civil wars in 1141 and 1216–17 – so did the killing reflect the entry of ideology as well as personal clashes over power into a civil war? (The devotion of the reformists to controlling royal power and to observance of the Provisions as just and Christian implies this.) The savagery may also be due to Edward's personal vindictiveness, a trait seen throughout his career – as late as 1306–1307 he was having his foe Robert Bruce's brothers executed for treason and hanging captive 'high-status' rebel womenfolk up in cages for public exhibition.

Had a more competent Montfortian commander brought a substantial relief-force to aid Simon at Evesham, the latter's experience in battle might well have prevailed over Edward and the Marchers. At least, a defensive 'stand' by Simon outside the town and/or a Montfortian counter-attack from the east on Edward's left flank could have driven the Prince's forces into flight. Had Edward escaped back to the Marches, a joint offensive from Simon across the lower Severn and Llywelyn south-east from Gwynedd had the capacity to drive him overseas to link up with his mother, Queen Eleanor, and his uncle-by-marriage Louis IX in France. Given the number of French lords absent in Naples in 1265–6, a successful French invasion of England would have been problematic and even when Charles of Anjou had secured the 'Regno' his forces needed to establish new lordships and garrisons there to back up his precarious kingship. (In 1268 his Hohenstaufen challenger Conradin, Conrad IV's son, was to invade so the Italian war was not over.) A challenge by Edward and Louis to the Montfortian regime was still a possibility, however, and Simon's next move after regaining the Marches would have had to be to besiege Pevensey Castle into surrender to deny the invaders a coastal base. The civil war could thus have ended with a long-drawn-out siege as in real life – but of royalist Pevensey, not of Montfortian Kenilworth (which only surrendered to Edward and Henry III in 1267). The real-life trajectory of events then saw the Principality of Antioch, one of the few remaining bastions of the Crusaders in 'Outremer', falling to Sultan Baybars in 1268 and the papacy launching a new Crusade so there would have been a brief 'window' for a Franco-royalist invasion of England before the Crusade took priority for Louis. Possibly Edward would have had to wait until the end of the Crusade, by which time Louis was dead (1270, in Tunis not Palestine). This also raises the issue of what would have happened if Henry III had died – as he did in real-life November 1272, aged sixty-five – with Edward still in exile and disgrace. Would the Church have tolerated the rightful heir being set aside as a 'traitor' to the Provisions of Oxford, which the papacy would surely have condemned? In an intensely legalistic age, depositions in Western Christendom were almost always proclaimed by the Pope – as with the Empire and Sicily – not a king's 'subjects', and no sane adult Western European monarch who had inherited a state by right was deposed by his subjects in this era. Simon and his followers setting Edward aside would surely have been resisted by a substantial section of the nobility, not least the Earl of Gloucester with his Marcher vassals, and would have led to a new civil war. The beneficiary of such an act would possibly have been Henry 'of Almain', the next legitimate heir after Edward (Richard of Cornwall just predeceased his older brother Henry III in 1272), as he had been on reasonable terms with Simon and had been allowed to negotiate for him with the papal legate in autumn 1264. Any attempt to elevate one of Simon's own sons, as the son of Henry III's sister Eleanor de Montfort, would have been a recipe for disaster and rebellion.

Chapter Five

Edward I, 1272–1307: A Series of Sudden Royal Deaths and 'Near Misses' – What if They Had Been Different?

The appearance of successful kingship

The impressive and intimidating presence of Edward I, nicknamed 'Longshanks' from his height, looms over thirteenth and early fourteenth century British history. He literally dominated his contemporaries as he was physically impressive and far more capable, statesmanlike, and good at knightly pursuits and war than his father Henry III and his son Edward II. His renowned savage temper and capacity for holding grudges were seen as desirable attributes for a king rather than the reverse, partly as these helped a ruler to intimidate potential and actual adversaries but also for their appropriateness in an age fond of using literary similes and visual heraldry – a king was meant to be like a lion, king of the beasts, and Edward's ferocious unpredictability showed his suitability for this role. Heraldically, the English royal arms were of three 'leopards' – not in the modern identification of the animal, but in the medieval sense of a lion 'couchant' (lying down) rather than standing. Like his great-grandfather Henry II, Edward was a vigorous and restless ruler of lands in both Britain and France, a wide-ranging traveller and a respected military commander, one of the dominant figures of contemporary Europe, who ruled for an impressive thirty-five years. Like Henry 'FitzEmpress', he was already the dominant figure of English political life before his accession at his ageing predecesssor's expense – he led the successful revolt against the de Montfort regime in 1265, restored order in the near-anarchy of the following years, and faced down his opponents but had the wisdom to accept (eventually) the need for compromise with the losing party in the recent civil war.

Unlike Henry, Edward also had the prestige of being a successful Crusader who was regarded as a faithful son of the Church rather than being responsible for the murder of an archbishop, and indeed succeeded to the throne when he was absent in the East assisting the embattled Kingdom of Jerusalem. Indeed, his decision to go to the Holy Land on Louis IX's Crusade in 1270 rather than stay at home to ensure a secure succession to his weakening father shows his combination of confidence and devotion to the 'holy' cause. His lack of the extensive lands that Henry II and Richard I had held on the Continent was balanced by his finishing off John's aborted work to make the English Crown dominant in the British Isles after the loss of Normandy. He conquered or confiscated all the remaining independent Welsh principalities in 1277–87 and made the most of a stroke of luck in the death without male heirs of Alexander III of Scotland in a freak accident in March 1286 to force the engagement of the latter's grand-daughter and heir Margaret to his own son and heir Edward – a plan to unite the two Crowns over 300 years before this finally happened in 1603. Margaret died in 1290, but Edward was accepted as the adjudicator of the assorted rival claims to the vacant throne and was able to ensure that the successful candidate of 1292, John Balliol (who held lands in England so was susceptible to blackmail by threats of confiscation), did homage as his legal vassal. Until now the kings of Scots had done their best to insist that the homage that they sporadically did to the kings of England – under duress – was only for their family lands held in England (especially the Earldom of Huntingdon), not due to their kingdom's subordination to England. Edward, keen to use his legal powers as well as his military machine to the utmost, put a stop to this ambiguity and made the Scots kingship his legal subordinate[1] – which meant that he could confiscate it in case of defiance.

In 1296 he annexed Scotland by deposing his vassal-king Balliol and subsumed Scots institutions into the kingdom of England as he had done with the Welsh states, and then defeated a widely supported insurgency under William Wallace and Sir Andrew Moray. The modern film-led revival of the Scottish cult of Wallace, with Edward cast as the arrogant upper-class English villain, tends to downplay the fact that the 'grass-roots' revolt in Scotland of 1297–8 was crushed by force and as of 1305–1306 Edward's armies and garrisons, backed by the majority of the Scots nobility, held most of Scotland, all of its south and east, and virtually all of its strongpoints as far north as Moray. The section of the nobility that he could not rely on was deported to England and English governors were imposed – including such greedy and resented 'colonial' administrators as his treasurer Hugh Cressingham, who the infuriated 1297 rebels murdered and flayed.[2] The rebels were initially successful against the larger and better-equipped English army due to a mixture of enthusiasm, numbers, capable military leadership, knowledge of the countryside, and blunders by the over-confident English generals, a series of advantages frequent for locally supported guerrilla armies, but were defeated at Falkirk in 1298 and ground down by ravaging and killing. The acquiescence of the war-weary populace and a nobility eager to protect their estates from ravaging was undoubtedly sullen and grudging – as in occupied Gwynedd, Powys, and Dyfed in Wales – and was probably unsustainable in the long term given the cost in finance and manpower. In hindsight, the use of a local 'quisling' king who could appeal to a large part of the Scots elite rather than outright occupation would have been wiser and Edward's successes of 1298–1306 were illusory. Edward III was to return to the policy of using a client-king with Balliol's son in 1333–41.

But as of 1306 Edward held the military advantage, and the surprise revolt by and coronation of Robert Bruce in spring 1306 was initially suppressed by quick action by the local English commanders who outnumbered his small army and drove him out of the Perth district into the wilds of western Atholl. There, a 'pincer' movement to help Edward by the local MacDougalls of Lorn (that section of the 'Clan Donald' of the Hebrides ruling mainland Argyll) saw Bruce's army intercepted in Strathfillan and heavily defeated. Indeed, the sequence of events that had led to Bruce's revolt and coronation had added to Edward's local support and potential for holding Scotland down. The rival dynasties of Bruce (lords of Annandale on the Borders) and Comyn (holding lands in Galloway and the Earldom of Buchan) both had claims to the vacant throne in 1292, which Edward had decided against, and the personal enmity of Robert Bruce (heir to his family claim since 1304) and John, the 'Red' Comyn, had been evident well before the latter was believed to have told the English that Bruce was plotting revolt in 1306. This led to Bruce stabbing Comyn to death in a confrontation in the Grey Friars church in Dumfries,[3] and the act irrevocably alienated the Comyns and their allies (including the MacDougalls) but also saw the international Church denounce and excommunicate him for violating the sanctity of a holy site. Even if Bruce succeeded in winning Scotland he would face the enmity of the Comyns and their allies, who in the event he had to drive out of their lands into England – and who provided the Balliol invasions of 1332–3 with invaluable manpower.[4] After Strathfillan the rebel survivors, led by Bruce himself, scattered and the English success was so complete that we do not know for certain where Bruce went in the following months, possibly the Hebrides or northern Ireland (traditionally Rathlin Island off the Ulster coast at one point). It is to this period that the legend belongs of Bruce hiding in a cave and contemplating giving up the struggle until he was inspired to fight on by seeking a patient spider at work – which is not recorded until the early nineteenth century.[5]

In practical terms, his main military support was now to come from the MacDougalls' rivals, the two other lines of 'Clan Donald' ruling in the Inner

Hebrides (Angus 'Og' of Islay and Christina Mac Ruari of Garmoran). The mainland Scots landed elite remained quiescent, for the moment. By the time of Edward's death in July 1307 he had landed in Galloway to launch a successful but still small-scale guerrilla war, which drove the infuriated English King to vow to destroy him and march north with a large army. Famously, sixty-eight-year-old Edward's body finally gave way during the march and he died in his tent at Burgh-by-Sands on the Solway Firth shore, within sight of Scotland but as far from destroying its independence as ever. He is supposed to have made his unmilitary son Edward (II) swear to continue the war and had his remains boiled so they could be carried at the head of his army, but the new King broke his word as soon as his father was dead and went home.[6] This seems to symbolize the turn of the tide in the rebels' favour, but as of July 1307 Edward seemed to hold all the political and military 'cards' in any open conflict and the war seemed likely to be long. Indeed, his military successes had included the capture of Bruce's refugee wife, daughter, and sister after Strathfillan – by local Scots allies not English soldiers, at the remote shrine of St Duthac at Tain in Caithness (a sign of his 'reach'). The new Scots Queen Elizabeth was safe from harsh treatment as her father was Earl Richard of Ulster, head of the de Burgh dynasty and an invaluable prop of Edward's regime in Ireland, so she was held hostage in a series of English nunneries as was Bruce's daughter (by his first wife), Marjorie. But Edward had contemplated putting the ten-year-old girl in a cage in the Tower of London until he was talked out of it, and one of Bruce's sisters and the indomitable Countess of Buchan (who had crowned him) were displayed in cages on the walls of northern castles. This calculated inhumanity to female non-combatants of noble birth went beyond the norms of the time, even if the Countess had committed 'treason' by crowning a rebel (in the place of her deported brother who would normally have done the task), and argues for an element of spite and contempt for chivalric behaviour, though it was not criticized by contemporaries. More in line with medieval norms, all of Bruce's brothers who were captured during the guerrilla war were executed as 'traitors' to their 'rightful sovereign' Edward.[7] This savagery may have been counter-productive in the long term, stimulating resistance and reprisal – but for most political 'actors' revolt would only occur when it seemed likely to succeed. Had Edward I been able to return to Scotland alive and in good health to continue his rounds of atrocities in 1307–1308, he would have been unlikely to have caught the refugee Bruce in the isolated hills and bogs of Galloway so the war would have continued. But, as with Edward III's military domination of the Lowlands as far as Inverness in the mid-1330s as long as he could operate there in person, the English collapse would have taken several years to unfold. The Comyns in Buchan had the manpower to hold up the Bruce army if the English had sent adequate military aid to them, but in real life had to fight alone and were overwhelmed and expelled.

As of July 1307, then, Edward was the most successful king of England within the British Isles to date and his achievements only started to unravel in Scotland in the next couple of years as Edward II clashed with his baronial elite and failed to send aid north to save the pro-English MacDougalls of Argyll and Comyns of Buchan from being overrun by Bruce and his Islesmen in 1308–1310. But there were a number of occasions when this 'narrative' of Edwardian triumph could have been prevented by accident or by human design. In an era of political or military success relying on strong, competent and committed leadership by an adult male ruler with elite support, a state's position dominating its own subjects and its neighbours could be slackened – temporarily or permanently – by the sudden loss of a strong leader and the substitution of a regency or an incompetent monarch. This mattered less if a governmental administrative 'machine' was complex, efficient, and accepted by its vassals as it could then continue to operate – as the French monarchy did when two kings died unexpectedly (Philip IV, in a hunting accident, in 1314 and Louis X in 1316) and a baby succeeded. But this was less so in England, at least as far as its domination of Scotland was concerned; the conquest of Wales was not affected by Edward I's death and Edward II's preoccupation elsewhere. In the cases of sudden alterations of English or Scots leadership in Edward I's time, the historical record would have looked rather different. These occasions were as follows.

Royal assassination – by the original 'assassins'? Acre, June 1272
It is a little-known fact that Edward might never have come to the English throne in November 1272, as a result of his involvement with Louis IX's Crusade in 1270. Unlike his father, Henry III, and his baronial rival Gilbert de Clare, Earl of Gloucester, the Prince took his Crusading vows seriously and so decided to take part in the French King's planned expedition to the Holy Land after the suppression of the de Montfort regime in 1265–7, despite the political and military risks of the heir to the throne leaving a country still insecure after a devastating civil war. The defeated sons of Earl Simon had held out in Kenilworth Castle well into 1267 while risings in their favour continued across the country and it was hit by a wave of brigandage, some of it by ex-soldiers with ideological motives or men foolishly deprived of their lands by the restored royal regime in a 'purge' of their foes in 1265–6. This unwise vendetta had added to the number of people prepared to take up arms against Henry III and Edward for their own self-preservation, and the vindictiveness of the royalist reaction was at odds

with that shown to the 'losers' in civil wars by the new king Henry II in 1154 and by William Marshal's regency for Henry III in 1217–19. It was reversed only after Earl Gilbert, a royalist as of 1265, had linked up with the 'Disinherited' holding out in the marsh-protected Isle of Ely (site of Hereward's heroic resistance to William I) and marched on London in spring 1267 to seize the mutinous city and demand pardons for those deprived of their lands. A near-civil war was avoided and the papal legate Ottobuono mediated a generous peace settlement with the 'rebels' being pardoned in the Statute of Marlborough,[8] and indeed Edward generously took ex-rebel captains into his personal service. He was also to travel around England putting down local brigandage in person, and supposedly took the formidable bandit captain Adam Gurdon into his service after admiring his mettle as they fought in hand-to-hand combat[9] – an act of personal chivalry to a foe reminiscent of the legendary Robin Hood, whose stories seem to have been emerging at this time. (One modern theory has it that 'Robin' was really one of the 'Disinherited', Roger Godberd.[10]) But the fact remains that Edward had mishandled the initial aftermath of the defeat of Earl Simon by excessive vengeance and harshness in autumn 1265, though he had learnt by his mistakes, and he had every reason to stay on in England with his father already over sixty and apparently in political eclipse and/or declining health. Earl Gilbert clashed again with Edward over their rival landed claims in South Wales after 1267, and failed to go on the Crusade as promised – apparently due to local Welsh resistance to the harsh governance of his lordship.[11] The usual procedure for a monarch (or effective ruler) about to go on Crusade but chary of leaving a rival behind was to insist that his associate either went with him, which Gilbert was supposed to do in 1270, or stayed out of England as Richard I endeavoured to require of John in 1189–90. At least Gilbert was not a dynastic threat unlike John had been, but as he had marched on London in 1267 Edward would have had an adequate excuse to insist that he and Gilbert must leave for the Crusade together or not at all.

Thus Edward had adequate excuses to stay in England, and his departure in spring 1270 was further delayed by the death of his mother's uncle Archbishop Boniface of Canterbury and the need to go to the city to arrange the election of his successor. When Edward set out for southern France in summer 1270 to join Louis, he arrived at the port of Aigues-Mortes to find that the King had already sailed – and that Louis' brother Charles of Anjou, King of Sicily (and Naples), had persuaded him to attack the Moslem emirate of what is now Tunisia rather than to go straight to Palestine. Any Moslem ruler could be counted a legitimate target for 'Holy War', and attacking and seizing the port of Tunis or requiring the Emir to 'sign up' as a Christian vassal would carry the Christian cause into North Africa, stop African ships raiding Sicily, and hopefully aid full Christian control of the straits between Sicily and Tunis to benefit both merchant shipping and military expeditions. The intimidated Emir would be forced to become a Christian vassal, and possibly even to convert. But, typically for the ambitious and unscrupulous Charles, it was to the direct benefit of his kingdom rather than of all Christendom, and in any case Louis (aged fifty-six) fell ill and died in his camp outside Tunis in August.[12] The question remains of whether Louis would have been persuaded to go straight to Palestine had Edward arrived at Aigues-Mortes in time, as the King's wife was Edward's aunt and he had been loyal to the English royals in their disputes with de Montfort. Edward was as forceful as Charles and would have insisted that the King's vow meant attacking the 'infidel' in the Holy Land, where the fall of Antioch in 1268 (see below) lent the campaign some urgency. Had Louis listened, his poor health might well have led to him dying in an epidemic anyway; there was one in the Christian camp when Edward arrived in Palestine in late spring 1271 in reality. But enough French commanders and troops would have been 'in situ' in Acre to give Edward valuable reinforcements for his 1271–2 campaigns even had Louis' son Philip (III) insisted on going home quickly to secure his throne when Louis died. Would Edward have been strong enough to tackle the waiting 'Mameluke' army (see below) in the field?

As events turned out, Louis died outside Tunis not in the Holy Land. The remaining French contingent that dominated the Crusading army was now led by the new King Philip III, an inexperienced young man without his father's passion for the Crusade who had been ill himself and decided to return to France. Thus when Edward arrived in Africa to join the army in November he found that Louis had died and Philip had come to terms with the 'infidel', at which he expressed his pious horror, and that the Crusade to Palestine would be postponed for three years. He had every reason to call off his own expedition and wait for the 1273/4 campaign, but he maintained that he would fulfil his vow unless the soon-to-be-elected new Pope forbade it, his father died, or a civil war broke out again in England.[13] None of this happened, though he did receive a letter from home early in 1271 saying that Henry had been seriously ill and advising him to return.[14] Henry's brother Richard of Cornwall was to die early in 1272 so was possibly also in poor health, and there was no vigorous adult royal male in England to take command – a worrying prospect only three years from the end of a civil war. Edward's cousin and close friend Henry 'of Almain', son of Henry III's brother Richard of Cornwall, did set out for home at Edward's request, but en route was shockingly murdered at Viterbo in Italy (in church) by the exiled sons of Simon de Montfort, now in papal service there, in an act of premeditated personal revenge for Simon's killing in 1265.[15] This would have excused Edward from going East on honourable grounds in contemporary eyes as he needed to hunt down the killers, but he left this to his subordinates and sailed on to Palestine. Thus, even had he left England as planned it was far from certain that he would arrive in Palestine – and be exposed to risk there.

The campaign: A damp squib

Edward arrived at Acre, the capital of the shrunken Kingdom of Jerusalem on 9 May 1271, the only senior leader of the late French King's Crusade to do so. The situation he found was desperate, as the Kingdom was under immense pressure from the aggressive new 'Mameluke' regime of Egypt, an elite corps of Turkish ex-slave guard officers which had ironically taken over that country in a coup during Louis IX's previous Crusade in 1250. The Kingdom of Jerusalem had never recovered from its loss of the eponymous Holy City to Saladin in 1187 and had finally lost it to a marauding army of 'Khwarizmian' (Central Asian) Turk refugees from the Mongols in 1244, but was now reduced even further to a string of coastal towns and fortresses under imminent threat of conquest. The combined Moslem state of Egypt, inland Palestine, and Syria, which the Mameluke officers had taken over from Saladin's family, the Ayyubids, in 1250 had reignited the 'jihad' to reconquer all of the Crusader states and had provided the necessary leadership, military expertise, and determination to exploit its latent resources. A series of capable military leaders had held power (and overthrown each other in more coups) since the 'junta' had overthrown Sultan Turan Shah during Louis' Crusade, and the current ruler was the most capable and brutal of them all – Rukn-al-Din Baybars, a talented and ruthless operator who had led the murder of his predecessor Qutuz shortly after that Sultan had defeated the Mongol invasion of Palestine at Ain Jalut ('Goliath's Springs') in Galilee in 1260. The weight of Mongol military power could have saved their putative Christian allies from the Mamelukes, albeit with the risk of them falling out later, and crushed the threat that Egypt posed to the Kingdom of Jerusalem as Louis had failed to do in 1250.

Had the Mongol general Kitbuqa won the battle Edward's small Crusade could have stood a chance of regaining some inland castles from a defeated and embattled Egyptian state, at least with Mongol help from an occupied Damascus. Instead, the Kingdom of Jerusalem was left facing a triumphant and determined Mameluke state, and in the 1260s Baybars proceeded to overrun its isolated castles and ports one by one with no chance of the Christians putting an adequate army into the field against him. In 1265

Caesarea, the last major port held apart from Acre, fell. In 1266 he overran Galilee, and in May 1268 he took the great port of Antioch, capital of the eponymous principality which the Crusaders had held since 1098. (Prince Bohemund still held onto his other fief at Tripoli.) Shortly before Edward arrived, in March 1271, he successfully besieged the greatest of the castles of the Order of the Knights of St John ('Hospitallers'), the still-surviving Krak des Chevaliers in the mountains above Tripoli. The improving Moslem siege-artillery battered the outer walls and gates until the defenders had to flee into the inner ring of fortifications, safe from all but the tallest siege-towers up a steep 'glacis' but short of supplies and men, and the surrender and evacuation was soon negotiated. With the Crusaders' inland castles now all lost only Edward's appearance – with the size of his contingent probably unclear to his enemies at first – saved Bohemund from an attack on Tripoli, and instead Baybars unilaterally called a truce and awaited developments.[16]

If the Crusade had gone according to plan the weakened government in Acre would have been reinforced by not only Edward in spring 1271 but by Louis IX and several thousand French troops that had sailed directly from Aigues-Mortes, not from Tunis via a stop in Sicily. A naval expedition from Aragon had also been expected under ageing King James I, but had been broken up by a storm. This force might have been large enough to march out against Baybars and force him to abandon his siege of the Krak des Chevaliers, had it arrived in time – though given his ruthless pragmatism he is likely to have avoided battle and returned to the attack once they had gone home. It was too late for a European expedition to make much difference in Palestine. Instead, Edward had to make do with aid from the titular sovereign of the Kingdom, King Hugh (III) of Cyprus, whose Lusignan dynasty had been installed in Cyprus by Richard I in 1192. (The previous ruler, Conradin the Hohenstaufen heir as grandson of the late Queen Isabella/Yolande, had never visited the Kingdom and had been executed by Charles of Anjou in 1268 for invading Naples.) Acre was a merchant city under the titular authority of the King, but it was in practice semi-autonomous like an Italian city-state and the loss of most of the inland fiefs had ruined the power of the King's local feudal nobility. The Venetian merchants in the city refused to abandon their trade with Egypt as Edward demanded, and he and Hugh could not force the restive Cypriot feudal nobles to commit themselves to a long campaign on the mainland.[17] All he could do was to follow the main military tactic of the papacy since the 1240s and call on the Mongols for help, as they had huge armies of ferocious steppe horsemen, were non-Moslems who had some high-ranking Christian subjects, and were the Mamelukes' long-term enemies. He sent ambassadors to the Mongols' state in Iran, the 'Ilkhanate', to ask their well-disposed young ruler, Abagha, to help. The latter had been tied up in a major war with his Mongol 'Jagatai Khanate' rivals in Central Asia until defeating their invasion at Herat in 1270, and was still too wary of them to do more than send a relatively small (by Mongol standards) force to raid Syria and distract Baybars. This was duly done and a column of Mongol horsemen rode south into the Orontes valley, causing the Mamelukes to evacuate their troops from Aleppo and fall back on Hama. But they were more interested in loot than battle and were wary of the latter since Ain Jalut; as Baybars advanced north from Damascus in November they retreated again.[18]

The Sultan's distraction by the Mongol raid enabled Edward to march his troops safely across Mount Carmel into Galilee, but he achieved little. He only had a few hundred men, and this was inadequate to take even a minor local Mameluke fortress (Qaqun). His force, now joined by his brother Earl Edmund of Lancaster and a second contingent from England, did succeed in ambushing some local Turcomans at Qaqun and killing up to 1500 of them plus their 'emir', seizing their animals – but these were nomads rather than 'crack troops' of the Mameluke army. He did not have a siege-train of artillery, and any siege would be reliant on starving out the defenders and would run the risk of a much larger Mameluke army arriving to relieve it. He had to withdraw again as a Moslem relief-force approached,[19] without tackling any of the fortresses that the Moslems had overrun in recent years, and would have needed a far larger army to risk anything more significant. Baybars then advanced with a large army on Acre to retaliate, but heavy rain prevented either side risking a battle and he retreated again.

The Acre merchants (backed by the naval 'super-power' Venice) were, however, chary of a war ruining their trade with Egypt and King Hugh lacked the legal authority to coerce the city's governing 'commune'. The government at Acre proceeded to negotiate a truce with Baybars with Charles of Anjou – who had hopes of adding Cyprus to his Mediterranean empire and was not well-disposed to King Hugh – mediating. Edward did not have the troops or the local influence to counter this, and his best hope was to return home to reinvigorate the sovereigns of Europe for another expedition with himself taking over King Louis' role as the champion of Christendom in the East. The truce was duly signed, for ten years and ten months, on 22 May; one later letter claims that Edward induced Hugh to agree to it but if he did it was only as a tactic to ensure peace until a new expedition arrived. Edmund of Cornwall and part of the English army now left for home, though Edward stayed on.[20] Usefully, one of the English contingent's accompanying clerics, Archbishop Visconti of Liège, had recently been elected pope (Gregory X) so he could act as 'cheerleader' for another Crusade in a few years. The vigorous new Pope's interest in obtaining Mongol help indeed involved an embassy to the 'Ilkhan's overlord, Kubilai Khan, in China, by the recently returned Polo brothers – which was to include their young relative Marco Polo.

The assassination attempt

It was at this juncture that Edward was nearly murdered by an assassin, on 16 June in his chamber at the royal palace at Acre. The would-be killer apparently sought an audience by claiming to be a native Christian, and suddenly lunged out at Edward with a poisoned dagger. Edward had quick reflexes and kicked him away, but was stabbed in the shoulder. A famous story had it that his wife Eleanor sucked out the poison, but this was first suggested a century later; an earlier source says that Edward's officer Otto de Grandison did it. Some poison must have remained or else the medical attention, from the skilled Templars, was clumsy, as an infection set in; the chronicler Walter of Guisborough says that the wound putrified and an English doctor had to cut away some flesh. (However, his account has Edmund present at the attack whereas in reality he had already sailed for home.[21]) The sources are unclear about the attacker's identity and motives, but some claim the man was a member of the fanatical 'heretic' Moslem sect of the so-called 'Hashishin', the original 'Assassins' (so-called from their taking hashish to embolden themselves for their suicidal attacks on prominent foes.) The main bases of the sect in Iran, around their headquarters at Alamut, had been cleared out by the Mongols in 1256 but a branch of the sect had long lived in the isolated Syrian coastal mountains north-east of Tripoli; their leader, the so-called 'Old Man of the Mountains', had been an occasional ally of the Crusaders and frequent foe of mainstream 'Sunni' Moslem rulers in Syria in the twelfth century. Their victims had included some Christian rulers deemed to be a threat, such as Count Raymond II of Tripoli (1152) and Conrad of Montferrat, the new King of Jerusalem (1192), but were more often Moslem. Indeed, in 1192 Edward's great-uncle Richard I had been suspected (by the French) of hiring the murderers of Conrad for his own devious purposes. The attacker may have been sent by the local Emir of Ramleh rather than the 'Old Man' and not even been a member of the 'Assassin' cult, but the attack bore their hallmarks. As he was able to gain admittance to Edward's chamber unsearched and the King's attendants were not expecting trouble he may have been a local employed at the palace; Edward was not naïve and was not usually careless.

The question of who sent the attacker is unresolvable, though the finger of suspicion must point at Baybars (at a careful 'second-hand' involvement?).[22] He had had time to assess Edward as a threat to him, and the current truce was only a temporary halt to hostilities; the English King might well return with a larger expedition in a few years and in any case he was clearly capable and committed to the war. The Sultan had also recently tried to hire the 'Assassins' in the mountains to intercept and liquidate one of the last lords of coastal Tripoli to defy his army, Bartholomew of Maraclea, whose rocky castle near Tortosa had defied him in 1271, by attacking him on his way back from a mission to the Mongols.[23] Baybars was quite capable of trying to remove Edward in a similar way, though when the attempt failed he hurried to congratulate Edward and deny all responsibility.[24] The Prince recovered after some weeks of danger – but what if he had not?

The potential ruler from November 1272 if Edward had been killed...?

As of June 1272, Edward's younger brother Edmund (born 1245) was en route home to England, where their father Henry III was to die on 16 November, aged sixty-five. His uncle Richard of Cornwall had already died in April, and the murder of the latter's eldest son, Henry 'of Almain', at Viterbo (which probably hastened Richard's end) left only Richard's second son, Edmund, as a 'reserve' adult male of the royal house in England. In addition, Edward's eldest son, Prince John, had died in August 1271 during his father's absence abroad – Edward supposedly mourned his father's loss more than John's and said that he could replace a son but not replace his father.[25] Edward's younger son, Henry, born in July 1268, was thus the next in line for the throne if Edward had been assassinated in June 1272, and England would have had another young king – even younger than Henry III, who had been aged nine on his accession in 1216. This would have entailed a regency by the 'next-in-line' adult male of the royal family, namely Edmund of Lancaster – who was back in England before Henry III died. But Henry, the putative 'Henry IV', died in real life in October 1274 at the Royal 'nursery' at Guildford Castle in Surrey; if this had occurred when he was king, Edmund would probably have succeeded as 'King Edmund'. Edward did have one daughter born in England (summer 1264), Eleanor, and a second born at Acre shortly before the murder attempt (Joan), but the accession of a small girl was unlikely given that there was no precedent for it and the attempt by Henry I to pass his throne to an adult woman had led to civil war. The rebel barons of 1216 had endeavoured to remove John in favour of his adult niece Blanche of Castile (Louis IX's mother), but had named her husband Prince Louis of France as the actual king rather than her or their infant son (Louis IX, born 1214). In legal terms, there were no hard and fast rules of inheritance in England – though a female could transmit a claim to a title to her husband or child and some contemporaries held and governed their estates by personal force of character, e.g. Isabella de Forz, Countess of Aumale and lady of the Isle of Wight. In practical terms, only a male could lead in war. If Eleanor was chosen there would have to be a regency and then a dispute over who was to marry her and rule on her behalf; it was simpler and safer to name an adult male as king instead. Given the recent shock of the murder of Henry 'of Almain' at Viterbo, another assassination in the royal family and the prospect of a disputed succession might well have caused Henry III to die, of shock, earlier than he did (16 November 1272).

What of Edmund's potential as king? Edmund 'Crouchback', as he was nicknamed, which may suggest a mild curvature of the spine (inherited by his distant descendant Richard III?), is a somewhat shadowy figure, loyal to and never challenging his more forceful elder brother Edward. (Ironically a story was to emerge in the coming century that he was really the elder of the brothers, probably propaganda by his ambitious descendants and totally unfounded.) Born on 16 January 1245 and so aged twenty-seven in 1272, he would have been the third king to have that name but probably been counted in official regnal records as 'the First' as the pre-1066 kings (including three Edwards) were not counted in the Angevin dynasty's regnal numbers. 'Edward the First' was in fact 'Edward the Fourth' – unlike in England the French kings reckoned their numbers from the ninth century. The choice of his ambitious and unrealistic father to receive the confiscated Crown of Sicily from the Pope in the 1250s (see previous chapter), he was a competent if uninspiring military leader who had spent the de Montfort ascendancy of 1264–5 in exile in France with his mother readying an army to invade. He returned after the battle of Evesham, was entrusted by Edward with the important role of driving the Kenilworth Castle rebels back inside the fortress and opening its siege in 1266, and on its surrender took over as governor. He was also granted the earldom and estates of Leicester, forfeited by de Montfort, plus the earldom and estates of Derby in the Peak District, which had been seized from the rebel Robert de Ferrers; this made him the King's chief vassal in the East Midlands. He then served as a commissioner on the panel that negotiated the humiliating Treaty of Montgomery with Llywelyn of Gwynedd in 1267, and in June 1267 received the earldom of Lancaster, with its estates, which made him dominant in the North-West. He was thus one of the greatest landowners in the kingdom, and was supposed to acquire the de Forz inheritance too (as custodian for his children) by marrying its heiress Avelina but her death without children (1274) prevented this. In spring 1271 he followed Edward on Crusade, and was en route home when the assassination attempt took place.

Assessing Edmund's potential as a king is difficult, but it is clear that he was as committed to the idea of Crusade as Edward; he was lined up to lead the next Crusade planned for c. 1276 by Edward and Pope Gregory and renewed his vow as late as 1287. He was also forceful enough on matters of his 'rights' to boycott the King's coronation in 1274, apparently in a sulk that he was not allowed to carry the great sword 'Curtana' in the procession to Westminster Abbey as should have been his duty as Great Steward of England. He served with credit in the King's invasion of Wales in 1277, leading one of the main armies in the expedition north from his own lands around Carmarthen to Llanbadarn to prevent the restive inhabitants of Dyfed aiding the main target, Gwynedd, and then erecting a new castle at Aberystwyth. In the 1282–3 Welsh rebellion he commanded in South Wales again, as he did in the south-east (as lord of the 'Three Castles' in the Monnow valley) in the next rebellion in 1294–5. In dynastic matters he was to marry again in December 1275 or January 1276, to Blanche of Artois, daughter of Count Robert and widow of King Henry of Navarre (who was also Count of Champagne). Blanche's daughter by Henry, Queen Joan/Jeanne of Navarre, inherited both Navarre and Champagne from her father in 1274 but was under-age, and so her new stepfather, Edmund, administered Champagne on her behalf in 1276–84. He handed it over to her and her new husband, King Philip IV of France, after her marriage in 1284. His regime was marked by a degree of harsh financial exactions, which led to riots at the town of Provins in January 1280, and this degree of belligerent demands on his full dues from his subjects may imply as forceful (and arrogant?) a nature as King Edward. His residence in Champagne also gave him useful 'leverage' within France by dealing with its elite, and as such he was Edward's choice for a number of important diplomatic missions to Kings Philip III and IV. He was to die in June 1296 at Bayonne in Gascony, during an expedition to retake the province after a French invasion.

Edmund's only notable blunders were in the diplomatic field, regarding his prestigious embassies to France in May 1293 and early 1294 to negotiate a settlement after 'low-level' maritime clashes between the two nations' shipping led to a risk of war. Philip IV of France was stoking up the tension by accepting appeals for 'justice' from the English King's subjects in Gascony, as was his legal right due to his being overlord of the province but a sign of ill-will as he and his forebears had not used this 'weapon' against the English Crown since the treaty of 1259 formalized the status of the duchy of Gascony as a French vassal. Philip now summoned Edward before his 'parlement' in Paris like any other vassal, with the threat of confiscation of Gascony if he did not turn up; Edward refused to humble himself (as was no doubt expected). Edward was keen to avoid war and bind both Kings to another Crusade, and Edmund's second embassy accepted a 'face-saving' proposal that the English hand over the principal towns and castles of Gascony to Philip's men as legally required and Philip would then hand them back, with honour on both sides satisfied. Edward would then marry the French King's half-sister Margaret to cement the peace deal. This was apparently suggested to Edmund's embassy in secret by Philip's stepmother, Dowager Queen Marie of France, on Philip's behalf, and Edmund accepted it as a solution and passed it on to Edward who agreed too; the towns and castles were handed over but Philip refused to return them and declared Gascony confiscated, precipitating war. This ruse suggests a degree of naivety on Edmund's part in trusting the Machiavellian Philip; but if so he was no more naive than Edward was in accepting the idea. Both were clearly men of more honour than Philip, and despite the latter having a reputation for keeping his plans secret he had not yet shown the full extent of his ruthlessness that he was later to show to his foe Pope Boniface VIII (assaulted and threatened by Italians on Philip's payroll) and the Templars (arrested en masse and burnt at the stake as heretics with their treasury confiscated).[26]

All this suggests that Edmund was much like his elder brother, and that a government led by him from November 1272 would not have been much different from that led by Edward. As he was lord of Leicester, Derby, and Lancaster as of 1272, these earldoms and their revenues would have been subsumed in the Crown and so added to its financial resources – unless granted out again to his sons or vassals. His military capabilities and Crusading interests were backed by conventional and generous piety, as he was probably the founder of the Franciscan friary at Preston in Lancashire; Blanche founded a nunnery of St Clare in Aldgate, London.[27] Whether his assuming the Crown would have made any difference to his choice of wife is unclear, though in any case Blanche was a useful dynastic 'catch' as a friendly Artois could act as an ally on the vulnerable northern flank of the Kingdom of France and be a conduit for English influence in Flanders in case of war with France. As stepfather of Queen Joanna of Navarre, Edmund would also have been able to install his nominees to govern it in 1276 until Joanna's marriage and so protect the southern flanks of Gascony from attack across the Pyrenees.

The fact that Edmund held the confiscated heartland of the defunct Welsh principality of Dyfed around Carmarthen (the basis for the later county) plus the 'Three Castles' in Gwent would have given him a personal interest in the protection and extension of royal power in Wales, but it cannot be said from this if he would have been as bold as Edward was in deciding to destroy Gwynedd as Edward did in 1283. The massive invasion of Wales in 1277 to restrict Prince Llywelyn's rule to the western parts of Gwynedd beyond the Conwy, confiscating the Eastern half of the principality and cutting Llywelyn's links to his vassals in mid-Wales, was, however, a repeat of John's invasion and confiscation of 1210 and Henry III's of 1240. These two previous Kings had endeavoured when possible to cut Gwynedd down to size and enforce royal vassalage of its ruler as a cowed feudal subordinate not an independent prince, and Henry III had showed interest in the early 1230s in overrunning central and southern Wales too (or at least depriving Gwynedd of its overlordship in favour of his English Marcher and Welsh loyalists).[28] A sustained campaign in the 1270s to expand the new King Edmund's lands in Carmarthen to control all of South-West Wales plus a forceful seizure of eastern Gwynedd was thus in line with past royal policies and Edmund's own interests as a local lord. Nor was it impossible that Edmund would have gone as far as Edward did in building new castles on the coast of western Gwynedd, such as Caernarfon, or confiscating low-lying and accessible Anglesey (Mon) and building Beaumaris Castle, which would serve to keep Llywelyn on the defensive. The builders of Edward's castles in real-life were led by a Savoyard master-mason, Master James of St George, and Edmund (the son of a half-Savoyard mother and inheritor of his great-uncle Peter of Savoy's eponymous palace in London) would have been served by Savoyards as Edward was. As assessed by modern experts, some of the castles may have been inspired by those Edward had seen on Crusade, and by Louis IX's fortified port of Aigues-Mortes – which Edmund had seen too.[29]

The confiscation of the principality of Gwynedd in 1283 is less certain from a King Edmund than is some sort of invasion paralleling the real-life one of 1277. The Welsh rebellion – not only in Gwynedd – which served as an excuse for the extinction of independence was preceded by relentless and probably deliberately provocative assertions of English legal procedure within Welsh lands, with Welsh litigants forced to plead before courts staffed by English judges who delivered 'rigged' verdicts. Even the prince of Gwynedd was forced to appear as a litigant, and any failure to appear could mean confiscation of estates for 'contempt of court'. This use of the law to extend English royal power via administrative 'fiat' and judicial persecution was clearly a personal initiative of Edward's, as he was a keen and obsessive legislator interested in the efficient implementation of all his administrative powers to the full.[30] It is unlikely that Edward's brother was as personally committed to this grand project, but the occasional glimpses we have of his acts as an administrator (e.g. the Provins riot) may indicate that he was just as keen to pursue his 'rights' so a 'committed' and active senior administrator (such as Robert Burnell, in real life the Lord Chancellor in the

1270s) could have suggested this extension of his legal 'reach' to him. This insistence on full use of all royal legal rights would have applied to all the King's vassals, not only in Wales, and would probably have led to attempts to enforce full vassalage on the King of Scots – which in real life Alexander III avoided at their 1278 meeting by only swearing allegiance to Edward for his lands held within England, not for his kingdom.[31]

When possible the English kings had endeavoured to enforce full vassalage on their Scots counterparts, as Henry II had done on William 'the Lion' after the latter was captured attacking Alnwick Castle in 1174; this sort of action could thus be expected when the next Scots king was in his English counterpart's power. In real life, the deaths of Alexander III in 1286 and his granddaughter Margaret in 1290 enabled Edward to act as head of the panel set up by the Scots regency to adjudicate the rival claims to the throne in 1292. The winner, John Balliol (who also held hereditary estates in County Durham in England), was forced to do homage to Edward explicitly as King of Scots – and when he (eventually) showed signs of trying to use the Scots alliance with France to pressurize England during the next Anglo-French war Edward invaded and deposed him.[32] It is unclear if Edmund would have gone so far as to confiscate Scotland and endeavour to merge it with England in 1296 rather than impose a new puppet king, as Edward showed a boldness of vision that went beyond the norms of contemporary politics. If Edmund had faced a leaderless Scotland in 1290 as Edward did and then awarded the crown to Balliol – the obvious heir under English precedents, as grandson of the eldest daughter of the late King William's brother Earl David of Huntingdon – he might well have 'played safe' on removing Balliol and replaced him with the heir of the next of Earl David's daughters, i.e. the eponymous father of Robert Bruce. 'King Robert', the Earl of Carrick in Scotland but also a landowner in England so wary of confiscations for disloyalty, would then have been succeeded by his son when he died in 1304, without any need for a bloody Scots civil war – and the elder Robert Bruce was a cautious man who fought for Edward I in the real-life wars of the late 1290s.[33]

But it is quite possible that Edmund, like Edward, would have jumped at the chance offered by the under-age Queen Margaret (born 1283) in 1286–90 to betroth her to his son and heir – Thomas, born c. 1278 – as Edward did in real life. A powerful neighbour or overlord using an under-age female queen as a device to create a 'union of crowns' was accepted contemporary policy, and the most blatant contemporary case of this involved Edmund's own step-daughter Queen Joan of Navarre (Countess of Champagne so a French vassal too) who King Philip III of France married off to his son and heir Philip in 1284. Edmund as king might also have used the fact that his new vassal Prince Llywelyn of Gwynedd only had one child, a daughter (Gwenllian), by his wife Eleanor de Montfort (who died in childbirth) to try to confiscate Gwynedd by insisting that the girl was betrothed to an English prince. This pair would then inherit Gwynedd when Llywelyn (born c. 1224) died, rather than the heir under Welsh law, Llywelyn's devious and untrustworthy brother Dafydd – and Edmund could insist on his feudal rights as overlord to choose Gwenllian's husband. It is, however, possible that Edmund might have used Dafydd, who had twice already plotted against Llywelyn and had allied himself to the latter's foe Prince Gruffydd ap Gwenynwyn of Powys in 1274, to overthrow Llewelyn at some point. This was particularly likely if the latter did not trust Dafydd to succeed him and turned to their brother Rhodri as his heir (or married Gwenllian to a man he did not approve of), as then England could enforce the weakening of Gwynedd by dividing it among rival heirs as it had done when Llywelyn's uncle Dafydd died in 1246. Llywelyn's brother Dafydd had sons as had Rhodri, so the royal line of Gwynedd would have continued but for an English intervention – the latter being likely at some point given local restiveness in Wales against the harsh imposition of English law after 1277 and thus a probable 'grass-roots' rebellion.

Scotland – what if Alexander III had not fallen off his horse in 1286? Or his heiress the 'Maid of Norway' had not died aged seven in 1290? Would there have been an Anglo-Scots union 300 years before 1603?
One of the most bizarre, tragic and avoidable incidents in the turbulent history of Scotland occurred on the night of 18–19 March 1286. King Alexander III, a capable forty-five-year-old ruler who had been on the throne since his father died during an invasion of the Hebrides in 1249, had lost his first wife Margaret of England, Edward I's sister – mother of his two sons, Alexander and David, and his daughter Margaret – in 1275. He had re-married on 15 October 1285 to another French noblewoman, Yolande of Dreux, daughter of a junior cadet of the French royal family, who was now pregnant. The question of the Scots succession was urgent, as Prince David had died aged nine in 1281 and Prince Alexander had died in 1283 aged twenty; their sister Margaret (born 1261) had been married off to Alexander's ally King Erik of Norway but had died in childbirth early in 1283, leaving a daughter also called Margaret (who was not heir to Norway, which was inherited by male descent). The 'Maid of Norway' was thus the heir to the Scots throne, as recognized in 1285. The King had no siblings, and apart from the 'Maid of Norway' his nearest heirs were the descendants of his grandfather William 'the Lion's younger brother, Earl David of Huntingdon (d. 1219), who had left three daughters. The elder two had

married into Anglo-Norman families holding lands in both Scotland and England – Balliol (originally de Ballieul) and Bruce (originally de Brus). There were also various descendants of illegitimate half-sisters and aunts of Alexander, the offspring of Alexander II (r. 1214–49) and William I (r. 1165–1214), but they would have to be legitimated to be acceptable to Church canon law.

The death of Alexander, March 1286: A freak accident changes history?

In fact, the lack of a son for a Scots king in his forties was not that unusual – Alexander had been born when his father Alexander II was forty-four and the latter had been born when his father William was fifty-four. William had lived to over seventy, his father King David to around sixty-nine, and his grandfather Malcolm III had been killed on campaign aged over sixty so there was every chance that Alexander would live for some years barring accidents. But the latter occurrence intervened – allegedly foretold by the poet Thomas 'the Rhymer' of Ercildoune (Earlston, Lothian), creator of the Scots version of the legend of Tristan and Isolde, a 'seer' who was supposed by legend to have seen a ghostly spectre at Alexander and Yolande's wedding-feast at Jedburgh Abbey portending doom.[34] On the evening of 18 March 1286 Alexander rode out of Edinburgh Castle after a council-meeting to take the ferry across the Firth of Forth and ride to his wife's current residence at Kinghorn on the Fife coast for the night, her birthday being the next day – a sign of his eagerness to be with his bride, and in such a hurry that he went without an adequate escort (or with enough rush-torches to light his way?). The journey was reasonably short, but his lack of precautions for the road along the Fife coast in a storm was somewhat careless. He never arrived and seems from the chronicles' account to have become separated from his escort. Next morning he and his horse were found dead at the foot of an embankment on Kinghorn beach (there was no cliff at the site later marked as the location of this) after apparently losing his way in the dark and stumbling or being thrown.[35]

This avoidable accident left Princess Margaret of Norway, aged three and living with her father in Bergen, as the Queen of Scots and necessitated setting up a regency council (as had been done for Alexander himself aged eight in 1249). The decision appears to have been delayed into mid-April – until Yolande gave birth as she is presumed to have said she was pregnant. The baby died at birth or was lost in a miscarriage (if it existed). The avoidance of a politically dangerous dispute over the succession among the heirs of Earl David of Huntingdon – including several major lordly dynasties – thus depended on Margaret surviving to maturity and being married off successfully. There was the probability of her council's choice of husband for her being interfered with by the overbearing King Edward of England, who was her great uncle and who also claimed that the Scots kings were his vassals (and thus that he could decide on a female vassal's choice of husband under feudal law). There was also a threat to the prospect of a 'united front' to English meddling among the regency council, as the latter included members of the nobility with rival claims to the throne should Margaret die and one or more of them could seek English military help or money to defeat their rivals. These included the future King Robert Bruce's grandfather, Robert Bruce (V) the lord of Annandale (known as 'the Competitor' from his participation in the succession-dispute of 1290–2), son of Isabella the second daughter of Earl David of Huntingdon – genealogically junior to Earl David's first daughter's grandson John Balliol. He had apparently been recognized by Alexander II as next heir after the latter's son before 1249 (or so he claimed in 1291).[36] As the son not the grandson of a daughter of David, he could claim to be closer in blood to the late King; and he had supported Edward I and his father in arms at the battle of Lewes in 1264. He was in his early seventies; his son Robert (VI), father of the future King, was Earl of Carrick by right of his marriage to its heiress, Countess Marjorie, daughter of the late Earl. She was later supposed to have been so enamoured of him when he returned from Crusade to tell her that his comrade, her first husband, had died that she locked him up until he agreed to marry her. (This story is confused as in fact it had been his father, not he, who was the Crusader in 1270; but their marriage appears to have been without the King's permission and so was challenged at the time).[37] The principal rivals of the Bruces were John Balliol (the heir of Earl David's eldest daughter Devorguilla), as mentioned earlier, and the head of the powerful Comyn dynasty of Buchan and Galloway, John 'the Black' Comyn, lord of Badenoch in southern Moray and married to a cousin of Edward I. The Comyns were descended from a daughter of King Donald 'Ban' (deposed 1097), King David's uncle. All of these families had been among the ambitious Anglo–Norman 'incomers' to Scotland in the early twelfth century, imported by King David from England to act as props of his rule with lands and offices. The Bruces and Balliols had extensive lands in northern England; the 'Competitor' was to choose to be buried on his English estates, not in England, and Balliol was heir to the lordship of Barnard Castle in county Durham. There were also lords on the council with no claim on the throne and more probability of taking a stronger 'line' with Edward, such as the hereditary 'High Steward' and lord of Renfrew and Lennox, James Stewart (ancestor of the later Stuart kings).

But the existence of rival factions and potential English allies among a Scots regency council was not unique for 1286 or a sign of instability and inevitable civil war, even with the existence of an ambitious and aggressive Edward I as the nation's nearest neighbour with no distractions of Welsh wars as in the late 1270s and 1282–3. The nobility of England and Scotland was part of an 'international' culture of European chivalric nobles with many ties of blood, marriage, and friendship across borders that extended to France too. Ambitious lords or younger sons 'on the make' had come to England with Duke William in or after 1066 and built up dynasties, and had then moved on to invade parts of Wales in the mid-1070s to 1090s and tackle Ireland after 1169. Thanks to invitations from King David (married to the Countess of Huntingdon, William I's great-niece, a former resident in exile at William II's court after 1093, and holding lands in Cumbria from both England and Scotland) as heir and King of Scots, numerous Anglo-Normans had moved into Scotland after c.1105. They had brought with them the Anglo-Norman systems of government, warfare, Church, economic development, urbanisation, and culture – all of which had served to regularize and stabilize the government, boost the monarchy's powers and prestige, increase tax revenues, and 'modernize' the country. As seen by the career of the de Montforts in England, it was not unusual for a family to have lands in and loyalties to the monarchs of more than one state.

Nor was English meddling in a Scots regency unusual or a sign of inevitable disaster. The nearest precedent for the situation of 1286, that of 1249 when a boy of eight (Alexander III) succeeded, had indeed seen a decade of feuding over the regency with another political polarization between two factions – one led by Alan Durward, a senior administrator and hereditary official married to Alexander's illegitimate sister, and Walter Comyn, lord of Badenoch. Durward had been accused of designs on the throne via his wife by the Comyns, and had relied on help from Henry III in gaining control of the regency council at the time of Alexander's marriage (aged ten) to the English King's daughter, Margaret, in December 1251. His new council had even included two English representatives to look after Henry's interests – and Henry, like Edward I in 1278, had tried unsuccessfully to bully the Scots King into doing homage for his kingdom during the festivities. Durward had been driven out of Scotland by the Comyns and taken refuge in England, going on Henry's expedition to Gascony for Prince Edward's marriage in 1254 to show his usefulness and then receiving English aid to seize Edinburgh Castle and Alexander in a coup in 1255. The Comyns had then driven him out in a counter-coup, kidnapping Alexander, in 1257; an uneasy stalemate with both sides represented on the regency council had eventually been patched up.[38] The prospect of feuding nobles with claims on the Crown fighting over control of an under-age sovereign and of the English King intervening was thus not new in 1286; and after Robert III died in 1406 Scotland was to see turbulent regencies for all six King Jameses plus Queen Mary. The prospect of Queen Margaret acting as a 'puppet' ruler for feuding nobles and a series of coups in her childhood and teens was thus no worse than what had faced Alexander III in the 1250s. Unlike in 1249–62, moreover, the new reign commenced with a truce among the contending dynasts holding for four years and no armed gatherings to intimidate the government or seize power.

The problem that faced Scotland was, however, accentuated in 1286 by Margaret's sex, as whoever she married would be expected to hold the reins of power and lead the nation's armies in war. A female had never reigned in Scotland, and when Malcolm II died without sons or brothers in 1034 it was his daughter's son, King Duncan (of Shakespearian fame as Macbeth's 'victim'), who took the throne, not one of his (probably two) daughters. The most obvious contender for a ruling queen as the nearest genealogical heiress to the Crown had been the 'original' of 'Lady Macbeth', King Macbeth's wife, Gruoch, as the representative of the superseded line of Malcolm III's cousin Kenneth III, when Duncan was killed in battle by her husband in 1040. If her husband Macbeth (Mac Beatha, 'Son of Life') had any claim to the throne for himself, this was either due to his mother being a younger daughter of Malcolm II (which is only stated by later sources) or due to his father, Findlaech, 'Mormaer' (Earl) of Moray, being descended from an eighth century king of Dalriada. However, it was Macbeth who took the throne after the battle of Spynie and when Duncan's son Malcolm III (who had relied on an English army to take power) killed him in Moray in 1057 the family claim passed to her son by her first marriage, Lulach – who Malcolm then killed too.[39] Whoever Margaret married would have the real power in Scotland, and her residence at her father King Eric's court in Norway in 1286 meant that she was under his authority and he would be seeking a husband for her that would aid Norway as well as Scotland politically. As she was only three it was impractical for the Scots regency to insist that she was sent to Scotland immediately, and Eric might well refuse. Edward also had an interest in the marriage as he did not want a prince or noble from a state hostile to England leading Scots armies across the Border – though as yet the 'Auld Alliance' between Scotland and France had not been created and past Scots kings had sought their brides from the Anglo-Norman or French provincial aristocracy if no princesses were available. Edward was Margaret's next male kin to Eric, as her late grandmother's brother.

The threat thus arose of Edward I negotiating to arrange Margaret's marriage to a candidate suitable to England with Eric, circumventing the need to win over a majority of the Scots council for his choice of husband.

However, the political need for him to be absent from England in Gascony in 1286–9 to deal with French encroachment delayed a crisis. Indeed, the Scots regency in 1286 was clearly not anticipating the possible threat that soon materialized with Edward trying to marry Margaret to his son and unite the two realms; nor was Edward quick to intervene. The regency sent the Bishop of Brechin to him as he made his way across France to Gascony in late spring 1286, following this with a second ecclesiastical mission that caught up with him in Gascony; they were apparently asking for his advice and goodwill. This does not indicate any fear of what Edward was planning – and Edward's reply was probably that the Scots monarchy must recognize him as its feudal overlord before he would aid them.[40] So as of 1286 he had other priorities, namely Gascony, and was endeavouring to win the homage that Alexander had refused to do in 1278. This did not change quickly, and the apparent manoeuvrings of the Bruce dynasty to gain Anglo-Norman allies in Northern Ireland and some form of military 'demonstration' against the authority of the regents were no more than the expected 'jockeying for position' of a major noble faction in an emerging struggle for influence in a regency.[41]

Eric of Norway, in possession of the child-Queen, was, however, more likely to be amenable to suggestions from the powerful international statesman Edward about Margaret's marriage than to the ideas of the weaker Scots monarchy – whose relations with Norway had been strained for centuries due to rival claims to the southern Hebrides. The latter, originally part of the pre-Viking era kingdom of Dalriada that formed part of Scotland in the 'union' of the 840s, had been settled by Scandinavians in the ninth century and ruled by dynasts of part-Norwegian descent, and at times the kings of Norway had used expeditions to enforce direct rule. King Edgar of Scots, David's elder brother, had formally ceded the Hebrides to Norway in 1098. It had only been lost by Norway after the failure of the final Norwegian naval expedition to the Hebrides and Clyde estuary by Eric's grandfather, King Haakon IV, in 1263 (culminating in the Battle of Largs); Scotland had annexed the area in 1266. Orkney and Shetland were still Norwegian, and were to remain so until mortgaged to Scotland in a marriage-treaty in 1469. Was Eric's goodwill to the Scots regency guaranteed, or would he prefer Edward's interests to theirs? Notably, Eric launched negotiations for Margaret's marriage while she was still under his guardianship – to maximize his 'leverage', rather than waiting for her to return to Scotland? But we have no certainty of who first raised the possibility of Margaret marrying Edward's only surviving son and heir, Edward of Caernarfon (born in April 1284). It may have been Edward, or possibly even the regency in Scotland.[42] If it was the latter, they must have hoped that Edward's resulting close involvement in their affairs would guarantee a stable government for the regency and warn off potential challengers – such as the Bruces? – who would now face English troops.

As seen in 1251–62, an English presence on the regency council and active English backing for the regime in Edinburgh were not unprecedented – though Henry III's backing had not saved firstly Durward and later the Comyns from overthrow by rivals. Possibly the regents hoped that they could speed up Eric's reluctance to send his daughter to Scotland by enlisting Edward's backing, and the engagement of Margaret to Prince Edward was necessary for this purpose – or even considered that they could back out of the marriage later when their regime was secure and Edward was embroiled with France again? If they were sincere, there would be a risk of Margaret being required to live long term in England and Edward maintaining his close involvement in Scots politics for his lifetime; in 1287 he was forty-eight and in robust health and his father had lived to sixty-five. The Scots' offering Margaret to Prince Edward would have been safer had he not been the heir to the English throne – his elder brother Alfonso had died in autumn 1284, months after he was born. (Thus, the legend that Edward I offered his new-born heir Edward to the Welsh as their Prince at Caernarfon in 1284 is inaccurate – the Prince was not his heir then.) But would Edward I have insisted on Margaret marrying his heir, not a younger son?

While Edward was still in Gascony in spring 1289 Eric sent envoys to him proposing that Margaret be married to Edward of Caernarfon. This is the first sign of the plan being considered – but it does not indicate if the Scots regents prompted Eric, or if Edward suggested it. The children were cousins so the papacy would have to grant legal exemption from the usual ban on such marriages and Edward's diplomats – backed by his Savoyard/Italian links – could gain this easier than remote Norway's. Edward's Savoyard retainer Otto de Grandison duly went to Rome for this in spring 1290.[43] Whoever thought of the original idea for a 'union of crowns' for England and Scotland, Edward made the most of it to extend his influence northwards. A man of vast ambitions and willing to take risk for political advancement, he may have been thinking of this solution ever since Alexander's two sons died in 1283, or at the latest when Queen Yolande failed to give birth to a son in spring 1286. It played into his hands in any case by providing for his permanent influence over Scotland and the removal of the latter's Queen to live in England with her husband.

The wife would be expected to follow her husband to his state, not the reverse, by contemporary 'mores', though it was unusual for a sovereign queen to marry a sovereign king (who would be expected to reside in his own country with her joining him there). A union of crowns, even a personal one where a treaty made it clear that both states were fully autonomous, was fraught with political difficulties and could lead to disaster if the marriage broke up acrimoniously. In 1128–35, Henry I's heiress Matilda had had to live with her husband Count Geoffrey of Anjou in his county rather than her husband coming to England – though he could not afford to leave his turbulent state anyway. Most ruling queens' husbands were royals of junior status, who could afford to leave their own states and come to assist their wives – such as Edward I's ancestor Count Fulk of Anjou, Geoffrey's father, who left his rule of Anjou to live in Palestine when he married the future Queen Melisende of Jerusalem (1129). The 'equal marriage' status of Queen Urraca of Castile and her husband King Alfonso I of Aragon, both ruling sovereigns of neighbouring states, after 1109 had been a disaster and soon ended in acrimony and separation. The precedents were thus not encouraging; but Edward I would have been expecting his daughter-in-law to spend most of her time in England under his thumb. No doubt the precedent of 1251 in putting English nobles on the Scots ruling council would have been insisted upon, to protect the English King's offspring's interests in Scotland.

Having secured full control of Wales by destroying the power of Gwynedd, creating English jurisdictional and administrative control of the Welsh heartlands, and annexing most of the native princes' lands in 1277–83, Edward now turned his attention to Scotland. This second large acquisition of a neighbouring 'Celtic' (the term was not used then) state would be by diplomacy and marriage, not conquest – but no doubt force would be used too if needed. With most of Ireland under the control of Anglo-Norman barons or semi-Anglicized Irish dynasts loyal to the English King at this 'high-water mark' of English influence in Ireland, all three main states of the British Isles would be under Edward's control. In terms of contemporary culture, it should be noted here that the hugely influential 1130s 'History' of Geoffrey of Monmouth presented a mythical picture of pre-Roman mainland Britain as originally one kingdom, founded by the Trojan refugee 'Brutus' and governed by his family – with the first kings of Scotland and Wales, Albanactus and Camber, as younger sons of the British royal house. In Geoffrey's version of history, after the Romans left Britain an 'empire' of all the island was then re-created by the chivalric paragon King Arthur, overlord of all the British Isles, Norway, and much of France – whose example clearly inspired Edward.[44] An Arthurian enthusiast who made a grand pilgrimage to Arthur's supposed burial-place at Glastonbury Abbey and rebuilt the 'tomb of Arthur and Guinevere' there in 1278, Edward staged Arthurian tournaments and regarded himself as Arthur's greatest successor;[45] the thirteenth-century understanding of Britain's past was that the Arthurian 'empire' and the pre-Roman 'realm of Brutus' were fact, not fiction. Ruling all of Scotland as well as Wales was thus seen as Edward's 'right' and the restoration of the realm of his ancestors. Thus the chance of marrying off Margaret to Prince Edward was vigorously pursued, and there was no chance that the Scots regents – no doubt alarmed at such a prospect – could talk the forceful English King out of it. Finding Margaret another husband was impossible without the backing of her father and guardian, King Eric, and this was not forthcoming. The only possible effective alternative candidate to an English one, which might give Edward pause for thought, was a French prince – and King Philip IV had only married in 1284 so his sons were infants and the marriage could not be carried out for years.

The talks continued after Edward returned to England, and the Scots regents sent their own representatives to join in; some of the regents came in person. (Whether the regency was united or some of its council had doubts over the plan is unknown.) Given the determination of Edward to secure the marriage, the Scots were bound to be sidelined by a combination of England and Norway and had to agree to what Edward and Eric wanted. The Treaty of Salisbury duly agreed that Margaret would come to Scotland or England before 1 November 1290 and then the details would be finalized; another, Anglo-Scots treaty at Birgham on the Tweed on 14 March 1290 ruled that both Edward and Eric would have to approve of Margaret's marriage and that their representatives would join the Scots regency council – the English involvement had a precedent from 1251. Scots independence was guaranteed by a second agreement at Birgham on 18 July, which formally confirmed the complete separation of the administrations of both kingdoms – in other words, there would be just a 'union of crowns' not a union of states. The Scots royal relics and muniments, symbols of Scots independence, were to be kept locked up in Scotland until Margaret had come to her kingdom and given birth to an heir[46] – a wise precaution as in real life when Edward abolished the Scots kingship in 1296 he notoriously carried them all off to London. (The coronation stone was installed for his line's use in Westminster Abbey, and was not returned officially until 1997 despite an earlier 'rescue', but some Scots prefer to think that Edward was fobbed off with a substitute.) The mention of an heir may well indicate that the regency's plan was that even if Margaret had to live in England, her heir would stay in Scotland – and Margaret would not leave Scotland until she had one? This personal not State union was the norm for other royal marriages of partners both ruling kingdoms, and was thus a major gain for the Scots – but it was not the way that Edward had governed Gwynedd after extinguishing its royal house by execution or deportation in 1283. Gwynedd had been incorporated into the English administrative and judicial system as a feudal estate of the English Crown, as also happened to those other, minor Welsh principalities incorporated into England by their rulers' deaths or dispossessions in the 1280s – and where a Welsh dynast's heirs survived, e.g. in parts of Powys, it was as an English landowner subject to the English Crown.[47] Were the Scots too sanguine about Edward's ruthlessness, or making the best of a poor negotiating 'hand'?

Edward may well have already hoped to incorporate Scotland legally and administratively into England after the marriage, given his actions after he deposed John Balliol in 1296. Notably, he endeavoured to get King Eric to send Margaret to him in England behind the Scots regents' back that summer of 1290, so that she would be in his hands and he could dictate all the arrangements. This amounted to double-crossing the regents, but luckily Eric refused to let Margaret sail and kept her in Norway until a Scots ship arrived for her.[48] Had he given way, Edward would have been in a strong position to marry Margaret off to Prince Edward at a time and with conditions of his choosing, and it is likely that he would have been anxious to keep her at court in England for his lifetime rather than letting her go 'home' as then anti-English Scots nobles could kidnap her. (Precedents of a Scots noble coup and royal kidnap to neutralize a pro-English regency existed from 1255 to 1257.) Margaret would have had to give birth to her children in England, and the Scots to wait until Edward decided that one of her offspring could live in Scotland – if he did so at all.

But it is possible that Eric sending Margaret to England instead might have resulted in her surviving the voyage to the British mainland, as she did not in real life. The voyage would have been on a more southerly route, to the Humber or the Thames rather than to the Forth via the Orkneys – though it would have been longer. Would Margaret have survived to adulthood and ruled Scotland, albeit *in absentia* and only in name until Edward died in 1307? If she had been ill when she landed as in real life, the monastic infirmaries of York or London or Edward's doctors would have had better remedies and facilities than those available for her in the remote Orkneys.

So what would have been different for Anglo-Scots relations if this ultra-complex crisis had not occurred – had Alexander not fallen off his horse or had he had a son (Alexander aged twenty-three or David aged fourteen) to succeed him? In a sense, the accident brought an end to 180 years of more or less amicable relations between the two nations, with a semi-Anglicized dynasty installed in Scotland from the time that King William II's armies replaced Donald 'Ban' with his nephew Edgar, son of Malcolm III and the English St Margaret, in 1097. David I, indeed, had been brought up in

England from 1093 to 1100 (and possibly longer) and was famous for introducing Anglo-Norman personnel, culture, spirituality, and methods of governance to his own country after he assumed the throne – and before that in Lothian as its governor, ruling it from around 1107 to 1124 along with Cumbria. The dynasty that he founded was often resident in the Borders, especially at his great foundation of Roxburgh Castle, and he built most of his Anglo-Norman-style abbeys there; the region was the heartland of prosperous twelfth and thirteenth century Scotland and Berwick was the country's principal port until destroyed by Edward I in 1296. David's family were close to their kin and wives in England, with David intervening in the civil war of 1138–53 to assist his niece Empress Matilda in person (as at Winchester in 1141) and his grandson William I using his mother's Warenne family surname. Alexander II led an army across England in 1216 to assist John's foes at the siege of Dover Castle. The relations between England and Scotland pre-1286 were not always good, as seen by the wars of the late 1130s and 1214–17 and by William I's assistance to Henry II's rebel sons in 1174, and English vassalage of Scotland was not invented by Edward I but was imposed by Henry II on the captive William (along with occupation of his main castles) in 1174–89. But conflicts were usually short and there was none of the prolonged fighting and embittering atrocities that were to occur after 1296. The Borders were rarely at peace after 1296, and the prosperous region of Tweeddale and the Merse was particularly ravaged; David's stronghold of Roxburgh frequently changed hands (as did Berwick) and was often held for decades by the English. James II was to be killed by an exploding cannon as he tried to retake it in 1460. The chaos and endemic bloodshed bred a 'gangster-like' Border society of clans of ferocious 'moss-troopers', such as the Armstrongs, who made their lives out of raiding the English and each other and operated an elaborate system of blackmail on their neighbours and defied the government. In turn, the lack of control or a regular army by a harassed Scots government led to the latter relying on more effective local landowners to keep order (supposedly) and take the lead in fighting the English – of whom the Douglases were the most prominent. The two branches of this dynasty (descended from Robert Bruce's great guerrilla-leader Sir James Douglas), the 'Red' Douglases in Lothian and the 'Black' Douglases in Annandale and Galloway, overshadowed the royal family in national politics at times. All this would have been different had the death of Alexander not led to endemic Border warfare and English attempts to take over Scotland, and the Borders in particular would have been a far more prosperous and better-governed place.

It is also safe to say that but for the Scots distractions after 1286 Edward I would have had to concentrate his energies elsewhere – with the 'caveat' that England had intervened before in Scots regencies so if the throne was occupied by an under-age ruler or subject to a succession-dispute at any point he could still have attacked. Scotland had been lucky before 1286 in that King William, who had had only daughters until the age of fifty-four, left a son of sixteen at his death in 1214 and this son (Alexander II) left a son in 1249. It could have been lucky again if Alexander III's son Alexander (IV) had succeeded as an adult in March 1286 or at a later date, though Edward I was quite likely to try to bully him into marrying one of his daughters and/or making him pay homage at a future date. The English kings had now reduced Wales to submissiveness after the 1294–5 rebellion and no king from 1210 to 1394 bothered to intervene in Ireland in person, so a conflict with Scotland would be a welcome extension of the dynasty's power over all the British mainland in the legendary tradition of Edward I's hero 'King Arthur'. But Edward had had friendly relations with Alexander III in the 1260s and 1270s, and the probability arises that the conflict with France over Guienne in 1294–8 would have been his main business of military aggression – without the distractions of real life in overthrowing John Balliol in 1296 and putting down rebellion after 1297. Would Edward have been able to concentrate on reconquering Guienne by force rather than having to accept it back by papal-mediated treaty in 1299 as in real life? Could he then have declared it independent of France and ended the problematic requirement to do homage to the King of France for it? This would have had major results for improved Anglo-French relations after 1299, as the kings of France would not have had the 'weapon' of being able to declare the province confiscated in case of any dispute with England. But it would not have prevented the wars resulting from Edward III's claim to the French throne after 1328, assuming that an Anglo-French 'rapprochement' around 1300–1308 involved Edward I's son marrying the daughter of Philip IV (Isabella) as in real life. Nor is it clear that avoidance of the cost of campaigning in Scotland after 1296 would have led to such a lower tax-burden on England that the constitutional conflict of 1297 was avoided (see section on Edward I's 1297 accident). Edward I was a man of restless ambition and feverish energy, and if he had had no Scots war in 1296–8 he was capable of calling up a much larger army than in real life to tackle France, raising heavy taxes, and so sparking off protests.

Margaret's death and after: What if she had lived and the union proceeded?

As it turned out, Margaret sailed for Scotland from Bergen that summer in any case, but she may have been ill by the time she sailed. She was only seven, and Eric's delay in despatching her may have had a medical as opposed to political cause. Were the Scots envoys too anxious to sail quickly whatever her health so that a delay did not mean Edward sending more ships to kidnap her? Her condition deteriorated on board ship, and when the latter reached Orkney she had to be taken ashore at Kirkwall to recuperate. Possibly she had caught pneumonia, as conditions on board medieval ships were primitive and warmth was not easy to secure without starting a dangerous fire; the North Sea can be very cold at night even in August. In any event, she died at Kirkwall on 26 September 1290,[49] leaving the Scots throne vacant with no obvious successor. Even before news reached the assembly of nobles waiting for her at Perth that she had died it appears that Robert Bruce the elder turned up to join them with a large armed affinity and uncertain intentions, possibly intending to threaten the others into accepting him as king and crowning him quickly (the coronation site at Scone was conveniently close) should Margaret have died. Bishop Fraser of St Andrews wrote urgently to Edward to ask him to come north and 'hold the ring' among the probable contenders for the Crown, and to support the rightful candidate – who was not mentioned, but the Bishop did refer favourably to a possible request for Edward's help from John Balliol so he probably backed him.[50] A separate appeal was made by representatives of the 'Seven Earls' who claimed legal precedents from ancient Scots history to decide on the identity of the new king, criticizing the role and intentions of the regency.[51] But as Edward journeyed north his wife, Eleanor of Castile died, so the devastated King's priority was her funeral and memorial arrangements – the last of the grand 'Eleanor Crosses', marking where her cortege rested overnight on its route to London, still survives at Charing Cross. His formal adjudication of the rival claims to the Scots Crown followed in 1291–2 – with the contenders all required to accept him as overlord of Scotland in return for being allowed to submit their claims to the panel that he headed.[52] This neatly circumvented the Scots' attempt to delay submission by alleging that only a king of Scots could judge whether or not the claim to overlordship was legal.

The indications from the Treaty of Birgham are that the Scots, caught facing Edward's determination to carry through the marriage and/or prepared to gamble on it to secure his backing for the regency's stability, wanted Margaret to live in Scotland at least until she had given birth to an heir. Her husband Prince Edward would presumably alternate between living in England and Scotland, and do his duty to provide her with sons – though it would be his ever-controlling father who would ultimately decide on his actions. A domineering and at times violent man even in family life,[53] Edward I was to treat his unmilitary son's fondness for non-martial sports and crafts with irritation and banish his waspish Gascon confidant Piers

Gaveston, who he undoubtedly suspected of being a bad influence on his son. Their homosexual involvement has been assumed, though mainly by later playwrights (e.g. the Elizabethan Christopher Marlowe) not by contemporaries, but this is only conjecture; the most recent analysts reckon that the relationship was more of a sworn 'bond of brotherhood' in the tradition of David and Jonathan in the Old Testament.[54] Its passionate nature and Edward's hatred of those who forced the exile of his friend (1305 and 1310) and later killed him are less in dispute; Edward was clearly insecure and unable to put his political survival above personal attachments. Edward may have come to detest his father by 1307, but he was not 'unmilitary' as such; he was physically active and fond of riding, owning a stud-farm inSussex. To that extent he would have been congenial to the knightly Scots aristocratic elite – though they may have been as puzzled by his fondness for fishing and boating as 'un-knightly' as his father and literary commentators were. The extent of their tension before 1305 is debateable, though it is possible that the oaths to carry on the Scots war that his father extorted from him and the nobility represent the King's fear of their lack of will for long-term warfare. By the early 1300s Prince Edward, married to Margaret, may have been keen to get away from his father's court and reside in Scotland to assert his independence – or to save his friend Gaveston from exile by the suspicious King?

The relationship between Margaret and her husband Edward (II) could not have been worse than that Edward had with his real-life wife Isabella of France, whom he married in 1308. She eventually deserted him to return home after he became close to the venal Marcher baron Hugh Despenser – and she overthrew him in an invasion with her lover Roger Mortimer in 1326. The royal couple were certainly mutually antagonistic by the early 1320s, though it is only speculation that this was due to a homosexual relationship between Edward and Despenser as opposed to the latter's political hold over her husband and arrogance. Her part in Edward's presumed murder is less certain.[55] Edward was at least bisexual rather than exclusively homosexual as he was able to give his wife four children in real life, and possibly both he and Margaret would have regarded themselves as victims of the overbearing Edward I and allied against the ageing King. Would they have been more compatible than the real-life couple of Edward and the strong-willed, unscrupulous Isabella – or would Margaret's possession of a loyal corps of Scots nobles willing to back her against England have led to her abandoning her husband if he neglected her for Gaveston? The latter drove the angry English nobles, who he teased with unpleasant nicknames, to have him exiled in 1310 and when he returned to murder him – would the same have happened to him in Scotland? Edward's unstable and disastrous handling of the English noble elite – based on his reliance on two successive unpopular monopolizers of his patronage, Gaveston and then Despenser – may well indicate that he would have fallen into the same 'trap' as co-ruler of Scotland in the 1310s. A later Scots king who turned to 'non-elite' favourites and antagonized the great magnates, James III, ended up deposed and murdered (1488).

Given the likely timescale of events, Edward I would have been impatient to have his son married and Margaret tied to his dynasty in case the Scots regents tried to back out of the marriage – especially if she was still resident in Scotland as of 1294 when he went to war with France, a possible Scots ally then as in real life. Edward had married at fifteen in 1254 for consummation of a vital diplomatic alliance, and in similar circumstances his grandson Edward III was to be married at fourteen in 1328. The impatient Edward I would have been eager to have the marriage consummated, at the age of puberty, to prevent any legal efforts to invalidate it by 'treacherous' Scots nobles with French help. The youngest medieval English royal marriages that soon produced children involved fourteen-year-old males (the future Henry IV, 1381) and thirteen-year-old females (Margaret Beaufort, 1456). The Scots Queen (born 1283) would be old enough to have children around 1296–7, and Edward I's son would be fourteen in summer 1298; the marriage could be expected to take place around then. But it is likely that if at all possible Edward I would have removed Margaret to England – if necessary by kidnapping her – before then to keep her out of the hands of anti-English nobles, and that the Anglo-French war would have seen some rapprochement between critics of submission to Edward's requirements and the French monarchy which threatened revolt in Scotland. In real life, the timid John Balliol was humiliated by Edward's intensive imposition of legal submission as an English vassal, having to appear in English courts and being forced to attend on his overlord in France, and was constrained into a French alliance by his nobles; Edward invaded and deposed him (1296). Margaret would have been tied to the English alliance by her father-in-law, and probably English officials would have been sitting on the regency council until her marriage or her majority (1298–1300?) and even after that.

Any revolt against Queen Margaret would have been on riskier grounds than the real-life revolts against Edward I's direct rule after 1296, and it is unlikely that Edward I would have permitted her to return home as an adult so that she might be able to lead a revolt herself. If she had one child, Edward I was likely to insist that this offspring – heir to England as well as to Scotland – stay in England. But it is possible that once she had a younger child, installed at Edinburgh or Stirling Castle as a guarantee of Scots independence, this infant might be the focus of a kidnap-attempt and used as the figurehead of a Scots noble revolt as later the young James IV was to be used against his unpopular father James III in 1488 and James VI was used against Mary Stuart in 1567. This would be more likely if Edward I was still on the throne; his son was a less harsh and intimidating ruler and was quite likely to have permitted his wife Margaret to spend part of her time in Scotland to head off revolt. Assuming that Edward II became involved with his 'favourite' Piers Gaveston as in real life, that might have led his neglected wife to seek to return home to govern her own realm – leaving one son in England as its heir? The question of whether England and Scotland would remain united under one child of Edward II and Margaret or be divided between two is another matter – but the likely financial exactions and administrative interference of Edward I's nominees in even a nominally separate Scots realm would have been likely to arouse deep resentment.

Edward I is nearly killed in a riding-accident: Winchelsea 1297. Result – no prolonged war over Scotland? The situation as of spring 1297 – Continental war plus two military occupations
The hoodwinking of Edward I and his brother Edmund of Lancaster by Philip IV over surrendering the major towns and castles of Gascony in 1294 (see above) left the English King with the task of evicting the new French garrisons as an urgent priority when war broke out in 1294. As a result a major expedition was launched to sail up the Garonne and attack Bordeaux, but it failed to take the city and had to make do with the fortified towns of Bourg and Blaye. Bayonne was recovered later and the English held onto their positions on the lower Garonne and to the south on the Castilian border,[56] but without Bordeaux this was merely a 'holding-operation' and the French had the advantages of operating by land from central France instead of having to sail all their troops across the stormy Bay of Biscay at risk of the weather and French ports' shipping. The English suffered reverses in Gascony in 1295, while Philip IV called on naval help from his Mediterranean ally Genoa, a major sea-power whose huge 'carracks' and swift galleys dwarfed English ships and whose shipwrights now built new vessels for Philip in Normandy. English ports such as Dover were raided, though Winchelsea fought the attackers off, while released English prisoner-of-war Thomas Turberville (a Royal Household knight) turned out to be a French spy planning to assist an attack on the ill-defended Isle of Wight. Edward made the most of the alleged threat of national destruction by the French in his claims to Parliament in 1295, no doubt to encourage the members to pay large taxes, but the situation was undoubtedly serious and extending the English naval forces to protect the coast cost money and employed men that could have been spent on the Gascon war. The second expedition to Gascony, led by Edmund, in 1296

failed again to take Bordeaux and its commander died at Bayonne on 2 June, short of money to pay his debts.[57] Further reverses occurred early in 1297. Like Richard I in the 1190s, John in 1214, and later Edward III in the late 1330s, Edward sought to back up his Continental campaigns by enlisting a coalition of European allies against France, especially in the Low Countries and the Rhineland – which meant finding the money to pay them large subsidies to fight. Philip, however, outbid Edward for the support of the Count of Holland, and when Edward sought to interest Count Guy of Flanders in marrying his daughter to Prince Edward (which he could not have done if the boy was already engaged to a surviving Queen Margaret of Scotland) Philip bribed Guy to hand the girl over to him instead.[58] (This was technically legal as he was Guy's overlord.) A wool-embargo on exports to French dominions, which included their vassal-county of Flanders, and an offer of 100,000 'livres' for the first year of an English alliance and 200,000 'livres' for the second persuaded Guy to back Edward instead in 1297.[59] The Count of Bar (whose lands were east of central France) and Edward's Savoyard kinsmen were also paid to fight for England, and in May 1297 some Burgundian nobles signed up for subsidies too.[60]

But the costly and time-consuming French war was not Edward's only problem as of 1294–7. In the meantime the King had to deal with a major revolt across supposedly subdued Wales late in 1294, led by local princes of ancient royal blood (Madoc of Meirionydd in Gwynedd and Morgan ap Maredudd of Caerleon in Glamorgan) who could thus call on 'national' loyalty. The majority of Edward's new castles held out, though half-built Caernarfon was overrun, and thanks to the recent summons of Edward's feudal vassals to assemble for the French war he had troops ready to send to Wales instead. But the war entailed hard campaigning well into 1295 before all the attacked castles were relieved or recovered and the 'rebels' punished. Ominously, it appears that the lesser and greater magnates were mostly opposed to the proposed 'feudal' summons to muster at Portsmouth in autumn 1294 for a campaign in Gascony, with hints of the resistance to fighting overseas for the King's foreign interests that had met King John in 1205. So few landholders turned up at the muster that it had to be cancelled (though the Welsh rebellion prevented any clear indication of whether this was a full 'strike' or just 'foot-dragging' as the offenders later turned up to fight in Wales).[61] In spring 1295 a group of senior magnates led by the Earl of Arundel ignored summonses to assemble for the Gascon war, and the frustrated King ordered their debts to be called in but clearly could not coerce or coax them by force of personality.[62] Does this indicate that the cohesion of the English elite was fracturing, at least for an expensive French war that was not seen as essential to their interests?

The cost of all this campaigning was not easy to meet, given resistance to emergency taxation and loans from lay landholders and merchants alike in 1294–6 – the initial royal plan for taxation at the autumn 1294 assembly (Parliament?) had to be reduced.[63] One of the main Italian banks that Edward usually called on for loans (Riccardi of Lucca) went bankrupt. He resorted to his usual weapon of using State power for naked blackmail of potential lenders; having expelled the Jews and seized their assets in a previous financial crisis, he now required the resident Italian bankers in England to issue him large loans on pain of being expelled if they did not co-operate.[64] All this multi-faceted crisis indicates that the war that Edward launched to evict his vassal King John Balliol from Scotland in summer 1296 was an unwelcome strain to the English state. However, it was not Edward who opened hostilities, although his legal demands on and humiliation of Balliol in 1292–6 had gone beyond precedent and he seemed to be treating him as a normal feudal vassal rather than as a sovereign ruler; indeed his summonses of Balliol to appear in his courts and to do military service were a mirror of what his own 'overlord' King Philip was seeking to impose on him in Gascony.[65] His aggressive assertion of his legal 'rights' had also been seen in 'vassal' Gwynedd in Wales after 1277, and had sparked off similar resentment and revolt in 1282. Clearly Edward did not want to 'learn from his mistakes' in Wales or take a politically wiser course of not humiliating his vassals thereafter. On this occasion, it was the Scots nobility rather than Balliol who led the way in seeking alliance with Philip IV in 1294–5, and in 1295 they created a new council of state to take important executive decisions (e.g. allying with France), which effectively curtailed royal powers. This would imply a lack of confidence on their part that Balliol – afraid of having his lands in County Durham confiscated? – was not to be trusted to stand up to Edward.

As the Scots concluded their treaty with France Edward called a feudal summons of his army to Newcastle in March 1296, with a major force of up to 30,000 anticipated, and summoned Balliol too – whose refusal meant confiscation of his lands for treason to his lord. The Scots peers opened the war by attacking Carlisle, which was defended by an Anglophile Scots governor (ironically, future King Robert Bruce's father), but this was only anticipating an inevitable English attack. Once Easter was over the English King attacked and sacked Berwick, the largest mercantile port in Scotland, with the resulting massacre (the worst wartime atrocity on the English mainland since the Norman Conquest) no doubt arranged as a deliberate warning to the Scots of what lay in store for any resistance. The Scots army that had failed to save Berwick was defeated at Dunbar, though it appears that Balliol was not present and the casualty-list of nobles was small so probably only a section of the Scots army was involved; Edward then advanced unopposed across the Lowlands into Edinburgh and on to Fife and received the surrender of many leading castles, plus that of senior nobles who were deported to England (presumably to deprive future resistance of its expected leaders). Balliol endeavoured to negotiate his surrender and abdication in return for an earldom and lands in England, which Edward had offered to his previous great foe Llywelyn of Gwynedd in return for abdication, but was required to surrender unconditionally and did so. He was deliberately humiliated as he was ceremonially stripped of his kingly emoluments and even his heraldic 'tabard' (surcoat bearing his 'arms') in a series of staged events in major eastern Scots towns, culminating in his deposition. (Hence his later sobriquet, 'Toom Tabard' – 'Empty Coat'). Edward clearly wanted to show his foe's complete abasement, preventing him from rallying any support later, and the fate that met all who defied their lord, and once Balliol was deposed no new king was appointed to replace him. Scotland was annexed to England and all its separate administrative and judicial bodies were closed down, with the regalia, coronation-stone, and royal archives – anything portable that symbolized Scotland as a state, in fact – being removed to England. The Scots nobility were summoned to a Parliament at Berwick – rebuilt as an English town – to swear fealty to Edward as King of Scotland (and England?), with their submissions recorded on the so-called 'Ragman's Roll'.[66] The precise legal status that Scotland now held is unclear, but if it was still thought of as a 'state' it was in union with England under one ruler and was not to be governed by a council and administrators chosen exclusively from its own nationals (at least at first). This may have been a 'security measure' for wartime to ward off 'treachery' aided by the French rather than a long-term plan, and Edward's political decapitation of the nobility by deportations and obtaining hostages was effective in preventing most of the remaining elite joining any revolt. (He clearly ignored the lower orders, which provided the leadership of the 1297 revolt in the form of minor landowners William Wallace and knight Andrew Moray). The effective annexation paralleled what Edward had done in Wales in 1283–4, and English administrators were placed in charge of the new government – including the forceful and oppressive treasurer, Hugh Cressingham, who was to arouse intense resentment. To all intents, therefore, Scotland had ceased to exist as a political entity in July 1296.

The crisis of 1297: The context of Edward's presence at Winchelsea that August

The maintenance of a (small) 'army of occupation' backing up the English governor, Edward's cousin Aymer of Valence, and assorted garrisons in major ex-royal castles in Scotland in 1296–7 was thus added to the problems of the French war, Gascon campaign, Welsh garrisons, and subsidies to Continental allies to place England in a position of 'military over-stretch' and financial strain as of spring 1297. Worse, there were signs of fractures in the co-operation of the lay and ecclesiastical elites in England under the pressures of war and taxation, with the clergy refusing to agree to a tax proposed by the King at the Parliament at Bury St Edmunds in autumn 1296. They had a new leader as confrontational and fearless as the King in Archbishop Robert Winchelsey of Canterbury, and had already refused to increase a small grant of tax that the King regarded as inadequate a year before; now they had the papal bull 'Clericos Laicos' (which banned clerics from paying tax to fund lay governance) to back them up.[67] The Church council in London in January 1297 repeated the clergy's refusal to pay up all that was wanted or immediately with the bull as the perfectly valid reason – if they defied it they could be excommunicated by the Pope. The international Third Lateran Church Council of 1179 had, however, legalized the clergy paying tax to the lay power in a case of national danger, and the Archbishop pointed this out to the King as a way that both sides could 'save face' and reach a compromise. Instead Edward accused a clerical deputation of breaking their oaths of homage and said that that excused him from any obligations to them in return – thus unnecessarily exacerbating the crisis.[68]

Lay resistance to his demands followed at the next Parliament, led by the Earls of Norfolk (Roger Bigod) and Hereford (Humphrey Bohun) who both had personal grievances against the King over matters such as the military/ceremonial office of Marshal and debts (Bigod) and a dispute with the late Earl of Gloucester (Bohun). The ability of these normally quiescent nobles to stir up the other peers was worsened by the lack of other equally high-ranked earls to oppose them; Edward's brother Edmund of Lancaster and son-in-law Gloucester had recently died, Edward's cousin the Earl of Cornwall and the Earl of Lincoln were fighting in Gascony, and his other cousin Earl Warenne was military governor of Scotland. Another senior peer, Arundel, had already objected to fighting abroad. Despite this threat and the earlier opposition, Edward did not tread cautiously. The clergy had their lay fees and goods confiscated, with the proviso that they could halt this by paying a fine to the King equivalent to the tax of 'a fifth', which they had earlier refused to grant; most gave in to this naked extortion. The (lay) Salisbury Parliament then saw Edward explicitly asking his assembled lords to fight overseas, and a blunt refusal to his face by some of them – who Edward then threatened to deprive of their lands. According to one version, Edward told the defiant Norfolk (who was not actually at the meeting) to 'by God, go or hang' and the Earl replied coolly 'By the same oath, O king, I shall neither go nor hang'.[69] The story gives the flavour of both men's attitude even if it is only hearsay.

The impasse continued, delaying the intended Gascon campaign, while Edward proceeded to use his administrative powers to sell goods confiscated from those clergy who were refusing to pay up. It was a throwback to the 'State vs Church' confrontation of his grandfather John's reign, with belligerent Pope Boniface VIII as determined to use his authority as Innocent III had been then. Archbishop Winchelsey, an overlooked figure in English history, was as uncowed by secular threats as Becket had been in the 1160s and arranged a legal appeal to Rome against any new royal legal aggression. However, the danger of a repeat of the crises of the 1160s and 1200s faded (though not thanks to royal compromise). The majority of the clergy decided at their next assembly to vote to follow their individual consciences over paying the fines – which in practice meant that the King would obtain the money he wanted – while preserving the principle of obeying the papal bull and not granting taxation.[70] The lay confrontation was not so easy to resolve, as although Parliament had granted the required taxes in November 1296 the King's belated summons to all his feudal vassals to assemble at or send troops to London on 7 July for a Continental campaign met widespread resistance. The order did not state the destination or give any explanation for the campaign beyond the 'salvation and general advantage of the realm', with no mention of feudal fealty as usual;[71] possibly this added to suspicion of Edward's intentions. In reply, Norfolk, Hereford, Arundel, and other leading magnates held an armed rally in the Welsh Marches – the first sign of potential defiance or coercion of the King since 1267 and an echo of the Montfortian assemblies of 1258–64 to intimidate the government. They decided that they were too impoverished by past wars and taxes to fight overseas. However, the evidence suggests that most of the attendees (even Norfolk) did anticipate that they would have to serve abroad eventually and continued to make arrangements to collect their vassals as ordered by Edward, so it was a dignified protest rather than the start of a civil war. Once they had made their point Norfolk and Hereford did go to London – where a further quarrel with the King over the nature of their summons led to him sacking them as Marshal and Constable of his armies.[72]

The protesting barons of 1215 had had the support of the Archbishop of Canterbury (Stephen Langton) in claiming that the King had exceeded his powers, and now Winchelsey reportedly assisted the protesters by saying that an overseas expedition should be put off until Edward had reached agreement with the Church (to avoid Divine wrath?). Edward was unimpressed, but he and the Archbishop reached an accommodation whereby the confiscated 'temporalities' (lay possessions) of the Church of

Canterbury would be restored and Winchelsey duly presided at the swearing of fealty to the King's heir Prince Edward. (This ceremony meant that if the King died overseas his heir could immediately call on the lay and clerical elite's support.) Norfolk and Hereford turned up to swear too as was legally required of them as royal vassals, but not with the main body of the peerage –with the citizens of London, long-term allies of the royal family's opponents from 1215–16 and 1258–65.[73]

The Archbishop mediated between Edward and the two Earls and their faction, but the latter now refused to attend the first planned conferences and when a meeting was finally held at Stratford-le-Bow Hereford demanded the reform of assorted abuses of power and governmental practice while assuring his personal goodwill to Edward. The opposition was thus both coalescing into a body of objectors keeping its distance from the court – which might mean a military clash was being prepared – and drawing up a statement of aims as in 1215, 1258 and 1263–4. A list of 'Remonstrances' was prepared, which included the lack of a destination given in the summons to the muster, a refusal to campaign in Flanders as it was not in the King's realm and the nation was impoverished by taxes, the harsh application of assorted laws (e.g. the 'Forest Laws'), arbitrary confiscation of subjects' legal franchises, excessive taxes (e.g. on wool), and the threat of the King's subjects being reduced to serfdom by all his financial demands. Breaches of Magna Carta were cited.[74] The language used was in some cases vague and generalized and Edward could complain that he had not actually levied certain specific forms of tax that were mentioned, but its general import was to rally support against a government seen as oppressive and arbitrary – as had been John's before 1215. All this was taking place, as the 'Remonstrances' pointed out, against a background of rising revolt in Scotland, which made the extra burden of a war in Flanders risky and untimely. The arguments were politically sophisticated and not unreasonable.

Edward's 'hard line' against the Church continued, as when the next clerical Assembly met the clergy refused to grant the requested tax unless the Pope gave his approval first and Winchelsey excommunicated all who were attacking Church property (i.e. selling it off for non-payment of fines as per the King's orders). In reply Edward ordered a new clerical tax of a fifth on their property or a third on their 'spiritualities', which was not paid in an effective 'tax strike'.[75] This reaction was to be expected. Meanwhile, a new royal summons for a muster at Winchelsea later that summer, issued in less provocative or demanding terms and explicitly offering wages unlike the earlier summons, met a poor response.[76] A new tax of an 'eighth' was announced, possibly agreed by the current Parliament but if so by a body without any magnates in attendance so not fully representative of all the 'estates', and a 'prise' (seizure and forced sale) of wool was arranged to raise extra cash – with compensation to follow after the current campaign. As stated in the King's documentary explanation of his current position, which did not deny but apologized for his unusually heavy financial demands, he was only seeking this extra revenue due to a national emergency and was not spending it on his own court or garrisons.[77] But the counter-argument was that the campaign was a burden too far and unnecessary. It was a battle of priorities – with both sides in entrenched positions and unwilling to compromise, and echoes of 1215, 1258, and 1264.

On 22 August, when the King had already arrived at Winchelsea for the muster, Norfolk and Hereford led a group of knights to appear at the Exchequer – the seat of royal financial governance – in Westminster Palace and Hereford announced their grievances. The first section dealt with the issues raised already in the 'Remonstrances'; the second was that the King's latest taxes (an eighth and a 'prise' of wool) were illegal as they had not been approved by the King's subjects in Parliament, though he was prepared to accept that the authorities had issued the tax-demands without the King's prior approval to 'cover' the King's reputation.[78]

The accident on the cliff: what if it had been fatal? Or what if there had been no Scots revolt and Edward had thus managed to prise Gascony away from France permanently?

The reality, August 1297 and later
It was at this juncture that the King had a near-fatal accident on the hill at the town of Winchelsea – that is, the new fortified town that he had personally founded on the hill overlooking the Brede valley (then an estuary) as a replacement for the exposed port of 'Old Winchelsea' on the 'Levels' below which was being eaten away by the sea. A rising sea-level plus extreme weather events were as much of a threat on Romney Marshes in the late thirteenth century as seven centuries later, and the coast was sinking. At the time, the line of coast was probably some way out to sea from its current position in Rye Bay – and the effects of erosion have been so severe that although the area lost in the Late Medieval period has been exposed again no trace of the old town remains. The shifting sea-level was currently seeing the English Channel rise over marshes exposed since Roman times while the current carried coastal soil up-Channel to be dumped on the spit at Dungeness across the Bay. The coast was being eaten away with only soft soil underfoot, and the exposed coastal port of 'Old Winchelsea' had been battered by severe storms throughout the thirteenth century and was mostly

destroyed by one in 1287. The storm, coming after two other similar ones in 1250 and 1252 according to Matthew Paris, also blocked the mouth of the River Rother East of (Old) Romney to the North-East, causing the river to flow into a new channel down from the Isle of Oxney to Rye. Edward founded a new town on the clifftop a couple of miles inland from Old Winchelsea, and bought up the land involved. This town was more or less complete by 1297 – the 'grid-pattern' layout, based on those of new towns built in Gascony, is still preserved today but the town has shrunk so much that most of it is now fields rather than buildings. The Brede estuary below was used as a harbour, then being protected from the sea by a spit of land extending out north-eastwards to the site of the later Camber Castle (1530s).

It was while Edward was riding on the clifftop overlooking his ships in the Brede estuary, at the north end of the town, that his horse became startled by the wind moving the sails of a nearby windmill (the ruins of the successor of this were finally destroyed by the hurricane in 1987). It reared and nearly threw him at the edge of the cliff, but he was able to land safely as it leaped in the air on the hillslope and plunged down onto lower ground below. It landed on its feet to the surprise of observers, and the King escaped a nasty accident.[79] But he was within inches of disaster – what if he had been thrown down the steep hillside and killed, or rolled on? As events turned out, Edward sailed from Winchelsea to Flanders with his truncated army on 23 August, leaving most of the senior nobles and gentry behind in England where the confrontation between government and the Norfolk/Hereford faction continued. Technically Prince Edward, aged thirteen, was in command of the government and had the right to demand support by the oaths of fealty taken to him, but in practice his father's administrators and senior loyal peers were in political command. Indeed, the absence of the outspoken and confrontational King probably aided a peaceful resolution. A summons of assorted knights was called to meet the Prince at Rochester Castle on 8 September – 170 men on 20 August and 56 more on the 28th, all asked to bring weapons and horses so presumably ready to form a military force if needed to confront Norfolk and Hereford.[80] Meanwhile, a royal official went to Canterbury to order the Archbishop not to take any action against the King or his supporters, e.g. by excommunication. A Parliament was summoned to Westminster for the end of September, where the news of the defeat of the government's forces in Scotland by Wallace's rebels at Stirling Bridge served to reinforce royalist arguments that the King's claims of a national crisis were correct and security required a compromise or delayed solution not a 'showdown'. The 'opposition', however, demanded that a series of additions be made to the existing limitation of royal powers – especially over raising taxes – in Magna Carta. This document, 'De Tallagio', banned any 'tallage' or 'aid' unless it was granted by the consent of all citizens, from archbishops to freemen, and limited 'prises' (seizures of goods for sale) to those approved first by the victims. Other taxes were abolished, and all who had refused to go to Flanders were to be pardoned – a necessity given Edward's usual legal vindictiveness to opponents ever since 1265. In reply, the government agreed to issue a new statement of restrictions on royal financial exactions in a separate document ('Confirmaton Cartarum') but not to add this onto Magna Carta, to confirm the latter and the 'Forest Charter' (on ending pre-1215 abuses of forest law), and to ask the King to pardon those who had refused to go to Flanders. Aids, prises and so on were not to be raised in future without consent – though this did not explicitly state whose consent in detail or say that this had to be in Parliament.[81] This compromise was acceptable to both parties, and the King grudgingly gave it his assent at Ghent on 5 November; the campaign 'refuseniks' were pardoned but soon faced evidence of the King's continuing ill-will to their leadership in terms of future employment and the outcome of legal cases.

The political crisis was thus resolved without Edward's presence, and that probably aided a peaceful settlement and avoidance of the military demonstrations of 1262–3 and armed conflict of 1264–5. In any case, once he was abroad Edward seems to have regarded his campaign as the priority, although he had only around 800 cavalry and under 8,000 infantry to use due to the English boycotts.[82] (By contrast, the well-supported campaign to attack Scotland in 1298 was to have an army around 30,000 strong.) His presence in Flanders lacked the expected help of Adolf of Nassau, 'King of the Romans' (i.e. Holy Roman Emperor-elect) and his Rhineland troops, but it induced Philip to come to terms, with a truce being mediated by the archbishop-elect of Dublin and signed on 9 October 1297. Pope Boniface then mediated a long-term peace, with the Scots rebellion meaning that even if Edward had been able to use the domestic English reconciliation to issue summons and pay for a new army in 1298 he would have needed this to fight in Scotland first. As a result, Edward had no diplomatic leverage to use on Philip and had to agree to the Pope's decision that the 'status quo ante' be restored and he should resume his position as a French vassal for his rule of Gascony. (Boniface also commented on his naivety in 1294 in accepting Philip's ruse and handing over Gascony.[83])

Other possible outcomes
The Wallace/Moray revolt of 1297 thus played a role in Edward failing to have the time and resources in 1298–9 to retake Gascony by force and end its role as a vassal of France. His large army raised in 1298 had to be used against Scotland, where he had lost control of most of the country in a

genuine and widely supported 'people's revolt' (as made much of ever since by Scots writers and by film-makers). As a result, he had to accept what terms were available in France in 1298 – although it is possible that the unwillingness that many of his vassals had shown to fighting abroad in 1295 and 1297 would also have hampered him in 1298 (even if no Scots occupation had entailed lower taxes in England and so less unrest). This had long-term consequences in that future French kings could threaten to confiscate Gascony again and receive legal appeals from anti-English subjects there (as seen in 1337 and 1369–70). Without a Scots revolt in 1297, would Edward – fighting on one 'front', not two – have managed to reconquer Gascony or else led a Low Countries/German expedition south-west into Artois and Picardy in 1298, forcing Philip to negotiate on weaker terms? A 'thrust' from Flanders on Paris had failed in 1214, but then the English King had not been leading his army in person – and this was to be the major threat to French power for centuries to come, as seen in 1870, 1914, and 1940. Once Philip had handed Gascony back to save Paris, Edward could proclaim himself its sovereign ruler and end the burdensome vassalage to France – meaning that he and his heirs would not face appeals from his subjects there to French courts in future or demands to do homage. Would this have avoided the clashes between England and France that centred on the confiscation of Gascony? It would not have prevented the clashes from 1337 over Edward III's claim to all of France, but a lasting peace-treaty would have been easier had the Gascony issue not constantly been available as a weapon for the French Kings to use. Arguably, then, the long-term effects of Edward deciding to confiscate the Kingdom of Scots in 1296 and 'round off' his domination of the British Isles lost him a major chance of securing an Anglo-French settlement in 1298–9, by driving the humiliated Scots to rebel in 1297. But a word of caution should be added – if Edward had chosen a new King of Scots (Robert Bruce's father or John 'the Red' Comyn?) in 1296 this man might still have allied to France in a future Anglo-French war and faced invasion and deposition by a vengeful Edward. And even if Edward had secured full control of Gascony in 1298–9 the humiliated Philip IV or his heirs were capable of attacking it once England was in difficulties elsewhere.

The question of what would have happened had Edward been killed in the riding-accident at Winchelsea also has major implications for international history. In domestic terms, his thirteen-year-old son's regency government would have had to accept the demands of the Norfolk/Hereford faction to ward off an unwelcome armed confrontation and weld together the fractured nobility ready to take on the Scots in 1298. But the overall result would not have been far different from the Prince's advisers' agreement with the 'opposition' in real life. This involved banning controversial taxes, issuing documentary ratification of new restrictions on arbitrary rule, and promising more consultation on legislative measures – probably with the latter 'tightened up' to give a larger role explicitly to Parliament. The largest possible army would have marched into Scotland to rescue Earl Warenne's embattled regime as in real life, though not led by Edward I – the most experienced royal commander would have been Edward's cousin Earl Edmund of Cornwall not the genealogically senior Earl Thomas of Lancaster, his nephew.

The weight of numbers would have given it victory at Falkirk as in real life, and the surviving rebels would have been driven to resume an exhausting guerrilla war. But would Earl Edmund and Warenne have had the tenacity (or obsessiveness?) of Edward I in pressing on year after year for victory at all costs? Maintaining garrisons in the Lowlands and along the eastern coast to Inverness would have held down the countryside and intimidated the landed nobility into co-operation for a number of years, but not indefinitely. Would the unwarlike Edward II, fourteen in 1298 and probably reaching his majority in the early 1300s, have decided that he would rather cut back on this costly war (which he was unlikely to have led for long in person) and have recognized one of the rival contenders as King of Scots as his vassal? Restoring Balliol was unlikely, given his lack of interest in the Scots Crown after 1296 in real life – Pope Boniface insisted on having him handed over to the papacy in the Anglo-French treaty and he settled on his French estates. He never accepted offers from his partisans in Scotland to return home and head the rebellion, though their leaders as of 1300–1303 were still calling themselves his representatives. The most likely contender for the role of Scots vassal-king was the younger Robert Bruce, as the heir of the senior line from Earl David of Huntingdon; his father died in 1304. He showed no sign of eagerness to desert the winning English side in 1304–1305 in real life – for which he is still criticized by some nationalists – and when he did revolt was apparently driven to act prematurely by his rival John Comyn threatening to betray their plans to the English King. He had to leave the English court in a hurry and flee back to Scotland, and then murdered Comyn at an interview at Dumfries and claimed the throne. (Without this, Bruce might well have waited until Edward I died.)

Accordingly, it is likely that Robert Bruce would have been a vassal of the English kings by the early 1300s as in reality, and if he found Edward II's interest in the war flagging he would have 'lobbied' for the vacant Crown. However, Edward II was not a 'peace at any price' man despite the contrast between him and his father and his dislike of the most militant of his peers, the Earls of Warwick, Pembroke and Lancaster. He was persistent in holding out rather than negotiating his way out of the Scots quagmire as his military position collapsed in real-life 1310 to 1314, and was not quick to recognize political reality thereafter, so it could well have taken time for him to accept that he needed to abandon his claim to the Scots throne and recognize a client-king. The best that can be said in the Scots crisis is that he would have committed fewer atrocities than his father did – and annoyance at his abandoning his Scots claim in the mid-late 1300s could have given his nobles more cause for grievances against him.

In matters of Continental 'foreign policy' from 1297 onwards, would Edward I's sudden death have emboldened Philip IV to refuse to return Gascony at all? And the regency in England have had to accept this in a peace-treaty so they could concentrate on the Scots war? In that case, England would have been forcibly 'disengaged' from its French ambitions in 1299 not in 1453, and not even possessed the town of Calais; Edward II would only have held the small and indefensible county of Ponthieu, which Philip would have easily overrun. But would a future military king such as Edward III still endeavoured to reconquer Aquitaine to avenge this humiliation? The English monarchs were still attempting to reconquer and then to hold Normandy – lost in 1204 – as late as 1415–50, so the loss of Gascony need not have improved Anglo-French relations long-term. Continental warfare and dynastic claims were too ingrained in the English monarchy's priorities for the loss of Gascony in 1299 to be seen as 'final'.

Notes

Chapter One: The Norman State

1. Orderic Vitalis, *Historia Ecclesiastica*, ed. and tr. Marjorie Chibnall, 6 vols (Oxford 1969–80) book iv, pp. 94–6; William of Malmesbury, *Gesta Regum Anglorum*, ed. and tr. R.A.B. Mynors (Oxford University Press 1998) vol ii, pp. 337–8; John Le Patourel, 'The Norman Succession 996 – 1131' in *EHR* vol 86 (1971) pp. 225–34; John Beckerman, 'Succession in Normandy, 1087, and in England, 1066: the role of testamentary custom' in *Speculum*, vol 47 (1972) pp. 258–60; Frank Barlow, *William Rufus* (Yale UP, 2000 edition) pp. 40–50.
2. Orderic, vol iv, p.94; William of Malmesbury, *Gesta Regum*, vol ii, p. 468.
3. Ibid., pp. 59–60; Orderic, vol ii, p. 357.
4. Orderic, vol ii, ch. 358–60.
5. William of Malmesbury, vol ii, ch. 460.
6. See David Douglas, *William the Conqueror* (Berkeley UP, 1964) pp. 356–8.
7. William of Malmesbury, vol ii, pp. 360–3; Barlow, *William Rufus*, pp. 74–82.
8. Hermann of Tournai, *Liber de restoratione monastery Sancti Martini tornacensis*, ed. G. Waitz, in *Monumenta Germania Historia*, vol 14 (Berlin 1956) pp. 278–81. Frank Barlow believes this to be gossip rather than an accurate story.
9. Eadmer, *Historia Novorum in Anglia*, ed. Martin Rule (Rolls Series vol. 81, London 1884) pp. 121–4; Warren Hollister, *Henry I* (Yale UP 2001), pp. 128–30.
10. Eadmer, pp. 47–9; William of Malmesbury, vol ii, pp. 369–70.
11. Orderic, book v, pp. 284–8.
12. Florence of Worcester, *Chronicon ex Chronicis*, ed. B. Thorpe, 2 vols (London 1848–9), vol ii, pp. 31–2; Orderic, vol iv, pp. 270–2; *The Anglo-Saxon Chronicle*, tr. Michael Swanton (Dent 1996) p. 228.
13. Orderic, book vi, pp. 210–12.
14. See also Orderic, book iv, ch. 220 on Robert's incompetence and weak rule at a time when his brothers were not yet undermining him.
15. Orderic, book iii, p. 115.
16. William of Malmesbury, book ii, p. 467; Hollister, *Henry I*, pp. 33, 36–7; Charles David, 'The Claim of King Henry to be Called Learned' in *Anniversary Essays in Medieval History Presented to RHC Davis*, ed. H. Mayr-Harting and R. I. Moore (London 1985) pp. 45–55. For the idea of a Church career as Henry's destination, see Matthew Paris, *Chronica Majora* (Rolls Series 1872-83), vol i, p. 102 and vol ii p. 130.
17. Orderic, book v, p. 292; William of Malmesbury, vol ii, p. 378.
18. Abbot Suger, *The Life of King Louis VI*, ed. Wacquet, p. 102; see also discussion in D. Grinnell-Milne, *The Killing of King Rufus* (Newton Abbot 1968).

19. See Emma Mason, 'William Rufus and the Historians' in *Medieval History*, vol i (1991) pp. 6–22.
20. See also J. H. Round, *Feudal England* (London 1895) p. 72 on the de Clare connection of the group of men in attendance on the King when he was killed.
21. Orderic, vol v, pp. 284–8.
22. Ibid.; and Warren Hollister, *Monarchy, Magnates and Institutions in the Anglo-Norman World* (London 1986) pp. 62–4.
23. Order, book v, pp. 288–9.
24. See Barlow, *William Rufus*, p. 420 and n.
25. William of Malmesbury, vol ii, p. 378.
26. Orderic, book v, p. 292.
27. *The Anglo-Saxon Chronicle*, tr. Swanton, p. 237; Florence of Worcester, book ii, pp. 48–9.
28. Eadmer, p. 127.
29. Ibid., p. 125.
30. Ibid., p. 126.
31. Ibid, p. 127; William of Malmesbury, book ii, p. 471. On the Treaty of Alton: William of Malmesbury, p. 472, Florence of Worcester, vol ii, p.49; Orderic, book v, pp. 316–18.
32. Henry of Huntingdon, pp. 482, 594, 836–7; John of Worcester, *Chronicle*, ed. J. R. Weaver (Oxford 1908) p. 29; Hollister, *Henry I*, p. 316.
33. Ibid., pp.316–18.
34. William of Malmesbury, vol ii, p. 496.
35. Ibid., pp. 496–8; Orderic, book vi, p. 296; Eadmer, pp. 288–9; Henry of Huntingdon, pp. 466 and 594.

Chapter Two: Civil War: Stephen Versus Matilda

1. William of Malmesbury, vol ii, pp. 457–8; Orderic, vol vi, chs. 448; analysis in Hollister, *Henry I*, pp. 476–7.
2. Robert of Torigny, book ii, ch. 240; M. Chibnall, *The Empress Matilda* (Oxford 1991) p. 56.
3. William of Malmesbury, p. 3; John of Worcester, p. 27; Hollister, *Henry I*, pp. 309–10. On Geoffrey's destined role as Matilda's army-commander, see Orderic book vi, ch. 482; on resistance to Matilda's nomination by Bishop Roger of Salisbury, see Hollister *Henry IV*, p. 315.
4. William of Malmesbury, pp. 24–5; Chibnall, *Empress Matilda*, pp. 60–62.
5. Orderic, book vi, chs. 446–7.
6. *Gesta Stephani*, ed. K. Potter and R.H.C. Davis (Old Medieval Texts 1976) pp. 10–12.
7. Henry of Huntingdon, *Chronicle*, ed. Diana Greenway (Old Medieval Texts, 1996) p. 476; Hollister, *Henry I*, p. 323.
8. William of Malmesbury, p. 13.
9. Orderic, book vi, ch. 446.
10. Edmund King, *King Stephen* (Yale UP, 2010) pp. 54–6, 59–64, 130–35.
11. Ibid., p. 130 and n.
12. Ibid., pp. 79–81.
13. William of Malmesbury, chs. 63–4; *Gesta Stephani*, ed. K. Potter and R.H.C. Davis (Old Medieval Texts, 1976) chs. 88–9.
14. William of Malmesbury, chs. 40–43; John of Worcester, book iii, chs. 248–9; Orderic book vi, chs. 514–17.
15. William of Malmesbury, chs. 38–9.
16. Orderic book vi, chs. 484–5.

17. John of Worcester, chs. 242–3.
18. Henry of Huntingdon, chs. 708–709; John of Worcester, chs. 216–17.
19. William of Malmesbury, chs. 42–3.
20. *Gesta Stephani*, chs. 88–9; John of Worcester, chs. 268–9.
21. Orderic, book vi, chs. 520–23; John of Worcester, chs. 250–1.
22. Orderic, chs. 520–1.
23. *Gesta Stephani*, chs. 90–3.
24. See *History of William the Marshal*, book 11; David Crouch, *William Marshal* (London 1990), chapter 1.
25. *Gesta Stephani*, chs. 142–3; Henry of Huntingdon, chs. 742–3; William of Malmesbury, chs. 132–3.
26. King, *King Stephen* (Yale UP 2011), pp. 138–43.
27. Henry of Huntingdon, chs. 726–37; William of Malmesbury, chs. 84–5; Orderic, chs. 542–5; John of Hexham, 'Continuation of the Chronicle of Simeon of Durham', in Simeon of Durham, *Opera*, book ii, ed. T. Arnold (Rolls Society 1882-5) vol ii pp. 307–8.
28. Henry of Huntingdon, chs. 718–19.
29. See note 15.
30. Orderic, book vi, chs. 546–51.
31. Robert of Torigny, p. 132.
32. *Gesta Stephani*, chs. 118–19.
33. Chibnal, *Empress Matilda*, p. 100.
34. Henry of Huntingdon, chs.744–5; Gervase of Canterbury, vol I, pp. 128–9; *The Chronicle of Waltham Abbey*, ed. Leslie Watkiss and M. Chibnall (Old Medieval Texts 1994) pp. 78–81; *The Chronicle of Ramsey Abbey*, pp. 331–2.
35. Gervase of Canterbury, vol I, p. 155; *Gesta Stephani*, chs. 238–9.
36. Chibnall, *Empress Matilda*, pp. 101–3; also Chibnall, 'The Empress Matilda and Church Reform' in *Transactions of the Royal Historical Society*, 5th series, vol 38 (1988) pp. 114–17.
37. John of Worcester, chs. 296–7; *Gesta Stephani*, chs. 124–5.
38. Ibid, chs. 118–35; William of Malmesbury, chs. 100–105; John of Worcester, chs, 298–303; Henry of Huntingdon, chs. 102–5; also Rosalind Hill, 'The battle of Stockbridge 1141' in *Studies in Medieval History Presented to R Allan Brown*, ed. C. Harper-Bill et al. (Woodbridge 1989) pp. 173–7.
39. William of Malmesbury, chs. 126–31.
40. William of Malmesbury, chs. 742–3.
41. Chibnall, *Empress Matilda*, pp. 109–12.
42. William of Tyre, book xvii, chs. 13–14, pp. 779–83.
43. *Gesta Stephani*, ch. 142; Gervase of Canterbury, vol. I, ch. 141; John of Hexham, in Simeon of Durham, chs. 322–3.

Chapter Three: The Collapse of the 'Angevin Empire'

1. William of Newburgh, *Historia Regnum Anglicanum*, ed. R. Howlett in *Chronicles and Memorials of the Reigns of Stephen, Henry II and Richard I* (Rolls Series 1884) vol i, pp. 112–13. Discounted by W. L. Warren in his *Henry II* (Methuen 1973) pp. 46–7.
2. J Broussard, *Le Comté d'Anjou sur Henri Plantagenet et ses Fils (1151–1204)* (Paris 1938) pp. 72–3; William of Newburgh, vol I, p. 114 on Henry's offer of Nantes to his brother.
3. Robert de Torigny, in *Chronicles and Memorials of the Reigns of Stephen, Henry II and Richard I*, vol iv p. 228; also B. A. Pocquet du Haut-Juisse, 'Les Plantagenets et la Bretagne' in *Annales de Bretagne*, vol liii (1946) pp. 1–27. On John in Ireland, Giraldus

Cambrensis, *Opera*, ed. J. S. Brewer, J. F. Dimmock, and G. F. Warner, 8 vols (Rolls Series 1861–91) vol v, pp. 388–95 and Roger of Howden, *Gesta Regni Henrici Secundi*, ed. W. Stubbs, 2 vols (Rolls Series 1867) vol I p. 339.

4. Roger of Howden, *Gesta* vol I, pp. 5–6; Roger of Howden, *Chronica*, ed. W. Stubbs, 4 vols (Rolls Series 1868–71) vol ii, pp. 4–5; Robert of Torigny, p. 245; Gervase of Canterbury, *Historical Works*, ed. W. Stubbs, 2 vols (Rolls Series 1879–80) vol I pp. 219–20. On Henry the Younger's arrogance and quarrels with his father: Roger of Howden, *Gesta*, vol I, p. 42, *Chronica*, vol ii, pp. 41–5; Gervase of Canterbury, vol I, p. 242; Robert of Torigny, pp. 255–6; William of Newburgh, vol I pp. 169–70.

5. A. Richard, *Histoire des Comtes de Poitou 778–1204*, 2 vols (Paris 1903) vol ii pp. 150, 161; on Richard's refusal to do homage, Roger of Howden, *Gesta*, vol I, p. 292.

6. Gervase of Canterbury, vol i, p. 208 and vol ii p. 79; Robert of Torigny p. 240.

7. *The History of William Marshal*, ed. A. S. Holden, S. Gregory, and D. Crouch, 2 vols (2002), vol I, p. 101; R. J. Smith, 'Henry II's heir: the Acts and Seals of Henry the Young King 1170-83' in *EHR* vol cxvi (2001), pp. 297–326.

8. Giraldus Cambrensis, vol viii, pp. 295–6.

9. Roger of Howden, *Gesta*, vol i, pp. 308–12.

10. Ibid., p. 319; Roger of Howden, *Chronica* p. 288; Warren, *Henry II*, p. 611.

11. Roger of Howden, *Gesta*, vol ii p. 7. On Richard's possible homosexuality, see John Gillingham, *Richard I* (Yale UP 1999) pp. 265–6.

12. Giraldus, vol viii pp. 177–9; Roger of Howden, *Gesta*, vol I p. 297.

13. Ibid., vol ii, pp.70-1; *Chronica*, vol ii, pp. 365–6.

14. Giraldus, vol iv pp. 369–72; vol viii, pp. 282–3, 286–7, 294–9; Gervase of Canterbury, vol ii, pp. 447–9; Roger of Howden, *Gesta*, vol ii, pp. 67–71, *Chronica*, vol ii, pp. 363–7.

15. Gillingham, *Richard I*, pp. 234, 243–4.

16. Gillingham, p. 126.

17. Ibid., p. 123.

18. Gervase of Canterbury, vol I p. 435; *Radulfi de Diceto Decani Londoniensis Opera Historica* (Ralph of Diceto), ed. W. Stubbs, 2 vols (Rolls Series 1876) vol ii, pp. 57–8.

19. Roger of Howden, *Gesta*, vol ii, pp. 104–5; Ralph of Diceto, vol ii, pp. 73–7.

20. Roger of Howden, *Gesta*, vol ii, pp. 166–7.

21. Adam of Eynsham, *Magna Vita Sancti Hugonis*, ed. D. L. Doucie and H. Farmer, 2 vols (Edinburgh 1962) vol ii, p. 104; for a defence of John's piety, see Jim Bradbury, 'Philip Augustus and King John' in S. D. Church, ed., *King John: New Interpretations* (Boydell and Brewer 1999) p. 350.

22. E.g. Shakespeare, *King John*, Act 5 scene 7, concluding lines. See also Olivier de Laborderie, 'L'Image de Richard Coeur de Lion dans La Vie et La Mort du Roi Jean de Guillaume Shakespeare' in J. Nelson (ed.), *Coeur De Lion: History and Myth* (London 1992) pp. 141–65.

23. Roger of Howden, *Chronica*, vol iii pp. 288–90.

24. For the argument that the Norman barons were too financially exhausted by 1199 to want to pay or fight to defend Normandy, see J. C. Holt, 'The end of the Anglo-Norman realm' in *Proceedings of the British Academy* vol lxi (1975) pp. 223–65 and Holt, 'The loss of Normandy and Royal finance' in Church, *King John: New Interpretations*, pp. 117–36; also N. Barratt, 'The Revenues of John and Philip Augustus Revisited' in ibid, pp. 75–9. For a decrease in Norman revenues before 1199, see R. V. Turner, 'Good or Bad Kingship: the Case of Richard the Lionheart' in *Haskins Society Journal*, vol 8 (1999) pp. 73–8. For the view that it was mainly John to blame, see Frank McLynn, *Lionheart and Lackland: King Richard, King John and the Wars of Conquest* (Vintage 2007) pp. 320–23.

25. Ralph of Coggeshall, *Chronicon Anglicanum*, ed. J. Stevenson (Rolls Series 1875) pp. 152–3 on the 1205 barons' 'strike'.
26. William le Breton, 'Gesta Philippi Augusti' in *Oeuvres de Rigord et de Guillaume le Breton*, ed. H. Delaborderie (Paris 1882) pp. 212–18; W. L. Warren, *King John*, pp. 93–5; McLynn, *Lionheart and Lackland*, p. 310.
27. See *Annales Monastici*, vol i, p. 27 on the probable events of Arthur's killing. For the popular version, see Shakespeare, *King John*, Act four, scene 1.
28. Gillingham, *Richard I*, pp. 256–7.
29. Ralph of Coggeshall, pp. 94–6; Roger of Howden, *Chronica*, vol iv, p. 84.
30. Gillingham, p. 228.
31. Roger of Howden, *Gesta*, vol ii, pp. 236–7; Richard of Devizes, *Cronicon*, ed. and tr. J. T. Appleby (London 1963) pp. 60–61.
32. Roger of Howden, *Chronica*, vol iii pp. 206–7.
33. Ibid.; Ralph of Coggshall, p. 61.
34. Roger of Howden, *Gesta*, vol ii, pp. 90–91.
35. William of Newburgh, book iv, chapter 5.
36. Richard of Devizes, p. 6.
37. The main proponent of this theory is J. C. Holt.
38. E.g. song written down by Geoffrey de Vinsauf in *The Poetica Nova of Geoffrey de Vinsauf*, tr. M. Nims (Toronto 1963) pp. 28–31.
39. Ralph of Coggeshall, pp. 97–8.
40. Roger of Howden, *Gesta*, vol ii, p. 183; later also Jean de Joinville in his *Chronicle of the Crusades*, tr. M. R. B. Shaw (Harmondsworth 1963) pp. 304–5.
41. Richard of Devizes, pp. 46–7.
42. Gillingham, *Richard I*, pp. 231–2.
43. *Oeuvres de Rigord et de Guillaume Le Breton*, ed. M. F. Delaborde, 2 vols (Paris 1882–5) pp. 120–1.
44. Roger of Howden, *Gesta*, vol ii, pp. 229–30 and 236–7.
45. McLynn, p. 220.
46. Ralph of Coggeshall pp. 53–4.
47. Roger of Howden, *Gesta*, vol I, pp. 185–6, *Chronica*, vol iii, pp. 195–6; Ralph of Coggeshall pp. 54–6.
48. *Chroniques de St Martial*, ed. H. Duples-Agier (Paris 1874) p. 192.
49. Gillingham, pp. 235–7.
50. Roger of Howden, *Chronica*, vol iii, pp. 206–7.
51. Ibid., pp. 198–9.
52. Roger of Howden, *Gesta*, vol ii, pp. 132–8.
53. *Chronica*, vol iii, pp. 225–7.
54. Giraldus, vol viii, pp. 177–9.
55. Ralph of Coggeshall, pp. 180–84; Roger of Wendover, pp. 380–83.
56. Roger of Wendover, vol iii, p. 171.
57. William of Newburgh, vol i, p. 521.
58. Roger of Howden, *Chronica*, vol iv, p. 120; Kate Norgate, *John Lackland* (1902) pp. 76–7; F. A. Cazel and S. Painter, 'The marriage of Isabella of Angouleme' in *EHR*, vol lxiii (1948) pp. 85–6.
59. Warren, *Henry II*, p. 302.
60. On the de Braose executions by starvation: Ralph of Coggeshall p. 164. On the execution of the Welsh hostages, see *Brut y Tywysogion*, ed. T. Jones (Cardiff University Press 1955) pp. 89–92.
61. See J. Gillingham, *Richard I*, pp. 236 and 239.

62. See N. Barratt, 'The Revenues of King John' in *EHR* vol cxi (1996).

63. Gillingham, pp. 317–20.

64. John of Salisbury, *Materials for the History of Thomas Becket*, ed. J. C. Robinson (London 1859): *Epistolae*, vol v, p. 381.

65. Roger of Howden, *Chronica*, vol iv, p. 66.

66. Ralph of Diceto, vol I, pp. 383–4; Gervase of Canterbury, vol I, pp. 248–9; Roger of Howden, *Gesta* vol I, p. 72 and *Chronica*, vol ii, pp. 61–3; William of Newburgh, vol i, pp. 183–9; Herbert of Bosham, *Vita Sancti Thomae Archiepiscopi et Martyris*, ed. J. C. Robertson in *Materials for the History of Thomas Becket* vol iii, p. 92.

67. W. L. Warren, *King John*, pp. 171–2.

68. Matthew Paris recounts the story of how John sent an ambassador to the ruler of Morocco, An-Nasir of the Almohad dynasty, offering to turn Moslem in return for aid. Most modern historians discount this as gossip.

69. See C. R. Cheney, *From Becket to Langton: English Church Government 1170–1213* (Manchester 1956) p. 94; also Cheney et al., *Letters of Innocent III concerning England and Wales* (Oxford University Press 1967) p. 126. For the election dispute at Canterbury, see McLynn, pp. 372–3.

70. Warren, *King John*, pp. 171–2.

71. Pipe Rolls, 16 John (1214–15): pp. 215–16.

72. See *Annales Monastici*, vol ii, pp. 261 (blackmail over priests' concubines) and vol iv, p. 397 (demanding money from monks); also C. R. Cheney, 'King John and the Papal Interdict' in *Bulletin of the John Rylands Library*, vol xxxi (1948) pp. 304–11 and Cheney, 'King John's Reaction to the Interdict' in *Transactions of the Royal Historical Society*, 4th series, vol xxxi (1949) pp. 107–8; Chris Harper-Bill, 'King John and the Church of Rome' in Church (ed.), *King John: New Interpretations*, pp. 306–7.

73. See Cheney, ed., *Letters of Innocent III*, nos. 1013 (p. 169) and 1016 (pp. 169–70); also Roger of Wendover, vol iii, pp. 336–8 and C. R. Cheney, *Pope Innocent III and England* (Stuttgart 1976) pp. 374–80.

74. Cheney, *Letters of Innocent III*, pp. 212–16.

75. Elizabeth Hallam, *Capetian France 987–1328*, p. 188.

Chapter Four: Henry III and Simon de Montfort

1. For the two most notable instances of this, see Matthew Paris, vol v, pp. 515–16, 520–1, and 529–31 (political elite reaction to the cost of the 'Sicilian Business' under Henry III) and Michael Prestwich, *Edward I*, pp. 403–407 (elite reaction to the cost of Edward I's French war, 1294–7). The similar reaction to John's extortion in 1214–15 did not involve exclusively foreign policy.

2. *The Chronicle of Melrose*, intro. by A. O. and M. O. Anderson (London 1936) vol iv, pp. 209–13; R. C. Stacy, *Politics, Society and Finance under Henry III* (OUP 1987) pp. 182–200; C. Bemont, 'La Campagne de Poitou (1242–1243)' in *Annales du Midi*, vol 5 (1893) pp. 289–314.

3. *Chronicle of Melrose*, vol v, pp. 101–102.

4. Ibid., pp. 463, 475–6; also Margaret Howell, *Eleanor of Provence: Queenship in Thirteenth Century England* (Blackwell 1998) pp. 135–6 and 304. On Joan of Ponthieu, *Chronicle of Melrose*, vol iii pp. 327–8; *Foedera*, vol I, pp. 216–17; Howell, *Eleanor of Provence*, pp. 10–11.

5. *Foedera*, vol I pp. 217–18; Stacy, pp. 180–1.

6. For Isabella, see V. Nicholls 'Isabella of Angouleme: John's Jezebel' in S. D. Church, ed. *King John: New Interpretations* (Woodbridge 1999).

7. See D. Carpenter, 'The Fall of Hubert de Burgh' in *Journal of British Studies*, vol xix (1980) pp. 1–17.

8. On William of Savoy: *Annales Monastici*, ed. H. R. Luard, 5 vols (Rolls Series 1864–9) vol iii, pp. 493–5. On Eleanor, see *Flores Historiarum*, ed. H. R. Luard, 3 vols (Rolls Series 1890) vol ii, pp. 481–2. Also Annals of Dunstable in *Annales Monastici*, vol iii, p. 223.

9. J. R. Maddicott, *Simon de Montfort* (Cambridge UP, 1994) p. 1.

10. C. Bemont, *Simon de Montfort*, first edition (Paris 1884) p. 333; *Close Rolls 1227–31* (HMSO 1902 ff.) pp. 316, 543.

11. See M. Powicke, *The Thirteenth Century* (Oxford University Press 1962) p. 75.

12. Mathaei Parisiensis, Monachi Sancti Albani (i.e. Matthew Paris), *Chronica Majora*, ed. H. R. Luard, 7 vols (Rolls Series 1872–83), vol iii, pp. 411–12, 418.

13. Paris, *Chronica Majora*, vol iii, pp. 264, 369, 403–404; Annals of Dunstable, in *Annales Monastici*, vol iii, p. 144; *Calendar of Patent Rolls 1232–47* (HMSO 1906) p. 185.

14. Paris, vol iii, pp. 470–1, 475–6; Stacey, pp. 118–24; N. Denholm-Young, *Richard of Cornwall* (Oxford UP 1943) pp. 497–8.

15. Paris, vol v, p.235; *Chronicon de Lanercost*, ed. J Stevenson (Maitland Club 1839) p. 39.

16. Paris, vol iii, p. 566–7; Bemont, *Montfort*, pp.334–5; Stacey, pp. 126–7.

17. T. H. Turner, *Manners and Household Expenses of England in the Thirteenth and Fifteenth Centuries* (Roxburgh Club 1841) pp. xviii–xix; P Jackson, 'The End of Hohenstaufen Rule in Syria' in *BIHR*, vol lix (1986) pp. 20–36.

18. Bemont, *Montfort*, p. 334; *Calendar of Liberate Rolls: 1240–5* (HMSO 1916) p. 153.

19. Calendar of Patent Rolls 1232–47 (HMSO 1906 ff.) p. 314; Paris, vol iv, pp. 228–9, 231.

20. *Charter Rolls*, National Archives: C 53/36 mm. 1–2; C 53/37 mm. 1–7; C 53/38, m.11.

21. Paris, vol iv, p. 363, 366–8; vol v, pp. 6–8, 20–21.

22. NA: C 53/38, mm. 1–10; C 53/39, mm. 8–14; *Calendar of Close Rolls 1242–7*, pp. 268, 288, 326; *Calendar of Close Rolls 1247–51*, p. 249.

23. Maddicott, pp. 79–81; Paris, vol v, pp. 415–16. On Grosseteste rebuking de Montfort, Paris, vol iii, p. 479. On Fulk of Neiully and de Montfort's parents, see Monique Zerner, 'L'epouse de Simon de Montfort et la croisade albigose' in *Femmes – Mariages –Lignages, XII au XIV Siecle: Melanges Offerts à Georges Duby*, ed. J. Dufournet et al. (Brussels 1992) pp. 449–70.

24. F. Stevenson, *Robert Grosseteste, Bishop of Lincoln* (London 1889) pp. 269–75; also F. W. Southern, *Robert Grosseteste: the Growth of an English Mind in Medieval Europe* (Oxford 1986) pp. 244—6.

25. Paris, vol v, pp. 415–16.

26. C. H. Lawrence, 'The Letters of Adam Marsh and the Franciscan School at Oxford' in *Journal of Ecclesiastical History*, vol xlii (1991) pp. 218–19, 228–9; Bemont, *Montfort*, second edition (Oxford 1930) pp. 276–7.

27. David Carpenter, 'St Thomas Cantilupe: His Political Career' in *St Thomas Cantelupe, Bishop of Hereford*, ed. M. Jancey (Hereford 1982) pp. 60–63, 65–6. Also *Documents of the Baronial Movement of Reform and Rebellion, 1258–67*, ed. R. F. Treharne and S. J. Sanders (Oxford 1973) pp. 104–105, 200–201; *Chronicon vulgo dictum Chronicon Thomae Wykes, 1066–1288* (i.e. Thomas Wykes) in *Annales Monastici*, vol iv, p. 180.

28. Lawrence, 'Letters of Adam Marsh' p. 219, n.3; C. R. Cheney, *Medieval Texts and Studies* (Oxford 1973) p. 191; Bemont, *Montfort*, second edition, p. 41, n.2.; Maddicott, *Montfort*, pp. 85–6.

29. *Flores Historiarum*, vol ii, p. 227; Lanercost, pp. 39–40, 76–7; Paris, vol v, p. 1.

30. Paris, vol v, p. 290.

31. *Monumenta Franciscana*, ed. J. Brewer, R. Howlett, 2 vols (Rolls Series 1858–82) vol I, p. 111; Paris, vol v, pp. 116, 340–1; J. Richard, *St Louis: Crusader King of France*, ed. S. Lloyd (Cambridge UP 1992) pp. 283–4.

32. *Chronicle of Melrose*, pp. xix–xx, 136–44; *The Chronicle of William de Rishanger of the Barons' War: de Bellis*, ed. J. Halliwell (Camden Society 1840) pp. 6–7.

33. Bemont, *Montfort*, first edition, pp. 264–5; F. M. Powicke, *King Henry III and the Lord Edward*, 2 vols (Oxford 1947) vol I, pp. 208–114 on Gascony.

34. Paris, vol v, p. 93; Bemont, first edition, pp. 335–6 and 341–2.

35. Ibid, second edition, pp. 77–91; Paris, vol v, pp. 48 and 103–104; *Close Rolls of Henry III: 1247–51* (HMSO 1902 ff.) pp. 343–4; J. Ellis, 'Gaston de Bearn: a study in Anglo-Gascon relations, 1229–90', Oxford D. Phil thesis 1952.

36. Paris, vol v, pp. 277, 284; *Calendar of Patent Rolls 1247–58*, pp. 124, 132; *Close Rolls of Henry III: 1251–3*, pp. 203–5; Bemont, first edition, pp. 336, 342.

37. Maddicott, p. 116.

38. *Monumenta Franciscana*, vol I, pp. 127–8; *Foedera*, vol I, pp. 282–7; Bemont, first edition p. 340.

39. Bemont, first edition, pp. 337–43; *Calendar of Patent Rolls 1247–58*, p. 161.

40. Bemont, pp. 321–4, 340–41.

41. Paris, vol v, pp. 366, 371–2, 407, 415–16; Maddicott p. 121.

42. Matthew Paris, vol v, pp. 515–16; Howell, *Eleanor of Provence*, pp. 132–3.

43. Howell, Eleanor of Provence, pp. 131–4; E. L. Cox, *Eagles of Savoy: the House of Savoy in Thirteenth Century Europe* (Princeton 1974) p. 210; H. Ridgeway, 'The Politics of the English Court, 1247–1265, with special reference to the role of aliens', Oxford D Phil. Thesis 1983, pp. 163–6.

44. *Foedera*, vol I, p. 284; Paris, vol v, pp. 346—7; *Close Rolls 1251–3*, p. 449.

45. Paris, vol v, p 346–7.

46. *Les Registres de Alexander IV*, ed. C. Bourel de la Ronciere et al., 3 vols (Paris 1895–1953) pp. 89–90; S. D. Lloyd, *English Society and the Crusade, 1216–1307* (Oxford 1988) pp. 222–4.

47. Paris, vol v, pp. 475–82; for Louis IX's excuse over not returning Normandy, p. 483. On the investiture of Edmund, ibid p. 515, and *Foedera*, vol I, p. 316.

48. Maddicott, pp. 128–9.

49. Steven Runciman, *The Sicilian Vespers*, p. 61.

50. Powicke, *King Henry III and the Lord Edward*, pp. 374–5.

51. E. Jordan, *Les Origines de la Domination Angevine en Italie* (Paris 1909) pp. 536–8.

52. Steven Runciman, *The Sicilian Vespers: the Mediterranean World in the Thirteenth Century* (Cambridge UP 1958) p. 88.

53. Runciman, p. 62.

54. Michael Prestwich, *Edward I*, p. 10.

55. Maddicott, pp. 130–31 and 136–7.

56. *Calendar of Patent Rolls 1247–58*, p. 321; *Close Rolls 1253–4*, pp. 272–3.

57. *Calendar of Patent Rolls 1247–58*, pp. 411, 542; *Close Rolls 1254–6*, pp. 195-6.

58. Bemont, first edition, pp. 75–6.

59. Paris, vol iv, pp. 645–6 and vol v, pp. 649–60.

60. Labarge, *Montfort*, p. 136; Ellis, 'Gaston de Bearn...' pp. 391–2 and 395–9.

61. Paris, vol v, pp. 130–36, 634, 676–7; David Carpenter, 'What Happened in 1258?' in *War and Government in the Middle Ages; Essays in Honour of J O Prestwich*, eds. J. Gillingham and J. Holt (Boydell and Brewer 1984) p. 115, n.44.

62. *Flores Historiarum*, vol iii, p. 252.

63. Paris, vol v, pp. 73, 376–8, 494.

64. *Documents of the Baronial Movement*, pp. 268–79.
65. Paris, vol v, pp. 708–9; Carpenter, 'What Happened in 1258?', pp. 112–16.
66. Bemont, first edition, pp. 327–8; *Annales Monasterii de Theokesberia* (i.e. Tewkesbury) in *Annales Monastici*, vol I, pp. 163–6; Carpenter, pp. 106–16.
67. Paris, vol v, pp. 676–7, 689; Carpenter p. 116.
68. Carpenter, pp. 116–17; *Calendar of Patent Rolls 1247–58*, p. 627.
69. Ibid., p. 663; p. Chaplais, 'The Making of the Treaty of Paris (1259) and the Royal Style', in *EHR*, vol lxvii (1952) pp. 235–9.
70. Paris, vol v, pp. 295–6; *Close Rolls 1256–9*, pp. 294–6, 299; Rishanger, *de Bellis*, p. 9; *Flores Historiarum*, vol iii, p. 253; *Annales Monasterii de Burton, 1004–1263*, in *Annales Monastici*, vol i, p. 438.
71. *Documents of the Baronial Movement*, pp.76–91; p. Brand, 'The Drafting of Legislation in mid-thirteenth century England' in *Parliamentary History*, vol ix (1991) pp. 244–51 and 271–3.
72. H. G. Richardson and G. O. Sayles, 'The Provisions of Oxford 1258' in *Bulletin of the John Rylands Library*, vol xvii (1933) pp. 25–7; *Annales Monastici*, vol I pp. 171, 458. *Documents of the Baronial Movement*, pp. 72–3, 100–105.
73. *Annales Monastici*, vol I, p. 165.
74. *Documents of the Baronial Movement*, pp. 100–105, 112–13; *Calendar of the Patent Rolls 1247–58*, pp. 627–8.
75. Paris, vol v, p. 697; *Documents of the Baronial Movement*, pp. 258–9, 264–5; *The Chronicle of Walter of Guisborough*, ed. H. Rpothwell (Camden Series vol lxxxix, 1957) pp. 185–6.
76. *The Metrical Chronicle of Robert of Gloucester*, ed. W. A. Wright, 2 vols (Rolls Series 1887) vol ii, pp. 733–4; Rishanger, p. 8; *Flores Historiarum*, vol iii p. 252.
77. Lanercost p. 67; *Chronica Johannis de Oxenedes*, ed. H. Ellis (Rolls Series 1889) p. 225; Rishanger, pp. 16–17.
78. *New Dictionary of National Biography* article on de Burgh by F. J. West: vol viii, p. 780.
79. Paris, vol vi, pp. 410–16; R. F. Treharne, *The Baronial Plan of Reform 1258–63* (second edition, Manchester University Press 1971) pp. 106–7.
80. *Documents of the Baronial Movement*, pp. 112–15, 118–23; *Calendar of Patent Rolls 1247–58*, pp. 649, 654–5.
81. Paris, vol v, pp. 744–5; *Flores Historiarum*, pp. 424–5.
82. J. Richard, *St Louis*, p. 222; W. C. Jordan, *Louis IX and the Challenge of Crusade* (Princeton UP 1979) pp. 61–3, 158–71.
83. Powicke, *King Henry III and the Lord Edward*, p. 224 n.5; Maddicott, p. 173.
84. Paris, vol v, pp. 729–32; P. A. Brand, 'The Drafting of Legislation in Medieval England' in *Parliamentary History*, vol ix (1990) p. 262.
85. *Documents of the Baronial Movement*, pp. 122–31; Brand, pp. 251–64 and 273–85.
86. Paris, vol v, pp. 744–5; *Flores Historiarum*, vol ii, pp. 424–5.
87. D. Carpenter, 'The Lord Edward's Oath to aid and Counsel Simon de Montfort, 15 October 1259' in *BIHR*, vol lviii (1985) p. 231; *Treaty Rolls*, vol I (HMSO 1955) p. 48; Chaplais, pp. 244–5.
88. *Treaty Rolls*, vol I, pp. 49–51; Labarge, *Montfort*, p. 137; Ellis, 'Gaston de Bearn' pp. 397–9.
89. Documents of the Baronial Movement, pp. 204–5; Carpenter, 'The Lord Edward's Oath' p. 230.
90. Carpenter, pp. 229–35.
91. *Close Rolls 1259–61*, pp. 228, 235, 259, 267; *Documents of the Baronial Movement*, pp. 110–11, 164–9, 206–7.

92. Ibid pp. 170–71, 206–207; *The Baronial Plan of Reform*, pp. 214–15.
93. H. Ridgeway, 'The Lord Edward and the Provisions of Oxford (1258)' in *TCE*, vol I (1986) pp. 88–9 and 97–8; H. Ridgeway, 'The Politics of the English Court... ' pp. 336–46; Gervase of Canterbury, vol ii pp. 209–10; *The Baronial Plan of Reform*, pp. 193, 336–46.
94. *Flores Historiarum*, vol ii, pp. 446–8; *Annales Dunstabuli*, p. 214; Wykes, pp 123–4.
95. *Close Rolls 1259–61*, pp. 157–8; *Documents of the Baronial Movement*, pp. 180–2.
96. Ibid., pp. 206–209; *The Baronial Plan of Reform*, pp. 229–33; *Flores Historiarum*, vol ii, p. 449; E. Jacob, 'A Proposal for Arbitration between Simon de Montfort and Henry III in 1260' in *EHR*, vol xxxvii (1922) pp. 80–82: *Documents of the Baronial Movement*, pp. 104–105 and 258–9.
97. Chancery records: N A C 53/50, mm. 1–3; C 53/51, mm. 3–4; C 61/4, m. 1. *Flores Historiarum*, vol ii, pp. 254–5, 448, 456; Ridgeway, 'Politics of the English Court...', pp. 368–70;*Documents of the Baronial Movement*, pp. 212–13, 222–3. H. R. King, 'King Henry III's Grievances against the Council in 1261' in *Historical Research*, vol lxi (1988) pp. 231–42.
98. *Calendar of Patent Rolls 1258–66*, p. 97; *The Baronial Plan of Reform*, p. 246.
99. Ibid., pp. 249–50; *Documents of the Baronial Movement*, pp. 206–207; Wykes p. 124; Gervase of Canterbury,vol ii, p. 211; *Flores Historiarum*, vol ii, p. 456; *Calendar of Patent Rolls 1258–66*, pp. 126, 136; M. M. Wade Labarge, 'The Personal Quarrels of Simon de Montfort and His Wife with Henry III of England' in his Oxford B LItt. Thesis, 1939, pp. 51–60.
100. *Flores Historiarum*, vol ii pp. 463–4; *Documents of the Baronial Movement*, pp. 222–5, 236–7; *Calendar of Patent Rolls 1258–66*, pp. 145–50.
101. Gervase of Canterbury, vol ii, p. 211; *Flores Historiarum*, vol ii, p. 470; *Annales Londoniensis: Chronicles of the Reigns of Edward I and Edward II*, ed. W. Stubbs, 2 vols (Rolls Series 1882), vol I, p. 58.
102. *Baronial Plan of Reform*, pp. 267–9; *Close Rolls 1259–61*, pp. 489–90.
103. Baronial Plan of Reform, pp. 275–7; *Close Rolls 1259–61*, p. 497; *Close Rolls 1261–4*, p.125; *Calendar of Patent Rolls 1258–66*, pp. 178, 189, 191–3; *De Antiquis Legibus Liber Chronica Maiorum et Vicecomitum Londoniarum (Chronica Maiorum)* , ed. T. Stapleton (Camden Society 1846) p. 49; *Annales Dunstabuli*, p. 217; *Annales Monasterii de Oseneia, 1016–1347* (i.e. Oseney Abbey) in *Annales Monastici*, vol iv, p. 129.
104. Gervase of Canterbury, vol ii, pp. 214–21; M. Prestwich, *Edward I*, pp. 37–8; *Annales Dunstabuli*, p. 220.
105. *Chronica Maiorum*, pp. 52–3; *Annales Oseneia*, pp. 130–31; *Flores Historiarum*, vol I, p. 477; *Documents of the Baronial Movement*, pp. 295–6; *Baronial Plan of Reform*, p. 300; *Annales Dunstabuli*, pp. 217, 221; Gervase of Canterbury, vol ii, p. 217; Chaplais, pp. 241–2.
106. Prestwich, pp. 37–8; Denholm-Young, *Richard of Cornwall*, pp. 119–22; Maddicott, *Simon de Montfort*, pp. 225—6; *Annales Dunstabuli*, pp. 221–2; Gervase of Canterbury, vol ii, pp. 221–2; Rishanger, pp. 10—11; Wykes, p. 135; *Close Rolls 1264–8*, p. 512; *The Chronicle of Bury St Edmunds 1212–1301*, ed. A. Grasden (London 1964) p. 27; *Close Rolls 1263–4*, pp. 249–50, 369–70; *Chronica Maiorum*, pp. 53–5; Paris, vol iii, p. 28; E. F. Jacob, *Studies in the Period of Baronial Reform and Rebellion* (Oxford 1925) pp. 225–8; *Baronial Plan of Reform*, p. 387. D. Carpenter, 'King Henry III's "Statute Against Aliens": July 1263' in *EHR*, vol cvii (1992) pp. 925–44.
107. *Flores Historiarum*, vol ii, p. 481; *Chronica Maiorum*, p. 55; Gervase of Canterbury, vol ii, p. 222.
108. *Chronica Mairoum*, pp. 55–6; *Annales Dunstabuli*, pp. 222–3; Gervase of Canterbury, vol ii, p. 223.

109. *Chronica Maiorum*, p. 53; *Flores Historiarum*, vol ii, p. 484; and ibid. p. 481–2 for the attack on the Queen at London Bridge.

110. *Documents of the Baronial Movement*, pp. 110–11, 234–5.

111. Gervase of Canterbury, vol ii, p. 224; *Annales Dunstabuli*, p. 225; *Flores Historiarum*, vol ii, p. 484; *Baronial Plan of Reform*, pp. 319–20.

112. Gervase of Canterbury, vol ii, pp. 224–5; *Chronica Maiorum*, p. 57.

113. Ibid., p. 58; Gervase of Canterbury, ibid.; *Annales Dunstabuli*, p. 225.

114. *Chronica Maiorum*, p. 58; *Annales Dunstabuli*, p. 227; *Foedera*, vol I, p. 430; *Calendar of Patent Rolls 1258–66*, pp. 278, 284; Wykes p. 137; *Flores Historiarum*, vol ii, pp. 484–5.

115. *The Chronicle of the Monastery of Abingdon*, ed. J. O. Halliwell (Reading 1844) p. 15; Powicke, p. 456 n.2.

116. *Chronicle of Abingdon*, p. 15; Gervase of Canterbury, vol ii, p. 229; *Baronial Plan of Reform*, pp. 325, 330, 387; *Documents of the Baronial Movement*, pp. 264–5.

117. Gervase of Canterbury, vol ii, p. 231; *Annales Dunstabuli*, p. 226.

118. Gervase of Canterbury, p. 231; *Foedera*, vol I, p. 433; *Calendar of Inquisitions Miscellaneous: Volume I, 1219–1307* (HMSO 1916), nos. 610, 613, 632, 716, 776, 777, 841, 856, 895; *Documents of the Baronial Movement*, pp. 104–5, 280–87; Wykes, pp.133–4; Denholm-Young, pp.121–4.

119. *Documents of the Baronial Movement*, pp. 264–5; *Baronial Plan of Reform*, pp. 335–6.

120. Gervase of Canterbury, p. 232; Wykes, p. 139; *Documents of the Baronial Movement*, pp. 280–91.

121. Maddicott, pp. 258–9.

122. Powicke, pp. 454–5; R. F. Treharne, 'The Mise of Amiens, 23 January 1264' in *Studies in Medieval History Presented to F M POwicke*, ed. R. Hunt et al. (Oxford 1948).

123. *Chronica Maiorum*, p. 61.

124. *Annales Dunstabuli*, p. 61; *Flores Historiarum*, vol ii, pp. 486–9; Gervase of Canterbury, pp. 232–3; *Chron. Abingdon*, pp. 15–16; Wykes pp. 140–41, 144; Rishanger, pp. 44–5; also R. F. Treharne, 'The Battle of Northampton, 5th April 1264' in *Simon De Montfort and Baronial Reform: Thirteenth Century Essays*, ed. E. Fryde (London 1986) pp. 312–13.

125. Wykes, pp. 141–3.

126. David Carpenter, *The Battles of Lewes and Evesham, 1264/5* (Keele 1987) pp. 13–18; Wykes, pp. 147–8; *Chronica Maiorum*, p. 62.

127. Carpenter, pp. 17–23.

128. Rishanger, p. 27; *Documents of the Baronial Movement*, pp. 254–5.

129 Wykes, pp. 148–9; *The Song of Lewes*, ed. C. L. Kingsford (Oxford 1890) part ii, pp. 228–42; Carpenter, pp. 19–22; J. R. Maddicott, 'The Mise of Lewes, 1264' in *EHR*, vol xcviii (1993) pp. 588–91.

130. *Flores Historiarum*, vol ii, p. 495; Rishanger, p. 31; Oxenedes, pp. 221–2; Carpenter, pp. 26–7.

131. Wykes, pp. 52–3; *Flores Historiarum*, vol iii, p. 261; Carpenter, pp. 22–34.

132. *Flores Historiarum*, vol iii, p. 261; Wykes, pp. 152–3.

133. Nicholae Triveti, *Annales*, ed. T. Hoag (London 1845) p. 261; *Chronica Maiorum*, p. 63; *Annales Dunstabuli*, pp. 232–3; *Annales Londonienses*, p. 64.

134. *Flores Historiarum*, vol ii, p. 487 and vol iii, p. 261; Guisborough, p. 196; Triveti, p. 261; *Foedera*, vol I, part I, p. 442; *Calendar of the Patent Rolls 1258–66*, pp. 318, 321–2, 324, 331, 343, 364, 374; *Documents of the Baronial Movement*, pp. 290–93.

135. *Foedera*, p. 444; J. p. Gilson, 'The Parliament of 1264' in *EHR*, vol xvi (1901) p. 500; *Documents of the Baronial Movement*, pp. 295–9; N. Denholm-Young, *Collected Papers* (Cardiff 1969) pp. 152–9, 162–4, 244.

136. *Flores Historiarum*, vol iii, p. 262; *Documents of the Baronial Movement*, pp. 298–9.

137. Triveti, *Annales*, p. 261; *Flores Historiarum*, vol iii, p. 261.

138. *Documents of the Baronial Movement*, pp 108–109; *Baronial Plan of Reform*, pp. 182–5 and 204–209; C. H. Knowles, 'The Disinherited 1265–80: A Political and Social Study of the Supporters of Simon de Montfort and the Resettlement after the Barons' Wars', University of Aberystwyth PhD thesis, 1959, pp. 78–80.

139. *Foedera*, vol I, part I, p. 444; *Flores Historiarum*, vol ii, p. 499; *Calendar of Patent Rolls 1258–66*, pp. 360–2; *Chronicle of Melrose*, p. 125; *Chronicle of Bury St Edmunds*, p. 29; Howell, *Eleanor of Provence*, pp. 213–17; *Documents of the Baronial Movement*, pp. 294–301.

140. Wykes, pp. 156–7; Gervase of Canterbury, p. 239; *Flores Historiarum*, vol ii, p. 501.

141. Wykes, p. 155; Maddicott, *Simon de Montfort*, pp. 305–307.

142. Wykes, pp. 161–2; *Flores Historiarum*, vol ii, pp. 504–505.

143. Maddicott, pp. 319–21.

144. *Annales Monasterii de Waverleia* (i.e. Waverley Abbey), AD 1–1377, in *Annales Monastici*, vol iv, p. 358; Wykes p. 160; *Calendar of Patent Rolls 1258–66*, pp. 397, 409.

145. Guisborough, p. 201.

146. *Flores Historiarum*, vol ii, p. 504 and vol iii, p. 264; *Annales Cestrensis* (Chester Annals), ed. R. C. Christie (Lancs and Chshire Record Society, vol xiv, 1886) p. 93. On Edward's escape: *Annales Waverleia*, p. 262; Wykes, pp. 162–3; Robert of Gloucester, vol ii, pp. 756–8; D. C. Cox, *The Battle of Evesham: a New Account* (Evesham 1986) p. 6.

147. Wykes, pp. 165–8; Gusiborough, p. 199; *Annales Waverleia*, pp. 362–3; Triveti, pp. 264–5; *Annales Cestrensis*, p. 95; *Flores Historarum*, vol iii, pp. 2–3. Commentary in Maddicott, pp. 335–9.

148. D. C. Cox, 'The Battle of Evesham in the Evesham Chronicle', in *Historical Research*, vol lxii (1989) p. 341; *Chronicle Mailros*, ed. Stevenson, pp. 198–9; *Annales Londoniensis*, p. 68.

149. Guisborough, pp. 200–202; Rishanger, p. 45; *Chronicles of the Reigns of Stephen, Henry II...*, pp. 547–8; Lanercost, p.76; Oxenedes, p. 229; Wykes, pp 173–5, 180; *Annales Prioratus de Wigornia, AD 1–1277*, in *Annales Monastici*, vol ii, p. 455; *Annales Waverleia*, p. 363; Cox, ibid; Maddicott, pp. 340–343.

Chapter Five: Edward I, 1272–1307

1. *Edward I and the Throne of Scotland: an edition of the record sources for the Great Cause*, ed. E. L. G. Stones and G. G. Simpson, 2 vols (Oxford 1978) vol ii, pp. 260–68.

2. Guisborough, vol ii, pp. 298–303; Lanercost p. 190.

3. W. S. Barrow, *Robert the Bruce*, pp. 205–208.

4. Walter Bower, *The Scotichronicon*, ed. D. E. R. Watt (1991) vol vi, book xii, chapter 17: pp. 141–3.

5. The legend first appears in Sir Walter Scott's 'Tales of a Grandfather', five hundred years after the event, with no source named. For Bruce's exile, see Barrow, pp. 161–70.

6. *Chronicles of England, France, Spain and the adjacent Countries* by Sir John Froissart, tr. T. Johnes (1839) p. 38.

7. *Flores Historiarum*, vol iii, p. 24; Guisborough, p. 367; Rishanger, p. 229; *Documents and Records Illustrative of the History of Scotland*, ed. F. Palgrave (1837) vol I, pp 35–9; also E. Stones, in *Scottish Historical Review* vol lii (1973) p. 84 on Edward I's use of 'cages' as a punishment for 'high security' prisoners.

8. *Statutes of the Realm* (Record Commission, 1810) vol I, pp. 19-25.

9. Wykes, pp. 189–90.

10. For the theory of Roger Godberd as an inspiration for the Robin Hood legend, see David Baldwin, *Robin Hood: the Outlaw Unmasked* (Amberley 2011). The placing of 'Robin' in the 1260s was made by the Scots chroniclers Bower and Wyntoun; the placing of him in the 1190s was not made until c. 1500 by the Scots chronicler John Major.

11. Gervase of Canterbury, vol ii, pp. 249–50; Denholm-Young, *Richard of Cornwall*, pp. 146–7.
12. Elizabeth Hallam, *Capetian France 987–1328* (Longmans 1980) p. 222.
13. *Chronica Maiorum*, p. 131.
14. Rishanger, p. 68; *Close Rolls 1268–72*, pp. 397–8.
15. Powicke, vol ii, pp. 609–10.
16. For events in Palestine, see S. Runciman, *History of the Crusades, vol iii: the Kingdom of Acre* (Penguin, 1981 edition) pp. 309–32.
17. Guisborough, p. 208; G. Hill, *A History of Cyprus* (1948) vol ii pp. 168–70.
18. 'L'Estoire d'Eracles, Empereur', in *Recueil des Historiens des Croisades: Histoires Occidentaux* (Paris 1841–1906) vol ii, p. 461.
19. Prestwich, Edward I, p. 77.
20. Ibid., p. 78.
21. *L'Estoire d'Eracles*, p. 462; Wykes, p. 249; Guisborough, pp. 208–10; Rishanger pp. 69–70; Ibn al-Furat: *Ayyubids, Mamlukes and Crusaders*, ed. and tr. U. and M. Lyons (Cambridge 1971) p. 159.
22. Prestwich, p. 78.
23. Runciman, p. 334.
24. Ibid., p. 338.
25. Rishanger, p. 78.
26. For Edmund's career, see the *NDNB* article by Simon Lloyd, in vol. lxvii, pp. 756–60.
27. Ibid.
28. R. R. Davies, *Conquest, Co-Existence and Change: Wales 1063–1415*, pp. 247, 298–9.
29. Wykes, pp. 237–8.
30. See Michael Prestwich, *Edward I*, pp. 267–97, and coverage of Edward's treatment of Llywelyn of Gwynedd 1277–82 and John Balliol 1292–6.
31. *Calendar of Documents Relating to Scotland*, ed. J. Bain,4 vols (Edinburgh 1881–8): vol ii, no. 120.
32. Prestwich, pp. 470–76.
33. Barrow, pp. 69–71.
34. *Scotichronicon*, tr. Watt, vol v, book x, chapter iv: p. 419.
35. *Calendar of Documents relating to Scotland*, vol ii, no. 250.
36. Marion Campbell, *Alexander III* (House of Lochar 1999) p.15.
37. The basic story, without the detail of Robert senior having been on Crusade, is in John of Fordoun, *Chronicle of the Scottish Nation*, tr. W. F. Skene (1872) p. 299. The full version, with the Crusade detail, which appears to be inaccurate, is in Sir Alexander Dunbar, *Scottish Kings: a revised chronicle of the Scottish nation 1005–1625* (Edinburgh 1899) p. 67. In fact, it was King Robert's grandfather who was the Crusader.
38. Campbell, *Alexander III*, pp. 56–124.
39. *1040 and 1058 regicides: Annals of Ulster, excerpts in Chronicles of the Picts, Chronicles of the Scots and Early Memorials of Scottish History*, ed. W. F. Skene (Edinburgh 1867) p. 369. The 1057 regicide: excerpts from BL Harleian Ms. 4628 in ibid., p. 175.
40. A. A. M. Duncan, 'The Community of the Realm of Scotland and Robert Bruce' in *Scottish Historical Review*, vol xlv (1966) p. 189.
41. *Documents Illustrative of the History of Scotland* vol I, pp. 22–3.
42. See G. W. Barrow, *Kingship and Unity: Scotland 1000–1306* (Mercat Press 1981) p. 159.
43. *Calendar of Documents relating to Scotland*, vol ii, no. 368.
44. Prestwich, pp. 118–21; Roger Loomis, 'Edward I, Arthurian enthusiast' in *Speculum*, vol xxviii (1957) pp. 114–27; on the Glastonbury visit, *Historia de rebus Gestis Glastoniensibus*, ed. T. Hearne (1727) quoted in E. K. Chambers, *Arthur of Britain* (Sidgwick and Jackson 1927) pp. 280–81.

45. Loomis, op. cit.
46. *Documents Illustrative of the History of Scotland*, ed. Stevenson, vol I, pp. 162–73.
47. R. R. Davies, *Conquest, Co-Existence and Change*, p. 361.
48. Ibid., vol I, pp. 149, 186–93.
49. *Foedera*, vol I, part ii, p. 741.
50. *The Great Cause*, vol I, pp. 5–6; vol ii, pp. 3–4.
51. *Anglo-Scottish Relations 1174–1328*, ed. E. L. Stone (1965) p. 44–50.
52. Prestwich, pp. 364–5; *The Great Cause*, vol ii, pp. 32–41, 46–65.
53. H. Johnstone, *Edward of Caernarvon* (Manchester UP 1946) pp. 122–6 for Edward I's overbearing attitude to his son; NA: C 47/4/5, f. 47 v for his assaulting his daughter.
54. See *NDNB* article on Edward II by J. R. S. Phillips, conclusions: vol 17, p. 836; and C. Robinson, 'Was Edward II a Degenerate?' in *American Journal of Insanity*, vol lxvi (1909–10) pp. 445–64.
55. See Ian Mortimer, *The Greatest Traitor: the Life of Roger Mortimer, Earl of March, regent of England 1327–1330* (Pimlico 2003) pp. 185–95, 242–64.
56. Prestwich, pp. 382–7.
57. Guisborough, p. 262.
58. Prestwich, p. 288.
59. *Treaty Rolls 1294–1325: vol I*, ed. Pierre Chaplais (1925) pp. 108–12.
60. NA C 62/71; *Treaty Rolls*, vol I pp. 132–3.
61. Prestwich, pp. 381–2, 406.
62. Ibid., p. 407; N A E 159/68, m. 65.
63. Prestwich, pp. 401–402.
64. Ibid., pp. 402–403.
65. *Foedera*, vol I, part ii, p. 84; Guisborough, p. 243.
66. See Barrow, *Robert the Bruce*, pp. 77–8.
67. Prestwich, pp. 414–15.
68. Cotton, p. 318.
69. Guisborough, pp. 289–90; *The Chronicle of Bury St Edmunds*, pp. 138–9; H. Rothwell, 'The Confirmation of the Charters 1297' in *EHR* vol lx (1945) p. 25.
70. J. H. Denton, *Robert Winchelsey and the Crown, 1294–1312* (Cambridge UP 1980) pp. 126–7; Denton, 'The Crisis of 1297 from the Evesham Chronicle' in *EHR* vol xciii (1978) p. 574.
71. *Parliamentary Writs vol I*, pp. 281–2.
72. Denton 'The Crisis of 1297…' p. 576; Prestwich pp. 419–20.
73. Denton, *Robert Winchelsey*, pp. 131–2; *Documents Illustrating the Crisis of 1297–8 in England*, ed. F. Palgrave (1827) vol I pp. 106–7.
74. Ibid., pp. 141–2.
75. Ibid., pp. 110–15, 133–5; Denton, *Robert Winchelsey*, pp. 149–51.
76. *Documents Illuminating the Crisis of 1297–8 in England*, pp. 108–109.
77. Ibid., pp. 125–9.
78. Ibid., pp. 137–40.
79. *Nicholae Triveti Annales*, pp. 281–3; B L Additional Mss. 6343, ff. 160 and 397; William Durrant Cooper, *The History of Winchelsea, one of the Ancient Towns admitted to the Cinque Ports* (London 1850) p. 57.
80. Prestwich, *Edward I*, p. 425.
81. Documents, 1297–8, pp. 110–13, 155–60.
82. Prestwich, *Edward I*, pp. 392–3.
83. Ibid., pp. 396–9.

Bibliography

Primary Sources

Abbot Suger of St Denis, *The Life of Louis VI*, ed. Wacquet (Paris 1964).

Adam of Eynsham, *Magna Vita Sancti Hugonis*, ed. D. L. Dowie and H. Farmer, 2 vols (Edinburgh 1962).

The Anglo-Saxon Chronicle, tr. Michael Swanton (Dent 1996).

Annales Cestrenses: Annals of Chester, ed. R. C. Christie (Lancashire and Cheshire Record Society, vol xiv, 1886).

Annales Londoniensis: Chronicle of the Reigns of Edward I and Edward II, ed. W. Stubbs, 2 vols (Rolls Series 1882).

Annales Monastici, 5 vols, ed. H. Luard (Rolls Series 1864–9).

Walter Bower, *Scotichronicon*, ed. D. E. R. Watt (Edinburgh 1991).

Brut y Tywysogion, ed. T. Jones (Cardiff UP, 1955).

Calendar of Documents Relating to Scotland, vols 1–4, ed. J. Bain (Edinburgh 1881–8).

Calendar of Patent Rolls: 1232–47, 1247–58, 1258–66 (HMSO 1906 ff.)

Charter Rolls (National Archives).

The Chronicle of Bury St Edmunds 1212–1301, ed. A. Gransden (London 1964).

The Chronicle of Lanercost, ed. J. Stevenson (Maitland Club 1839).

The Chronicle of Melrose, intro. by A. O. and M. O. Anderson (London 1936).

The Chronicle of the Monastery of Abingdon, ed. J. O. Halliwell (Reading 1844).

The Chronicle of Waltham Abbey, ed. Leslie Watkiss and M. Chibnall (Old Medieval Texts 1994).

The Chronicle of William de Rishanger of the Barons' War: de Bellis, ed J. O. Halliwell (Camden Society 1840).

Close Rolls: 1227–31, 1242–7, 1247–51, 1251–3, 1253–4, 1254–6, 1256–9, 1259–61, 1268–72 (HMSO, 1902 ff.)

Documents and Records Illustrative of the History of Scotland, ed. F. Palgrave (London 1837).

Eadmer, *Historia Novorum in Anglia*, ed. Martin Rule (Rolls Series vol 81, London 1884).

Edward I and the Throne of Scotland: an edition of the record sources for the Great Cause, eds. E. C. Stones and G. G. Simpson, 2 vols (Oxford 1978).

Florence of Worcester, *Chronicon ex Chronicis*, ed. B. Thorpe, 2 vols (London 1848–9).

Flores Historiarum, ed. H. Luard, 3 vols (Rolls Series 1890).

Foedera Conventiones, Litterae et Acta Publica, ed. T. Rymer (Record Commission, 1816 edition).

Geoffrey Gaimar, *L'Estoire des Engles*, ed. Alexander Bell (Oxford UP 1960).

Geoffrey of Vinsauf, *Poetria Nova*, tr. M. F. Nims (Toronto 1967).

Gervase of Canterbury, *Historical Works*, ed. W. Stubbs, 2 vols (Rolls Series 1879–80).

Gesta Stephani, ed. K. Potter and R. H. C. Davis (Old Medieval Texts 1976).

Giraldus Cambrensis/Gerald of Wales, *Opera* (Works), ed. J. S. Brewer, J. F. Dimmock, and G. E. Warner, 8 vols (Rolls Series 1861–91).

Henry of Huntingdon, *Historia Anglorum*, ed. Diana Greenway (Old Medieval Texts 1996).

Herbert of Bosham, *Vita Sancti Thomae Archiepiscopi et Martyris*, ed. J. C. Robinson, in *John of Salisbury: Materials for the Life of St. Thomas Becket* (London 1859).

Hermann of Tournai, *Liber de restauratione monasterii Sancti Martini tornacensis*, ed. G. Waitz, in *Monumenta Germania Historia*, vol xiv (Berlin 1956).

The Letters of Innocent III (1198–1216) concerning England and Wales, ed. C. R. Cheney (Oxford UP 1967).

Jean de Joinville, *Chronicle of the Crusades*, tr. M. R. B. Shaw (Harmondsworth 1963).

John of Fordoun, *Chronicle of the Scottish Nation*, tr. W. Skene (Edinburgh 1872).

John of Salisbury, *Materials for the History of Thomas Becket*, ed. J. C. Robinson (London 1859).

John of Worcester, *Chronicle*, ed. J. R. Weaver (Oxford 1908).

Orderic Vitalis, *Historia Ecclesiatica*, ed. and tr. Marjorie Chibnall, 6 vols (Oxford 1969–80).

Matthew Paris, *Chronica Majora*, ed. H. Luard, 7 vols (Rolls Series 1872–83).

Ralph of Coggeshall, *Chronicon Anglicanum*, ed. J. Stevenson (Rolls Series 1875).

Ralph of Diceto, *Radulfi de Diceto Decani Londoniensis Opera Historica*, ed. W. Stubbs, 2 vols (Rolls Series 1876).

Recueil des Historiens des Croisades: Historie Occidentaux, vol ii (Paris 1841 ff.)

Richard of Devizes, *Chronicon*, ed and tr. J. Appleby (London 1963).

Oeuvres de Rigord et de Guillaume le Breton, ed. H. F. Delaborderie, 2 vols (Paris 1882–5).

The Metrical Chronicle of Robert of Gloucester, ed W. A. Wright, 2 vols (Rolls Series 1887).

Robert of Torigny, in vol iv of *Chronicles of the Reigns of Stephen, Henry II and Richard I*, ed. R. Howlett (see below).

Roger of Howden, *Chronica*, ed. W. Stubbs, 4 vols (Rolls Series 1868–71).

——, *Gesta Henrici et Ricardi*, ed. W. Stubbs 2 vols (Rolls Series 1867).

Scottish Annals from English Chroniclers, 500 to 1286, ed. A. O. Anderson (Stamford 1991).

Simeon of Durham, *Opera* (Works), ed. T. Arnold (Rolls Society 1882–5).

The Song of Lewes, ed. C. L. Kingsford (Oxford 1890).

The Chronicle of Walter of Guisborough, ed. H. Rothwell (Camden Series vol lxxxix 1957).

William of Malmesbury, *Gesta Regum*, ed. and tr. R. M. Thompson and M. Winterbottom, 2 vols (Oxford UP 1998).

——, *Historia Novella*, ed. E. King, tr. K. R. Potter (Oxford 1998).

The History of William Marshal, eds. A. J. Holden, S. Gregory, D. Crouch, 2 vols (Anglo-Norman Texts Society 2002).

William of Newburgh, *Historia Rerum Anglicanum*, ed. R. Howlett, in *Chronicles and Memorials of the Reigns of Stephen, Henry II and Richard I* (4 vols) (Rolls Society 1884–9).

Secondary Sources

Anniversary Essays in Medieval History presented to RHC David, ed. H. Mayr-Harting and RI Moore (London 1985).

Baldwin, David, *Robin Hood: the English Outlaw Unmasked* (Amberley 2011).

Barlow, Frank, *William Rufus* (Yale UP, 2000 edition).

Barrow, J. W. S., *Robert Bruce and the Community of the Realm of Scotland* (Edinburgh 1965).

——, *Kingship and Unity: Scotland 1000–1306* (Mercat Press 1981).

Bemont, C., *Simon de Montfort*: first edition (Paris 1884); second edition (Oxford 1930).

Boussard, J., *Le Comté d'anjou sous Henri Plantagenet et ses Fils (1151–1204)* (Paris 1938).

Broughton, B., *The Legends of King Richard I* (The Hague 1966).

Campbell, Marion, *Alexander III* (House of Lochar 1999).

Carpenter, David, *The Battles of Lewes and Evesham, 1264/5* (Keele 1987).

——, *The Minority of Henry III* (London 1990).

Cheney, C. R., *From Becket to Langton: English Church Government 1170–1213* (Manchester UP 1956).

Chibnall, Marjorie, *Anglo-Norman England, 1066–1166* (New York 1987).

——, *The Empress Matilda: Queen Consort, Queen Mother and Lady of the English* (Oxford UP 1991).

Church, S., *King John: New Interpretations* (Boydell and Brewer 1999).
Cooper, William Durrant, *The History of Winchelsea, one of the Ancient Towns admitted to the Cinque Ports* (London 1850).
Cox, D.C., *The Battle of Evesham: a New Account* (Evesham 1986).
Cox, E. L., *Eagles of Savoy: the House of Savoy in Thirteenth Century Europe* (Princeton UP 1974).
Crouch, D., *William Marshal* (London 1990).
——, *The Reign of Stephen, 1135–1154* (London 2000).
Davies, R. R., *Conquest, Co-Existence and Change: Wales 1063–1415* (Oxford UP 1987).
Davis, R. H. C., *King Stephen 1135–1154*, third edition (London 1990).
Denholm-Young, N., *Richard of Cornwall* (Oxford UP 1943).
Denton, J. H., *Robert Winchelsey and the Crown, 1294–1313* (Cambridge UP 1980).
Documents of the Baronial Movement of Reform and Rebellion, 1258–67, ed. R. F. Treharne and R. J. Sanders (Oxford UP 1973).
Douglas, David C., *William the Conqueror* (Berkeley UP 1964).
Gillingham, John, *Richard I* (Yale UP 1999).
Grinnell-Williams, Duncan, *The Killing of William Rufus* (Newton Abbot 1968).
Hallam, Elizabeth, *Capetian France 987–1328* (Longmans 1980).
Hill, G., *A History of Cyprus: vol ii* (Cambridge University Press 1948).
Hollister, C. W., *Monarchy, Magnates and Institutions in the Anglo-Norman World* (London 1986).
——, *Henry I* (Yale UP 2001).
Holt, J. C., *King John* (London 1963).
Howell, Margaret, *Eleanor of Provence: Queenship in Thirteenth Century England* (Blackwell 1998).
Johnstone, H., *Edward of Caernarvon 1284–1307* (Manchester UP 1946).
Jordan, W. C., *Louis IX and the Challenge of Crusade* (Princeton UP 1979).
King, Edmund, *King Stephen* (Yale UP 2011).
Labarge, M. W., *Simon de Montfort* (London 1962).
Le Patourel, J. H., *The Norman Empire* (Oxford UP 1976).
Lloyd, S. D., *English Society and the Crusade, 1216–1307* (Oxford UP 1988).
McLynn, Frank, *Lionheart and Lackland: King Richard, King John and the Wars of Conquest* (Vintage 2007).
Maddicott, J. R., *Simon de Montfort* (Cambridge UP 1994).
Mortimer, Ian, *The Greatest Traitor: the Life of Roger Mortimer, Earl of March and Regent of England 1327–30* (Pimlico 2003).
Nelson, J., *Coeur de Lion: History and Myth* (London 1992).
The New Dictionary of National Biography, ed. Colin Mathew (Oxford UP 2002).
Norgate, Kate, *John Lackland* (Macmillan 1902).
Powicke, F. M., *King Henry III and the Lord Edward*, 2 vols (Oxford UP 1947).
——, *The Loss of Normandy 1189–1204*, second edition (Manchester UP 1961).
Prestwich, Michael, *Edward I* (Methuen 1988).
Richard, A., *Histoire des Comtes de Poitou 778-1204*, 2 vols (Paris 1903).
Richard, J., *St Louis: Crusader King of France*, ed. S. Lloyd (Cambridge UP 1992).
Round, J. H., *Feudal England* (London 1895).
Runciman, Steven, *History of the Crusades: vol iii, The Kingdom of Acre* (Penguin 1981 edition).
——, *The Sicilian Vespers: a History of the Mediterranean World in the Thirteenth Century* (Cambridge UP 1988).
Southern, F. W., *Robert Grosseteste: the Growth of an English Mind in Medieval Europe* (Oxford 1986).
Stacey, R. C., *Politics, Society and Finance under Henry III, 1216–45* (Oxford UP 1987).
Stevenson, F., *Robert Grosseteste, Bishop of Lincoln* (London 1889).
Stones, E. L. G. (ed.) *Anglo-Scottish Relations, 1174–1328* (1965).

Treharne, R. F., *The Baronial Plan of Reform 1258–63*, second edition (Manchester UP 1973).
Warren, W. L., *King John* (Methuen 1961).
——, *Henry II* (Methuen 1973).
Weir, Alison *Eleanor of Aquitaine* (Pimlico 2000).

Articles
Bacharach, B., 'The Idea of the Angevin Empire', *Albion*, vol x (1978) pp. 293–9.
Barratt, N., 'The Revenues of King John' in *EHR* vol cxi (1996).
——, 'The English Revenues of Richard I' in *EHR* vol cxvi (2001).
——, 'The revenues of John and Philip Augustus Revisited' in *King John: New Interpretations*, ed. S. D. Crouch (Boydell and Brewer 1999), pp. 75–9.
Bates, D., 'The Character and Career of Odo, Bishop of Bayeux', in *Speculum*, vol l (1975) pp. 1–20.
Beckerman, S., 'Succession in Normandy 1087 and in England 1066: the role of testamentary custom' in *Speculum* vol xlvii (1972) pp. 255–60.
Bemont, C., 'La Campagne de Poitou (1242–3)' in *Annales du Midi*, vol v (1893) pp. 289–314.
Bradbury, J. M., 'Philip Augustus and King John' in ed. SD Crouch, *King John: New Interpretations* (Boydell and Brewer, 1999), p. 350.
Brand, P. A., 'The Drafting of Legislation in Mid-Thirteenth Century England' in *Parliamentary History*, vol ix (1990).
Carpenter, David, 'The Fall of Hubert de Burgh' in *Journal of British Studies*, vol xix (1980).
——, 'St Thomas Cantilupe: His Political Career' in *St Thomas Cantelupe, Bishop of Hereford*, ed. M. Jancey (Hereford 1982).
——, 'What Happened in 1258?' in *War and Government in the Middle Ages: Essays in Honour of JO Prestwich*, ed. J. Gillingham and J. C. Holt (Boydell and Brewer 1984).
——, 'The Lord Edward's Oath to Aid and Counsel Simon de Montfort, 15 October 1259' in *BIHR*, vol lviii (1985).
——, 'King, Magnates and Society: the Personal Rule of King Henry III, 1234–1258' in *Speculum* vol lx (1985).
——, 'Simon de Montfort: the First Leader of a Political Movement in English History', in *History*, vol lxxvi (1991).
——, 'King Henry III's "Statute Against Aliens": July 1263' in *EHR* vol cvii (1992) pp. 925–46.
Cazel, F. A. and Painter, S., 'The marriage of Isabella of Angouleme' in *EHR*, lxiii (1948) pp. 85–6.
Chaplais, Pierre, 'The Making of the Treaty of Paris (1259) and the Royal Style' in *EHR* lxvii (1952) pp. 235–9.
Cheney, C. R., 'King John and the Papal Interdict' in *Bulletin of the John Rylands Library*, vol xxxi (1948).
——, 'King John's Reaction to the Interdict in England' in *TRHS*, 4th series, vol xxxi (1949).
Chibnall, Marjorie, 'The Empress Matilda and Church Reform' in *Transactions of the Royal Historical Society*, 5th series, vol xxxviii (1988).
Davis, R. H. C., 'William of Jumieges, Robert Curthose and the Norman succession', *EHR* vol xlv (1980).
Ellis, J., 'Gaston de Bearn: a study in Anglo-Gascon Relations, 1225–90', Oxford D Phil thesis 1952.
English, Barbara, 'William the Conqueror and the Anglo-Norman Succession' in *Historical Research*, vol xxxiv (1991) pp. 221–36.
Gillingham, John, 'The Unromantic Death of Richard I' in *Speculum*, vol liv (1979).
——, 'Richard I and Berengaria of Navarre' in *BIHR*, vol liii (1990).
Gilson, J. P., 'The Parliament of 1264' in *EHR*, vol xvi (1901).

C. Harper-Bill, 'King John and the Church of Rome' in ed. S. D. Crouch, *King John: New Interpretations* (Boydell and Brewer, 1999).

Hill, Rosalind, 'The Battle of Stockbridge 1141' in *Studies in Medieval History Presented to R. Allen Brown*, eds., C. Harper-Bill, C. Holdsworth and J. Nelson (Boydell and Brewer 1989).

Hollister, C. W., 'The Anglo-Norman civil war 1101' in *EHR*, vol lxxxviii (1973).

——, 'The strange death of William Rufus' in *Speculum*, vol xlviii (1975).

Holt, J. C., 'The end of the Anglo-Norman Realm' in *Proceedings of the British Academy*, vol lxi (1975) pp. 223–65.

——, 'The loss of Normandy and Royal Finance' in ed. S. D. Crouch, *King John: New Interpretations* (Boydell and Brewer, 1999).

Jackson, P., 'The end of Hohenstaufen Rule in Syria' in *BIHR*, vol lix (1986) pp. 20–36.

Jacob, E. F., 'A Proposal for Arbitration between Simon de Montfort and Henry III in 1260' in *EHR*, vol xxxvii (1922) pp. 80–2.

Jourdan, E., *Les Origines de la Domination Angevine en Italie* (Paris 1909).

Knowles, C. H., 'The Disinherited 1265–80: A Political and Social Study of the Supporters of Simon de Montfort and the Resettlement after the Barons' Wars', University of Wales Aberystwyth PhD thesis, 1959.

Lawrence, C. H., 'The Letters of Adam Marsh and the Franciscan School at Oxford' in *Journal of Ecclesiastical History*, vol xlii (1991) pp. 218–29.

Le Patourel, J., 'The Norman Succession 996 – 1135' in *English Historical Review*, vol 86 (1971).

Leyser, K., 'The Anglo-Norman Succesion 1120-1125' in *Anglo-Norman Studies*, vol xiii (1990/1), pp. 225–41.

Lloyd, S. D., 'Gilbert de Clare, Richard of Cornwall and the Lord Edward's Crusade' in *Nottingham Medieval Studies*, vol xxi (1986).

Loomis, Roger, 'Edward I, Arthurian Enthusiast' in *Speculum*, vol xxviii (1953).

Mason, Emma, 'William Rufus: Myth and Reality' in *Journal of Medieval History*, vol iii (1977).

——, 'William Rufus and the Historians' in *Medieval History*, vol i (1991).

Moss, V. D., 'The Defence of Normandy 1193–8' in *Anglo-Norman Studies*, vol xxiv (2001).

——, 'Norman Exchequer Rolls' in ed. S. D. Crouch, *King John: New Interpretations* (Boydell and Brewer, 1999).

Pocquet du Haut-Jusse, B. A., 'Les Plantagenets et la Bretagne' in *Annales de Bretagne* vol liii (Rennes 1946).

Richardson, H. G. and Sayles, G.O., 'The Provisions of Oxford 1258' in *BJRL*, vol xvii (1933) pp. 25–7.

Ridgeway, H., 'The Politics of the English Court 1247–1265, with Special Reference to the Role of Aliens', Oxford D Phil thesis, 1983.

——, 'The Lord Edward and the Provisions of Oxford, 1258: a Study in Faction' in *TCE* vol I (1986).

——, 'King Henry III's Grievances against the Council in 1261' in *Historical Research*, vol lxi (1988) pp. 232–42.

Smith, R. J., 'Henry II's heir: the acts and seals of the Young King' in *EHR* (2001).

Treharne, R. F., 'The Mise of Amiens, 23 January 1264' in *Studies in Medieval History Presented to FM Powicke*, ed. R. Hunt, W. A. Pantin and R. W. Southern (Oxford 1948).

——, 'The Battle of Northampton, 5th April 1264' in *Simon de Montfort and Baronial Reform: Thirteenth Century Essays*, ed. E. B. Fryde (London 1986).

Turner, R. V., 'Eleanor of Aquitaine and Her Children: an Inquiry into Medieval Family Attachment' in *Journal of Medieval History*, vol xi (1988).

——, 'Good or Bad Kingship: the case of Richard the Lionheart' in *Haskins Society Journal*, vol viii (1999) pp. 73–8.

Wabe Labarge, M. W., 'The Personal Quarrels of Simon de Montfort and his Wife with Henry III of England', Oxford B Litt thesis 1939.

Zerner, Monique, 'L'epouse de Simon de Montfort et la croisade albigoise' in *Femmes-Mariages-Lignages, XII au XIV Siecles: Melanges Offerts à Georges Duby*, ed. J. Dufournet, A. Joris and p. Toubert (Brussels 1992).

Index